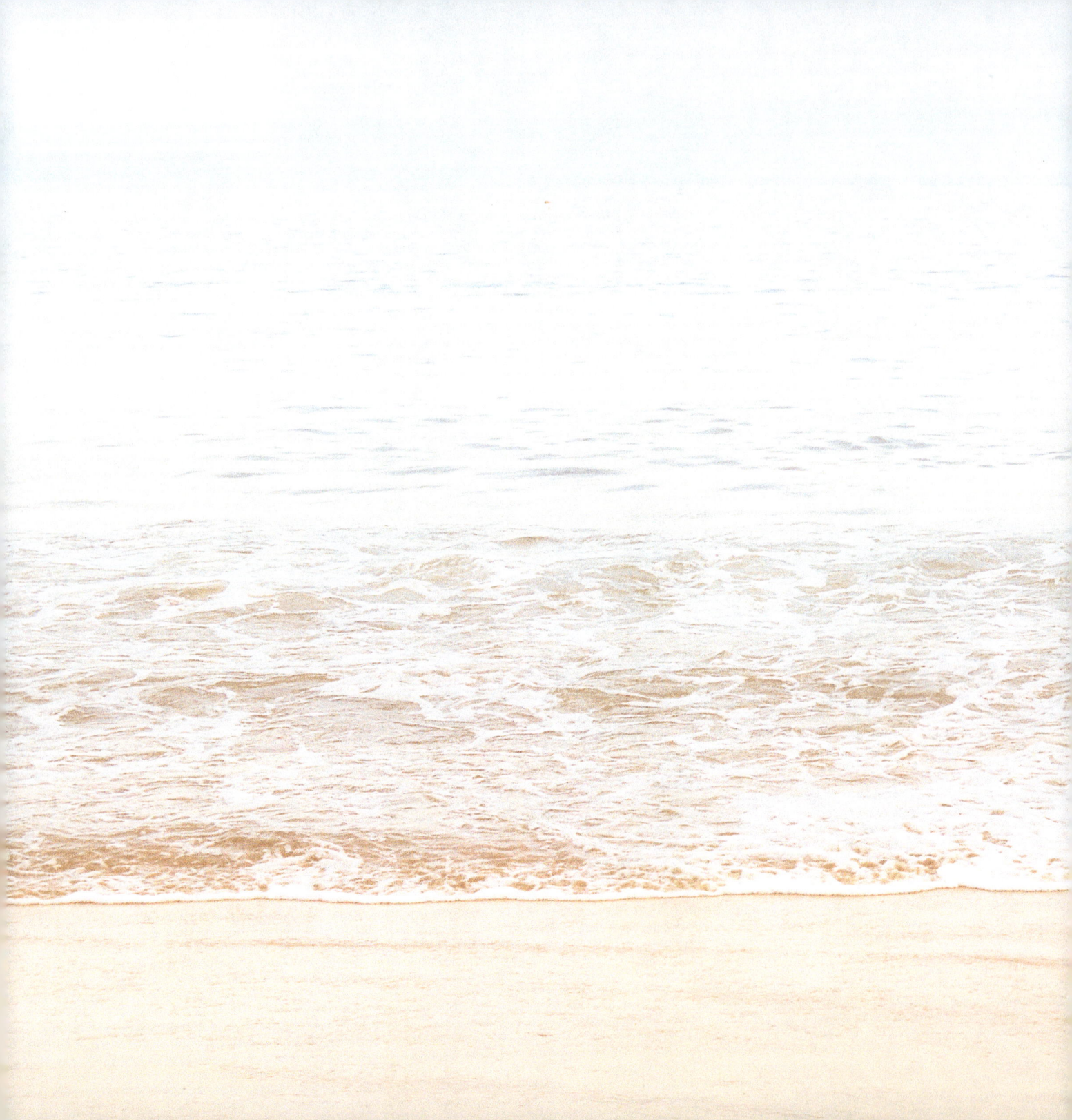

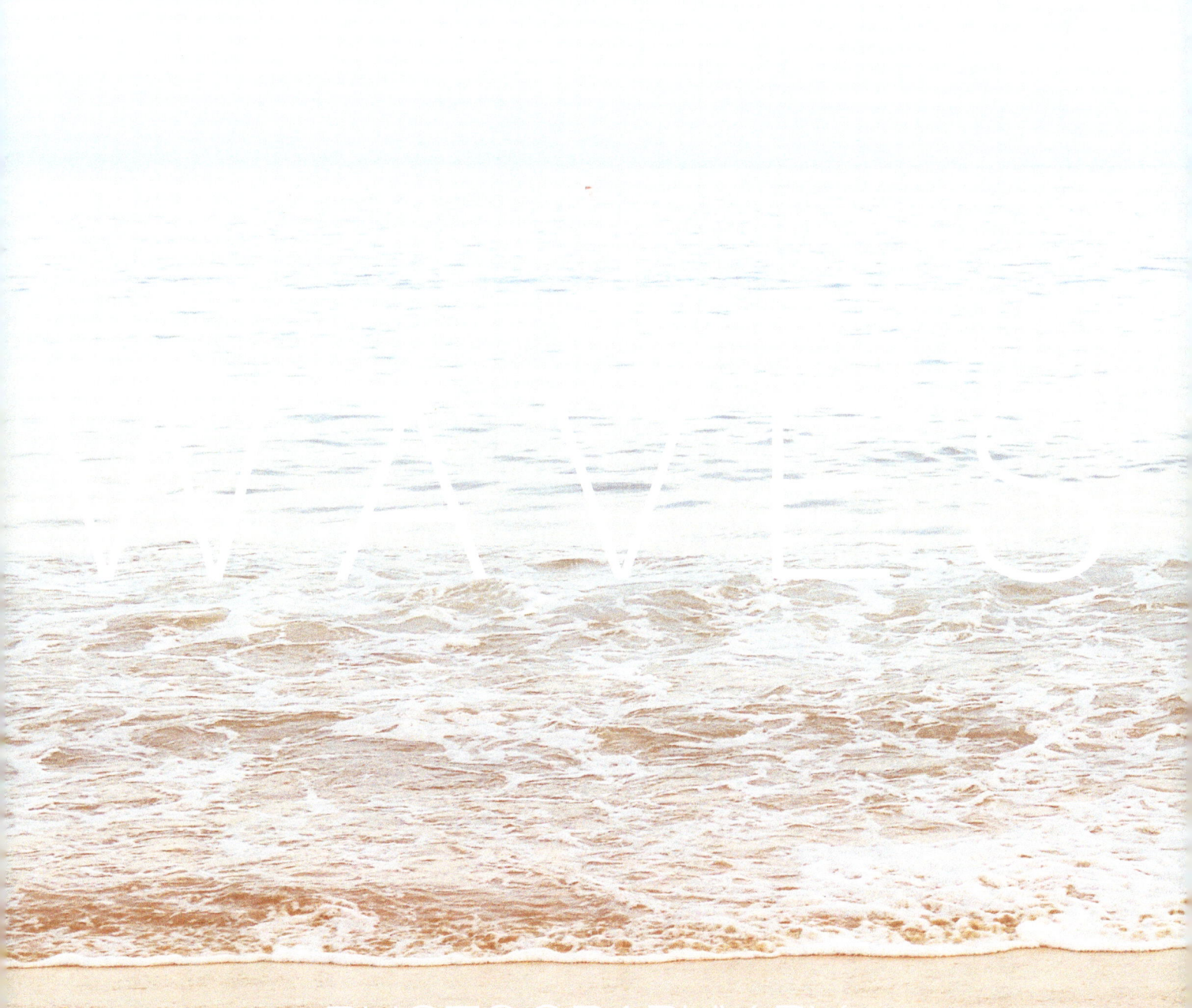

WAVES

PHOTOGRAPHY BY

J.M. WHITAKER

Published by Ink Spot Publishing | 2017
Glendale, CA
www. Scribbles And Ink Spots .com

"WAVES" First Edition
Photography by J.M. Whitaker

ISBN: 978-0-9980981-2-8

INTRODUCTION

This book is a series of photographs taken by me, mostly of the California coastline. The water and it's ability to reflect light and its multitude of colors has always been facinating to me. The photos you are about to see are aranged chromatically to reflect how the waves of the ocean change with waves of light.

I hope you enjoy these photos as much as I did taking them.

J.M. Whitaker

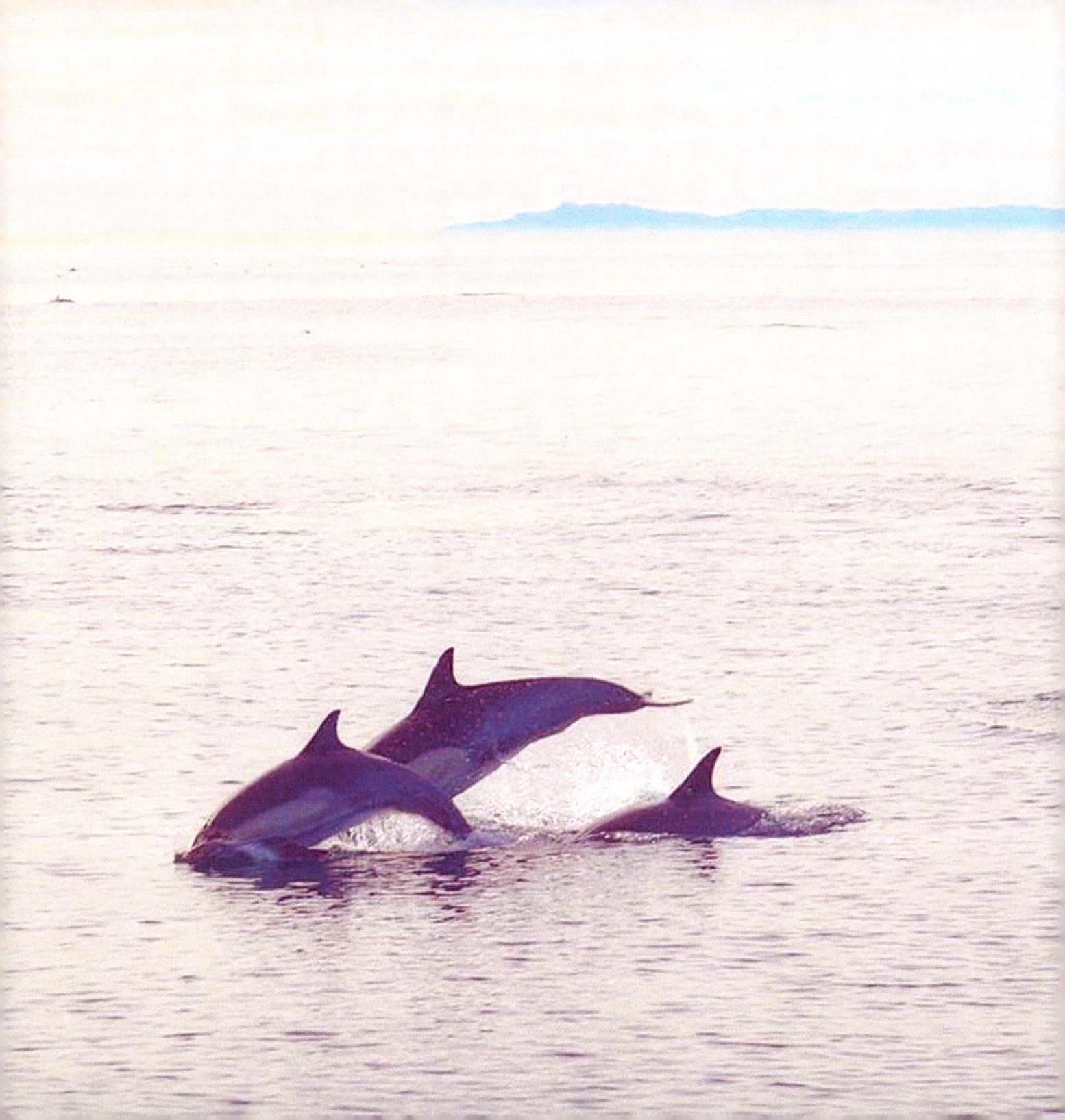

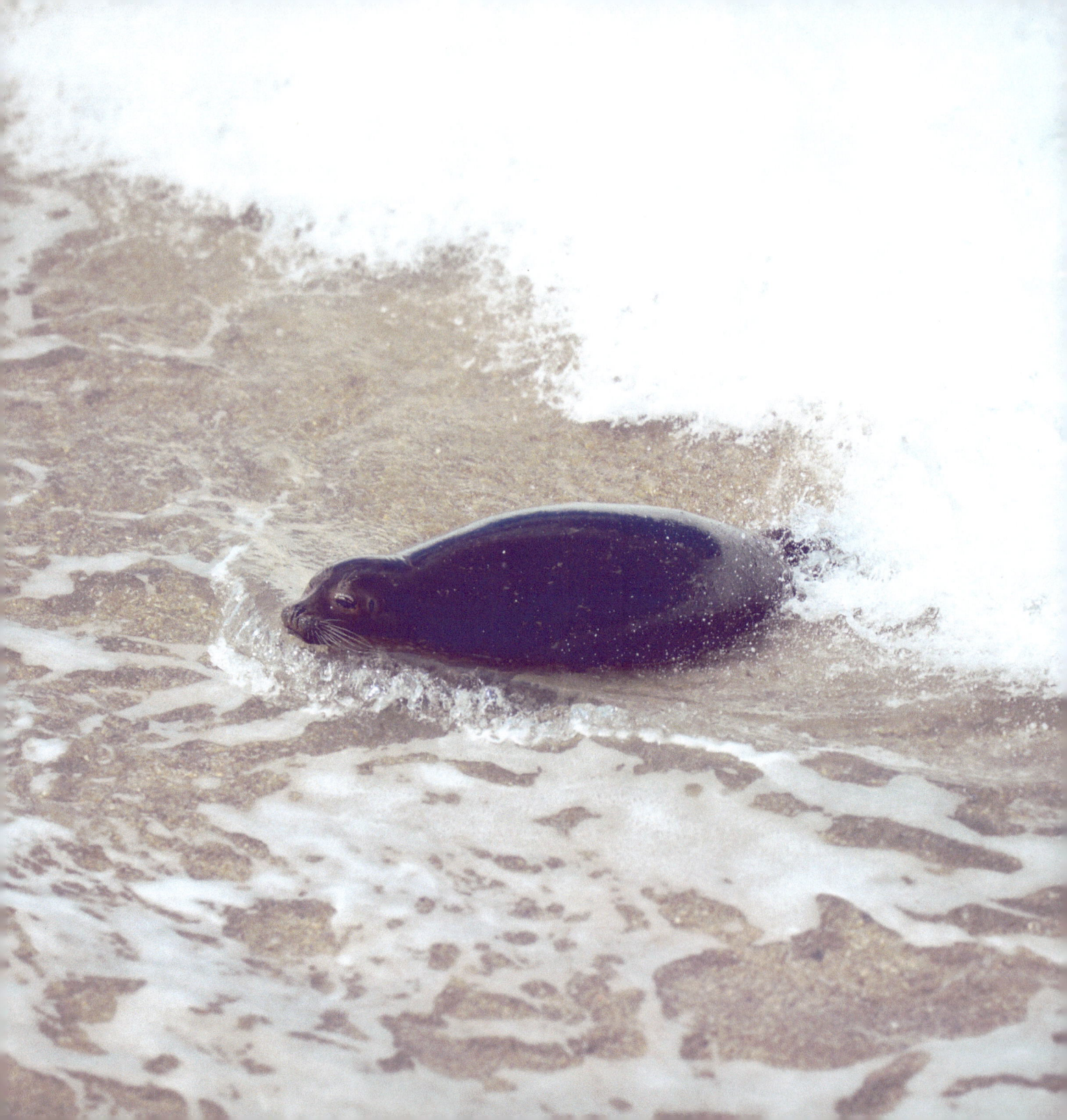

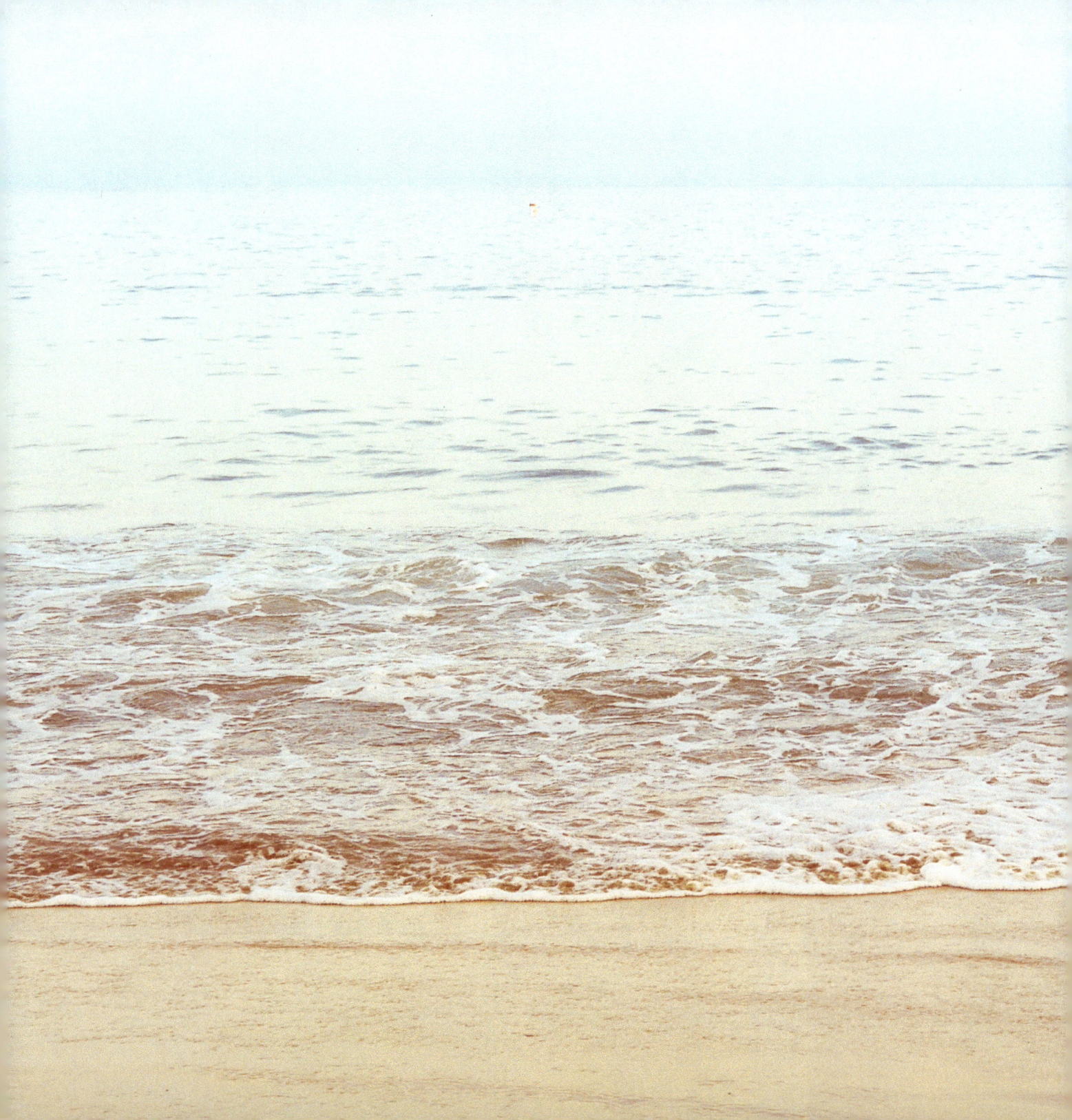

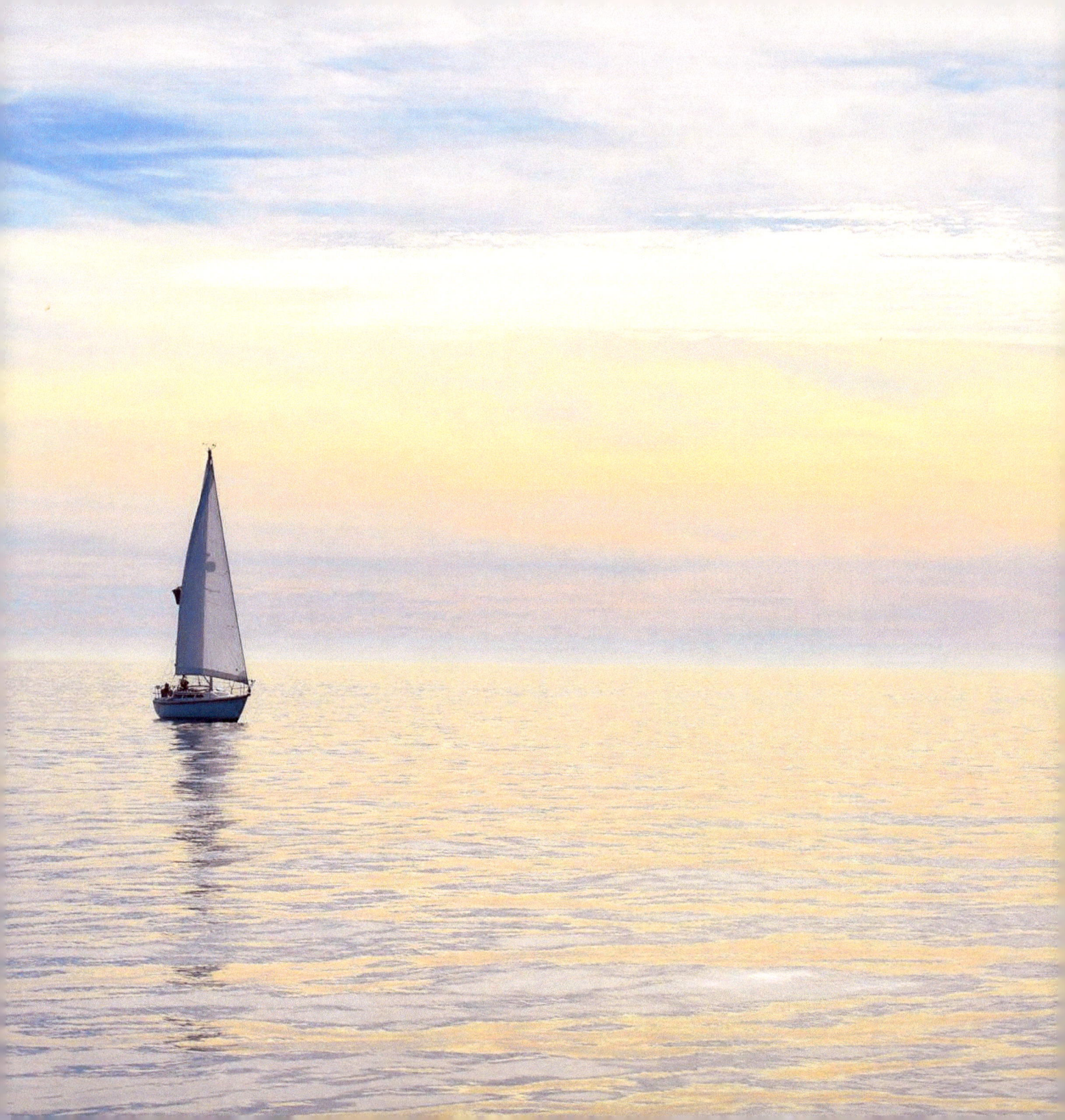

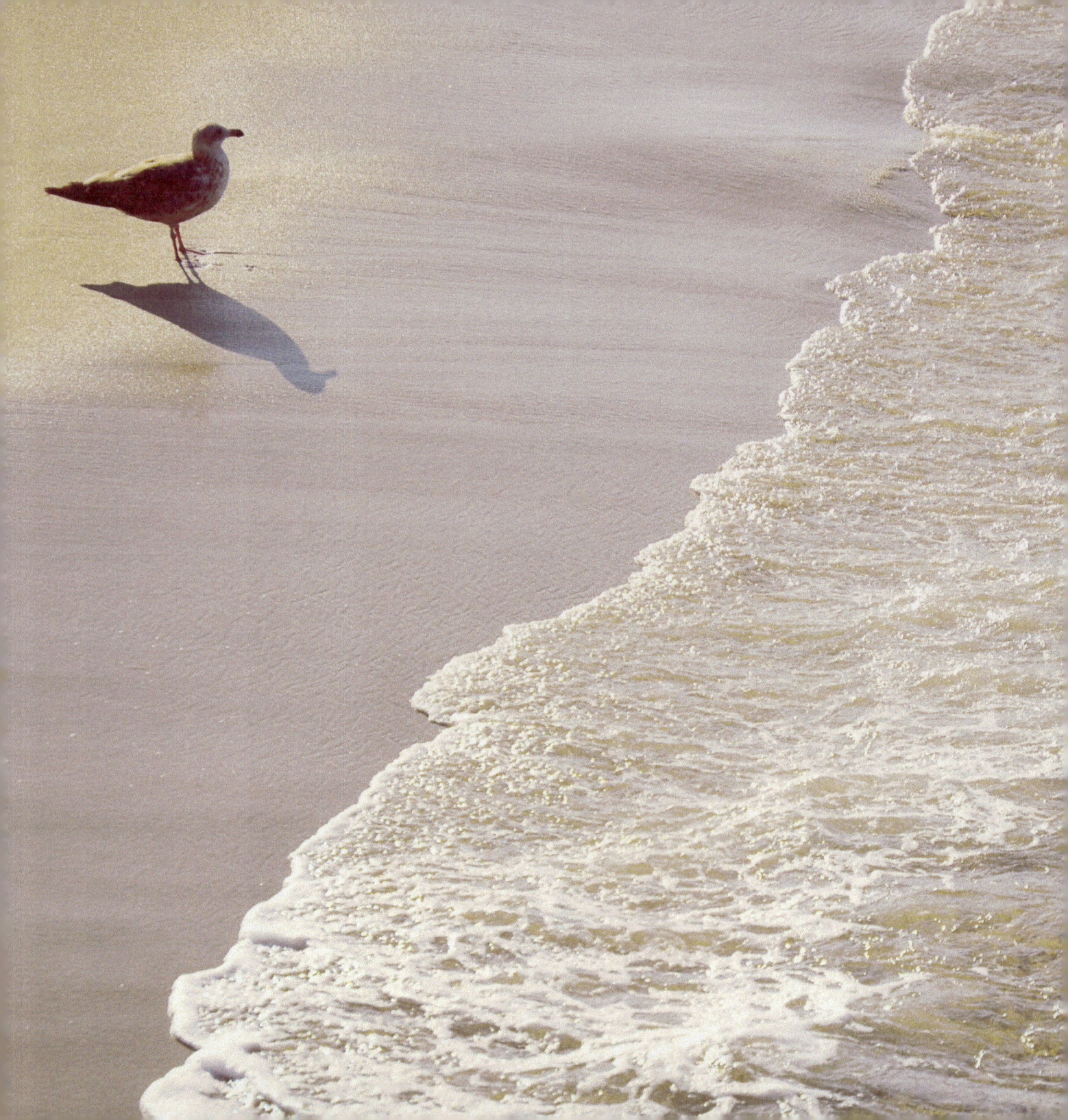

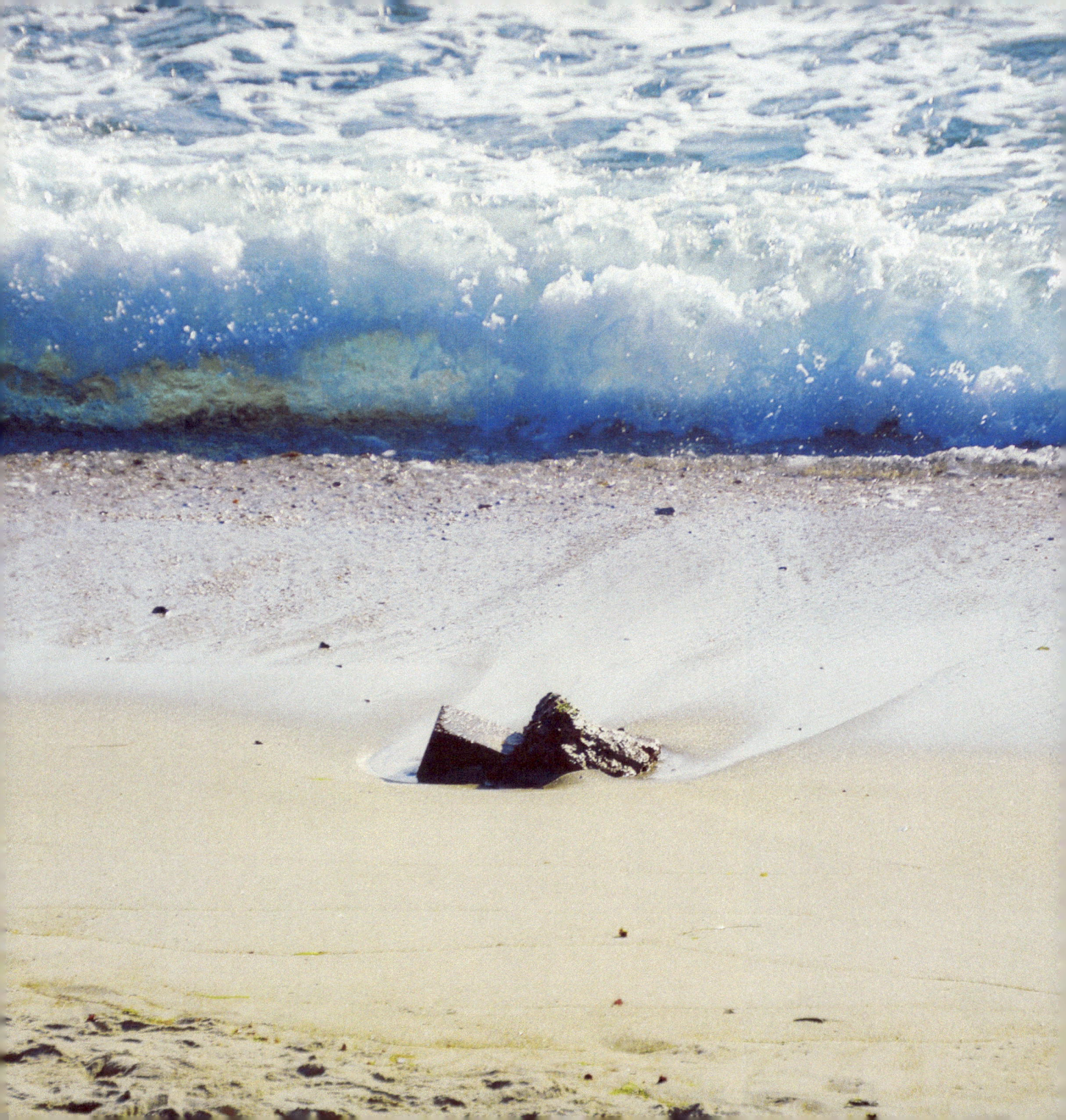

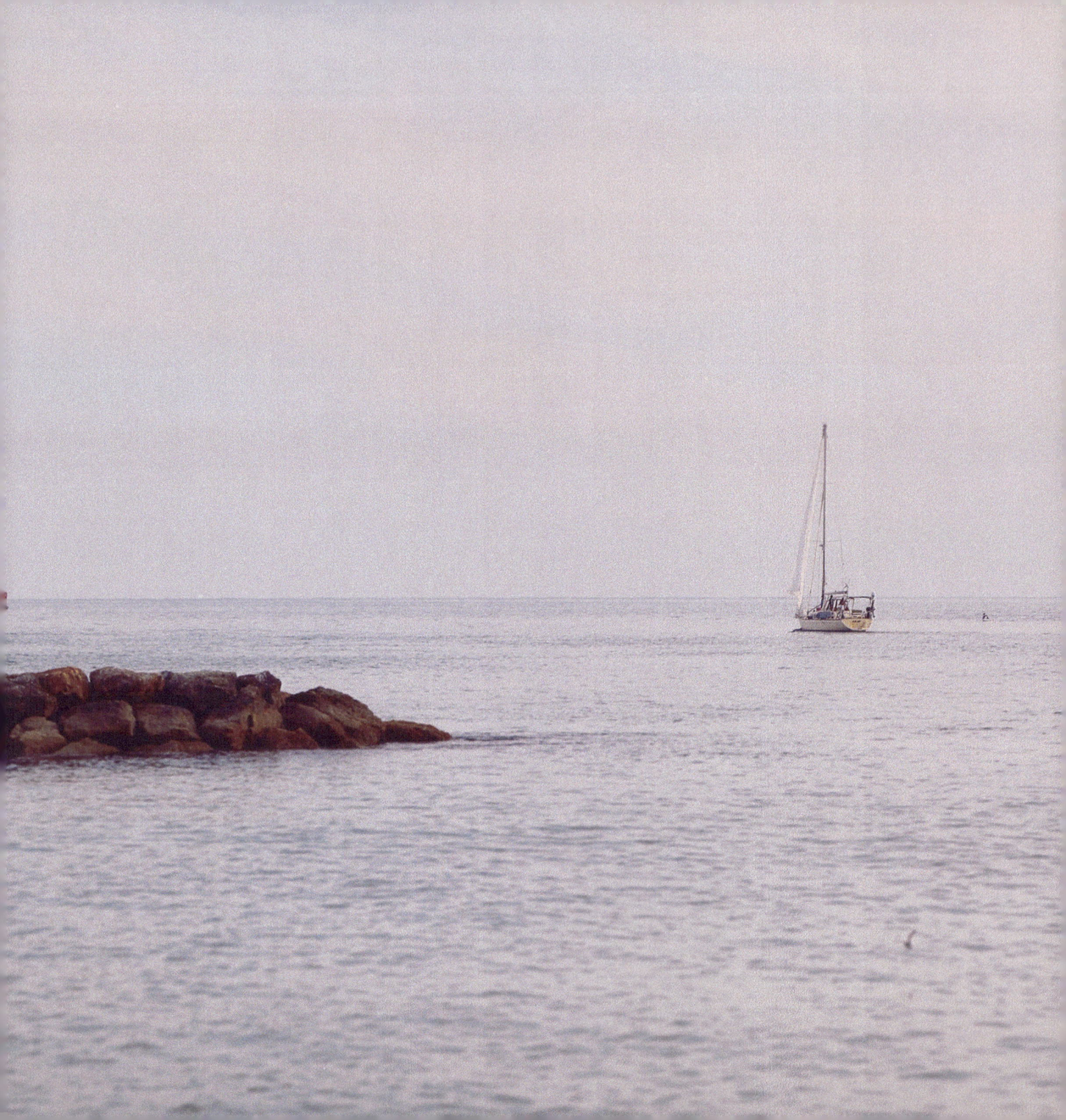

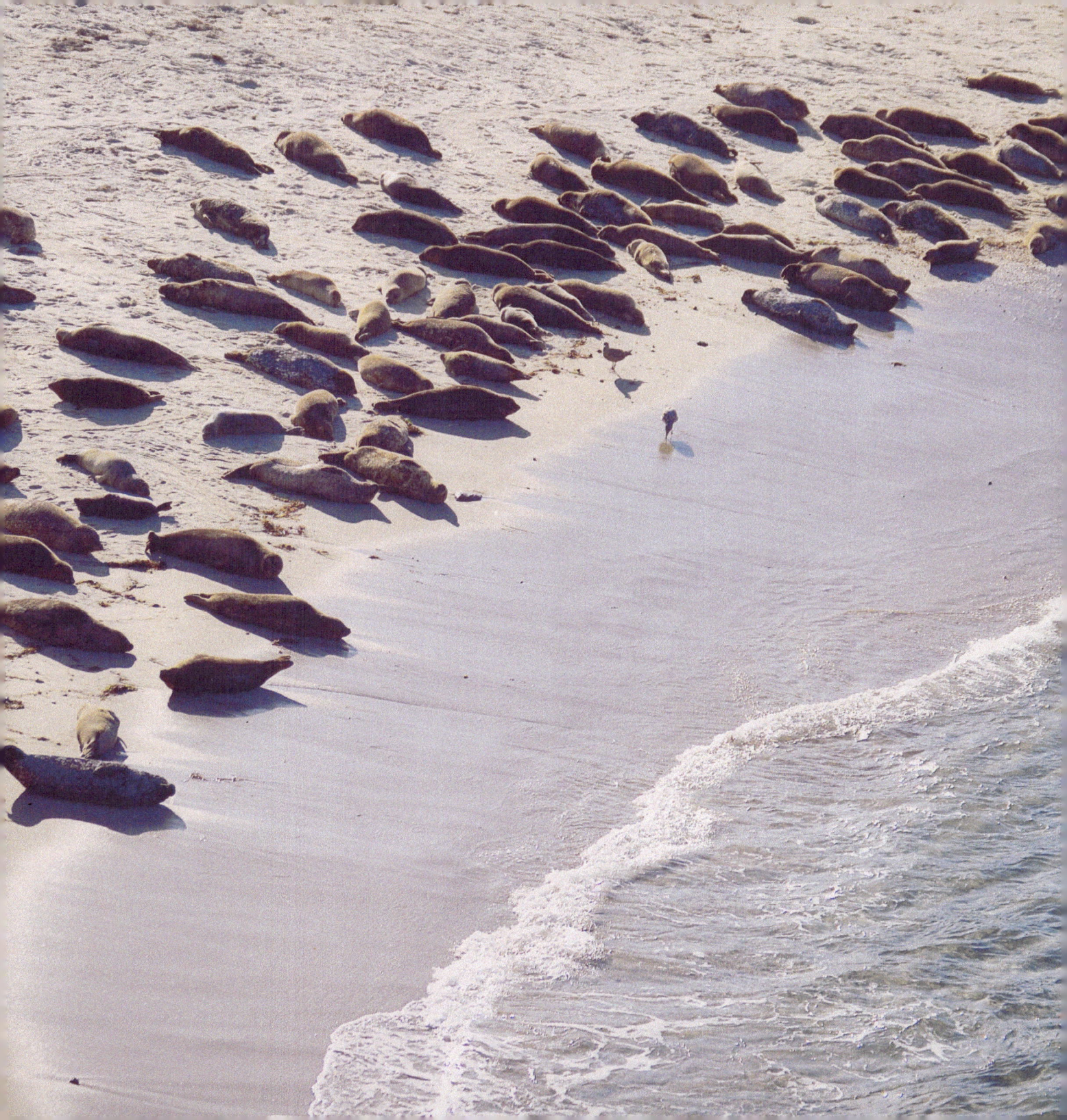

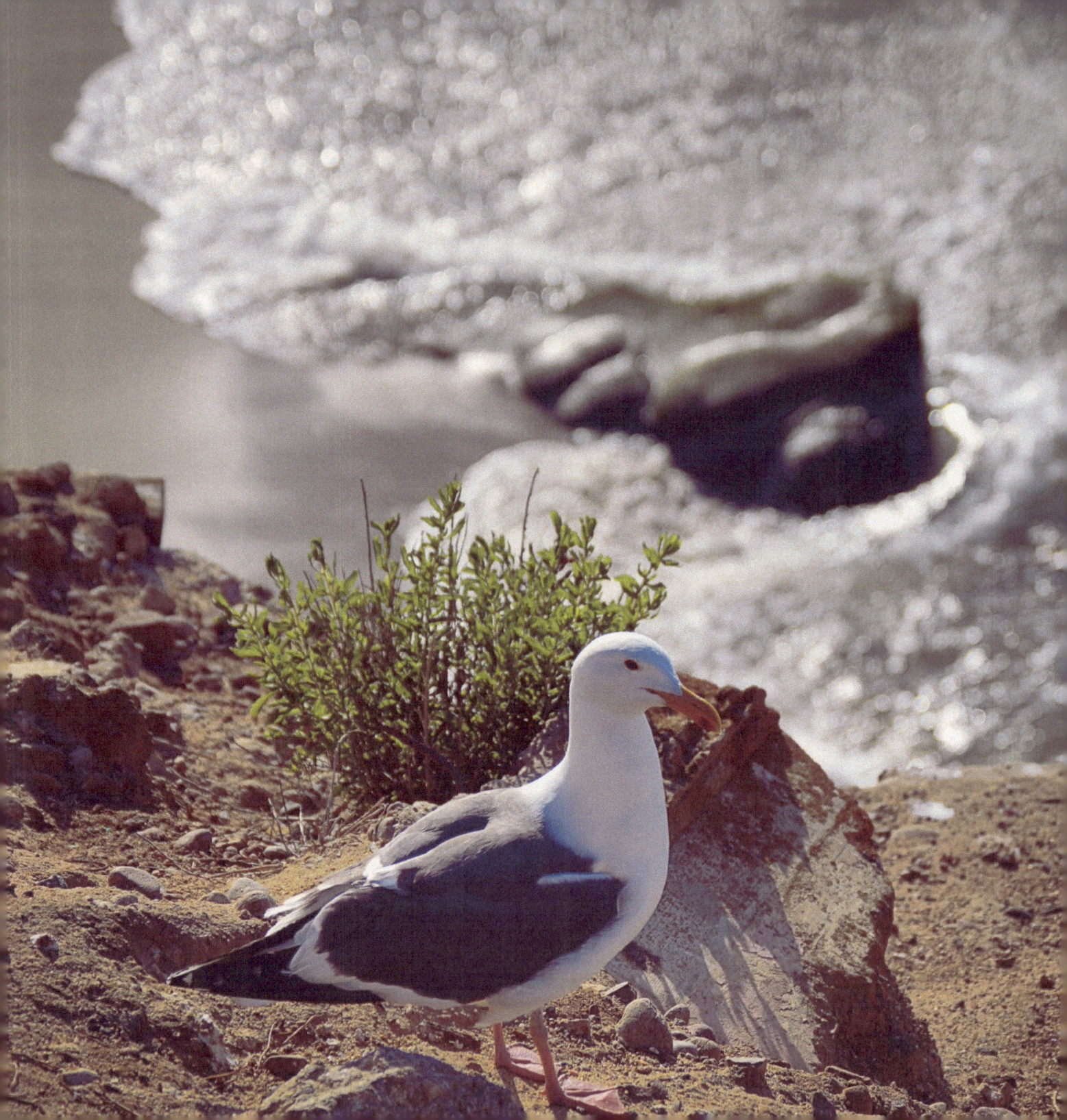

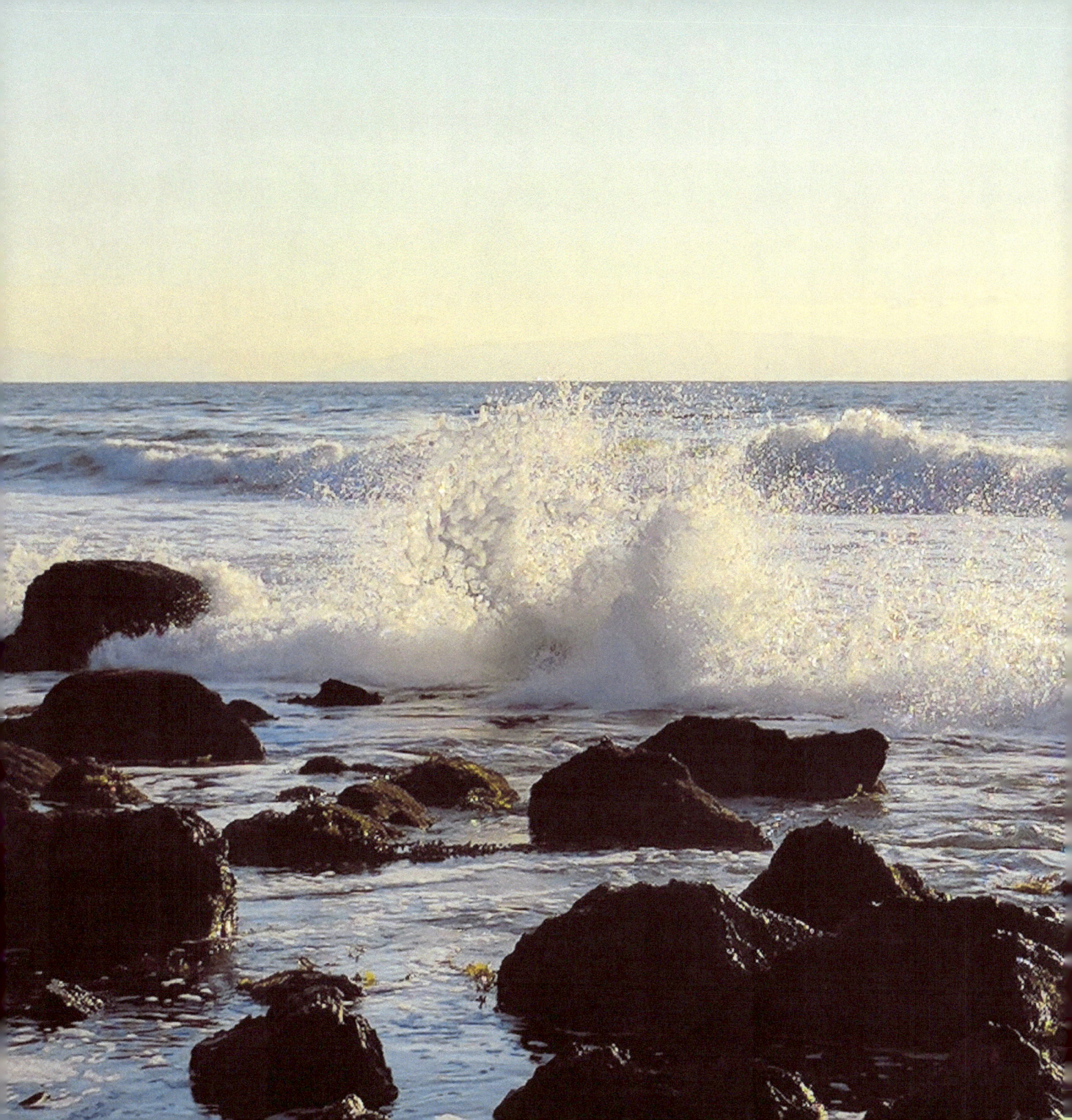

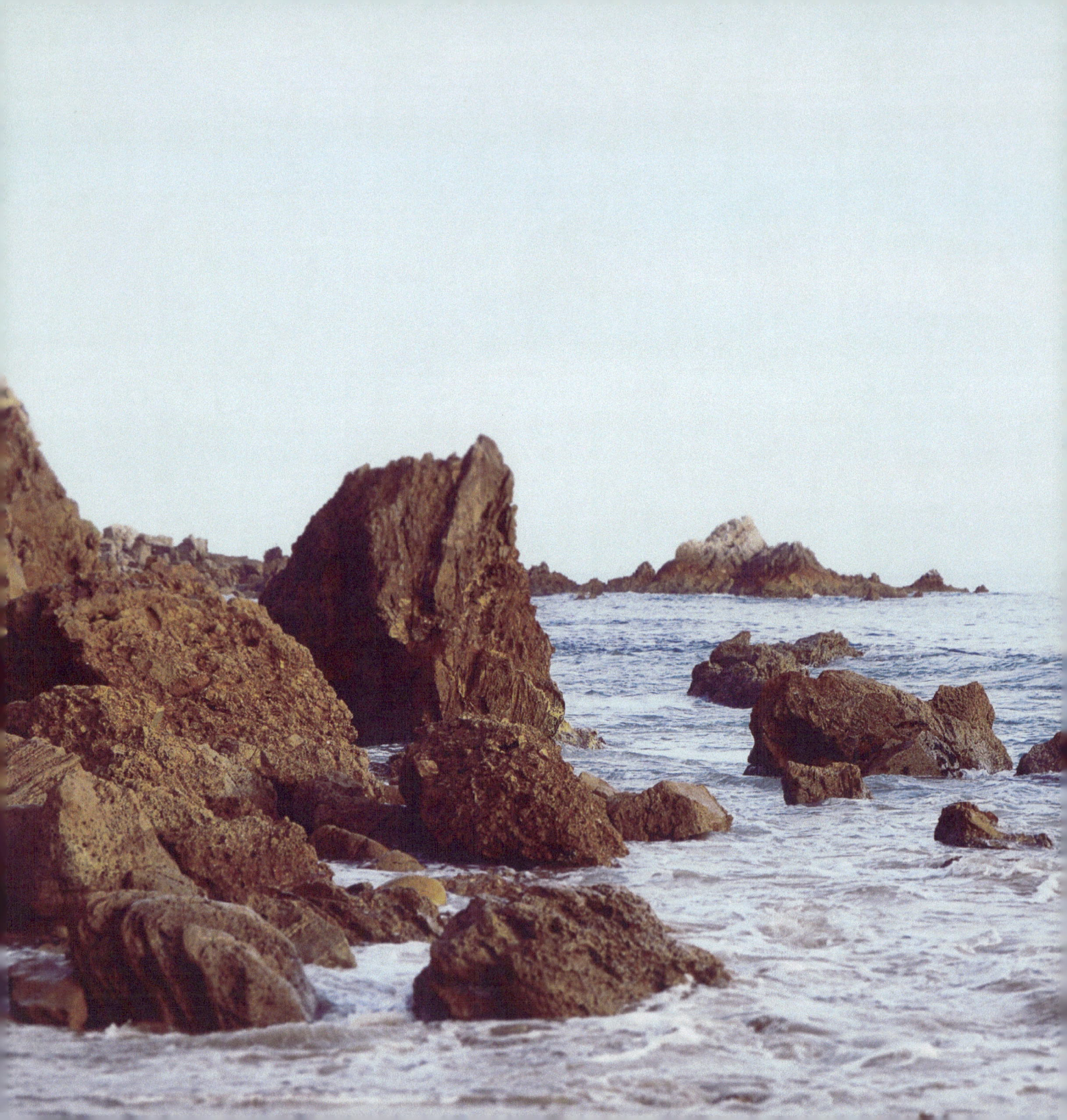

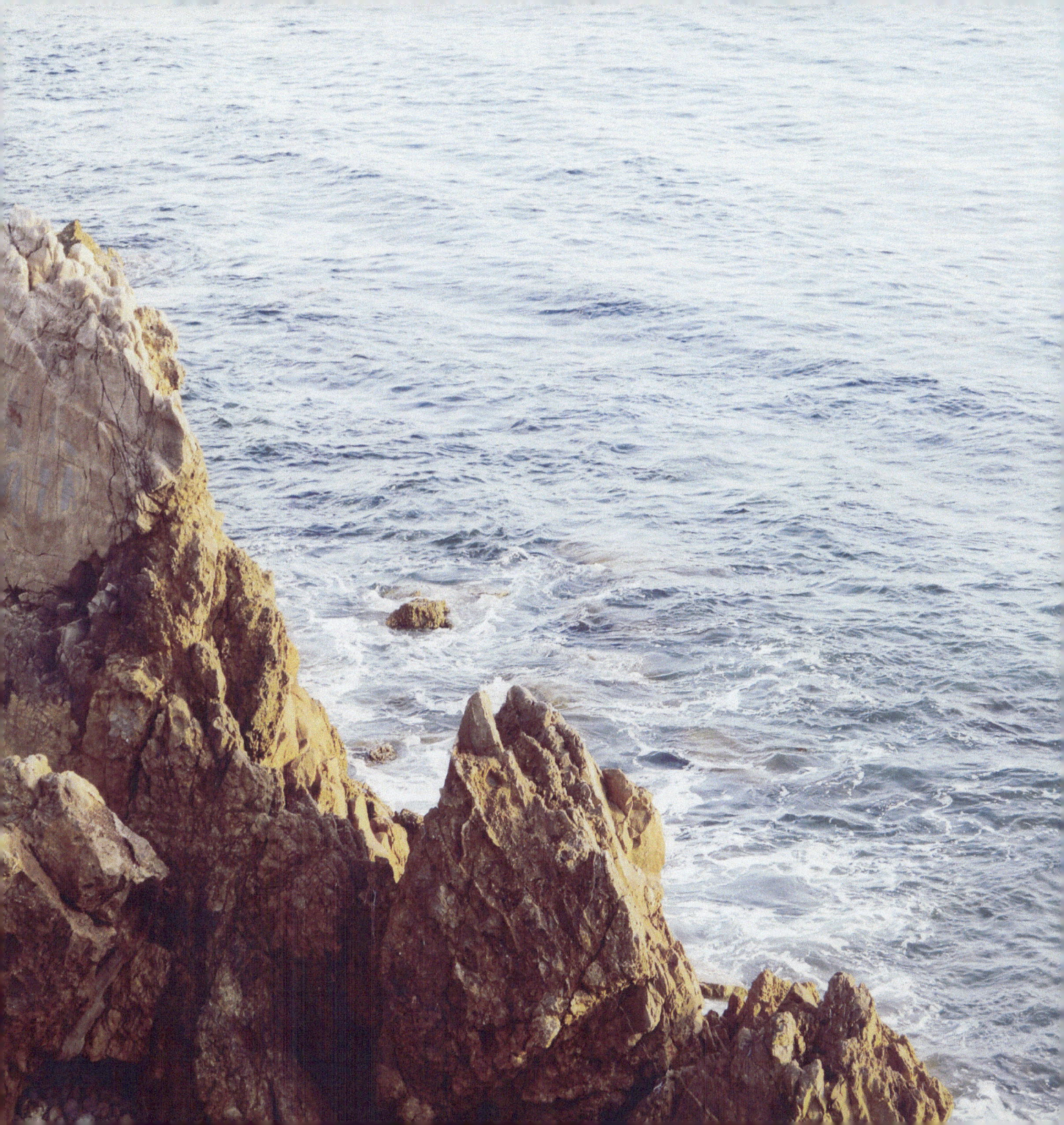

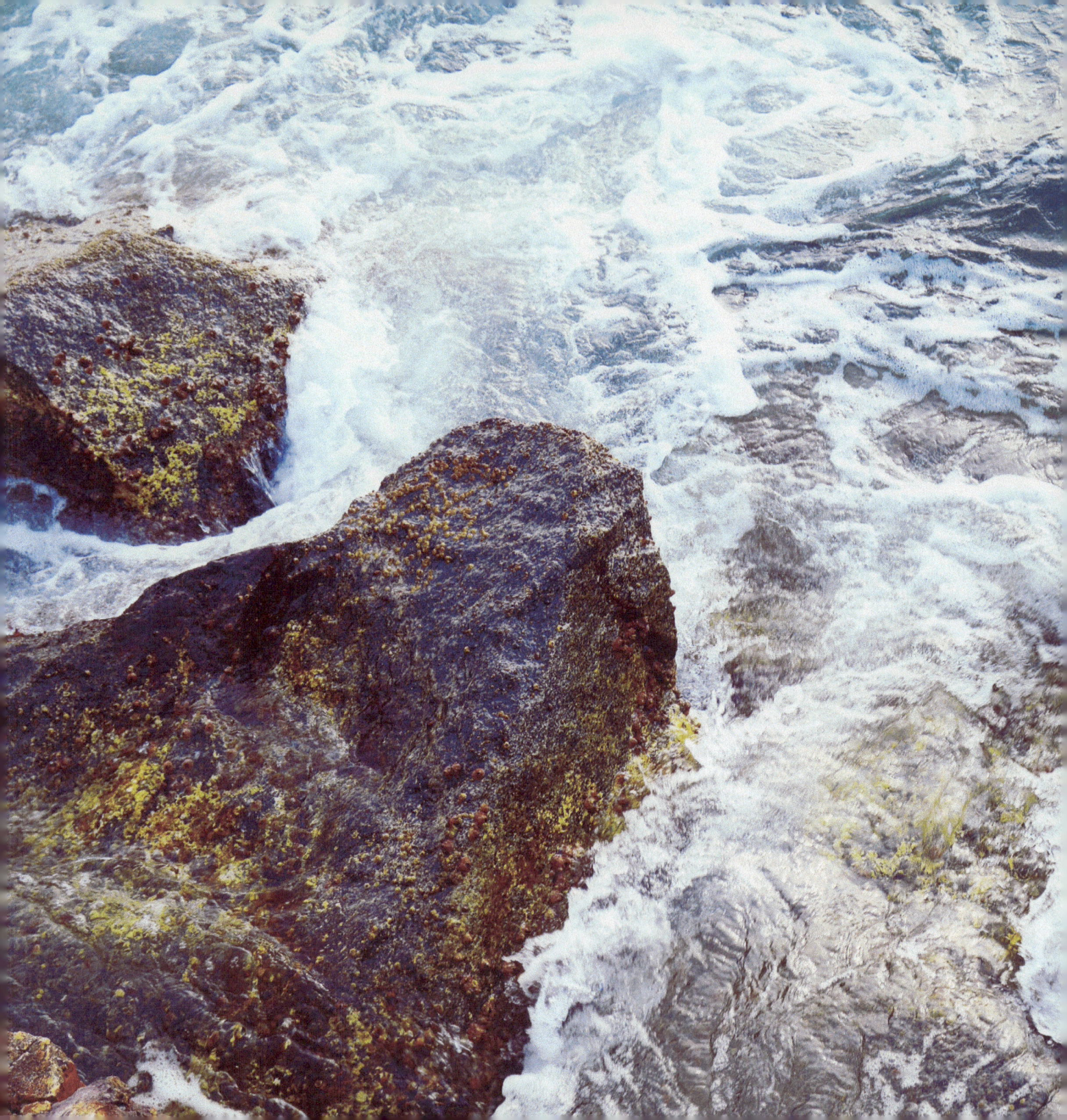

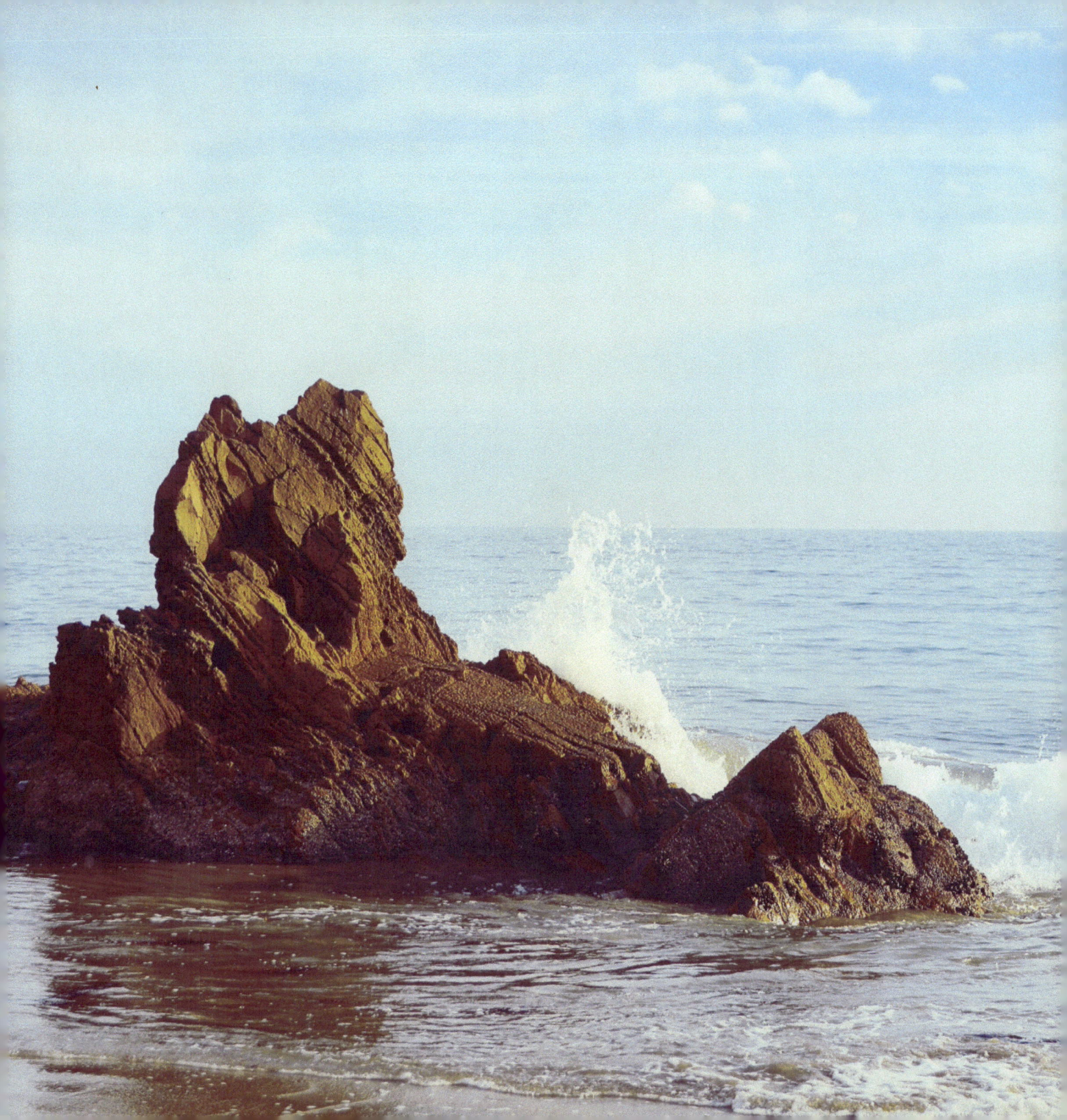

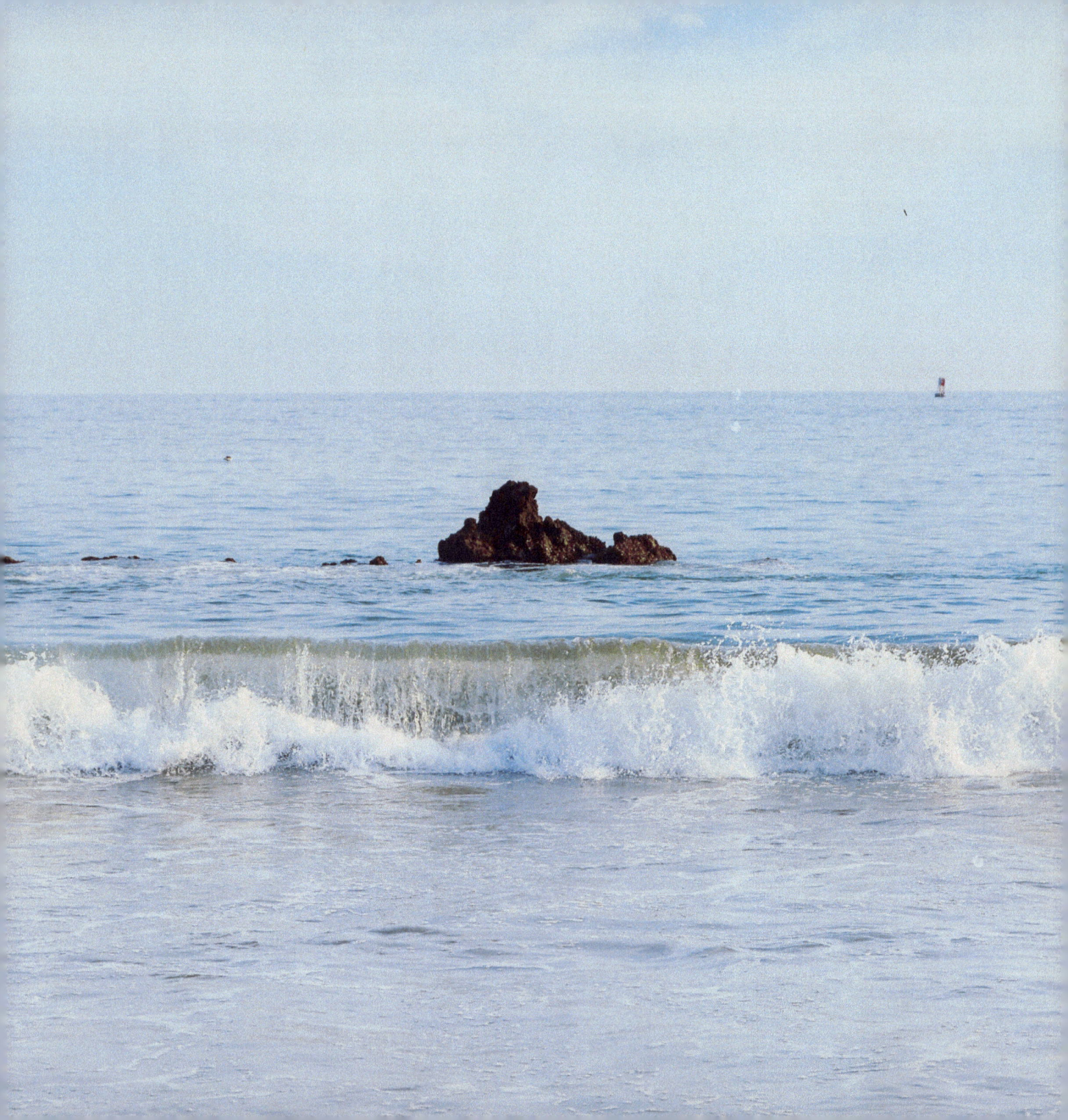

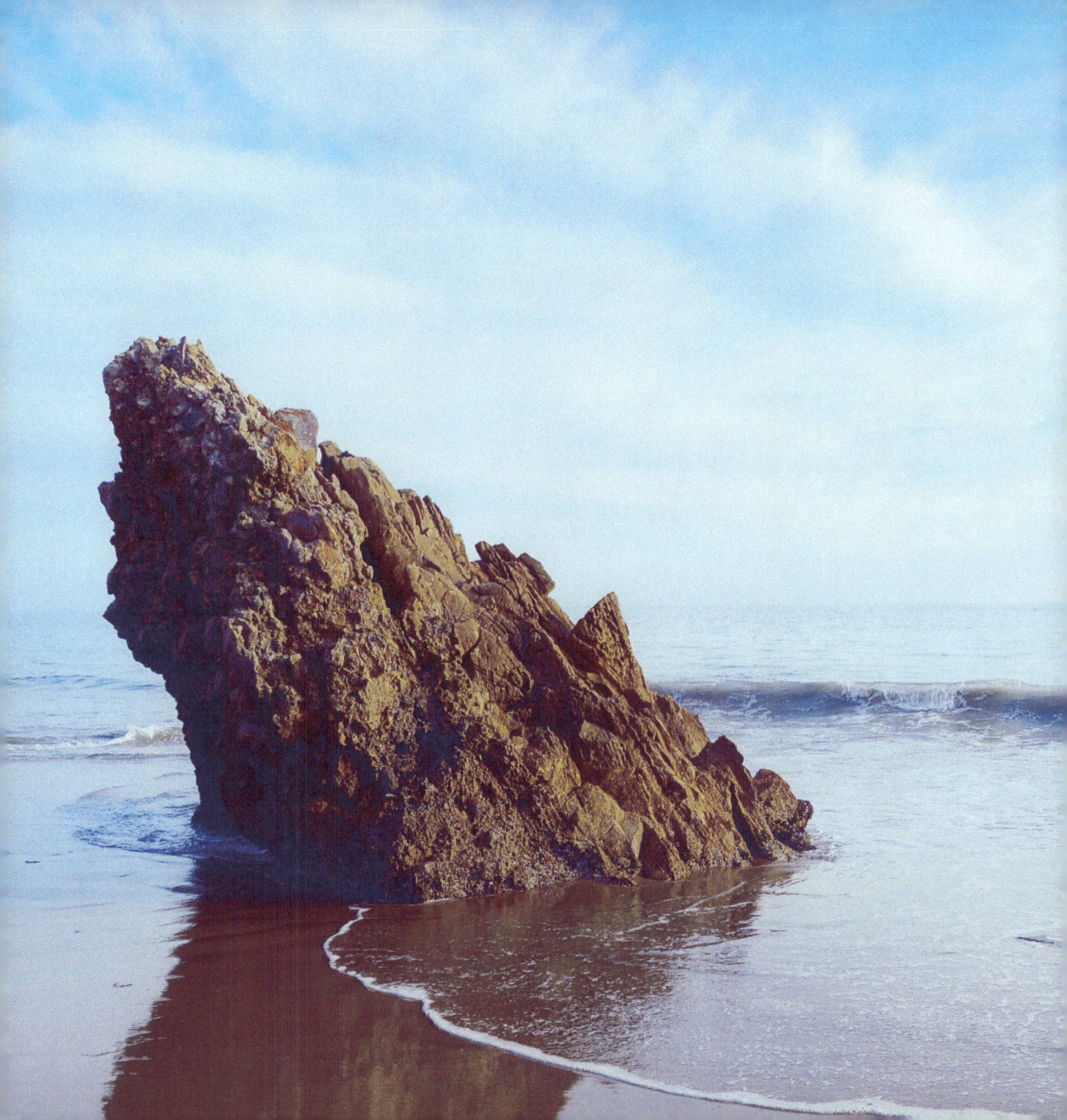

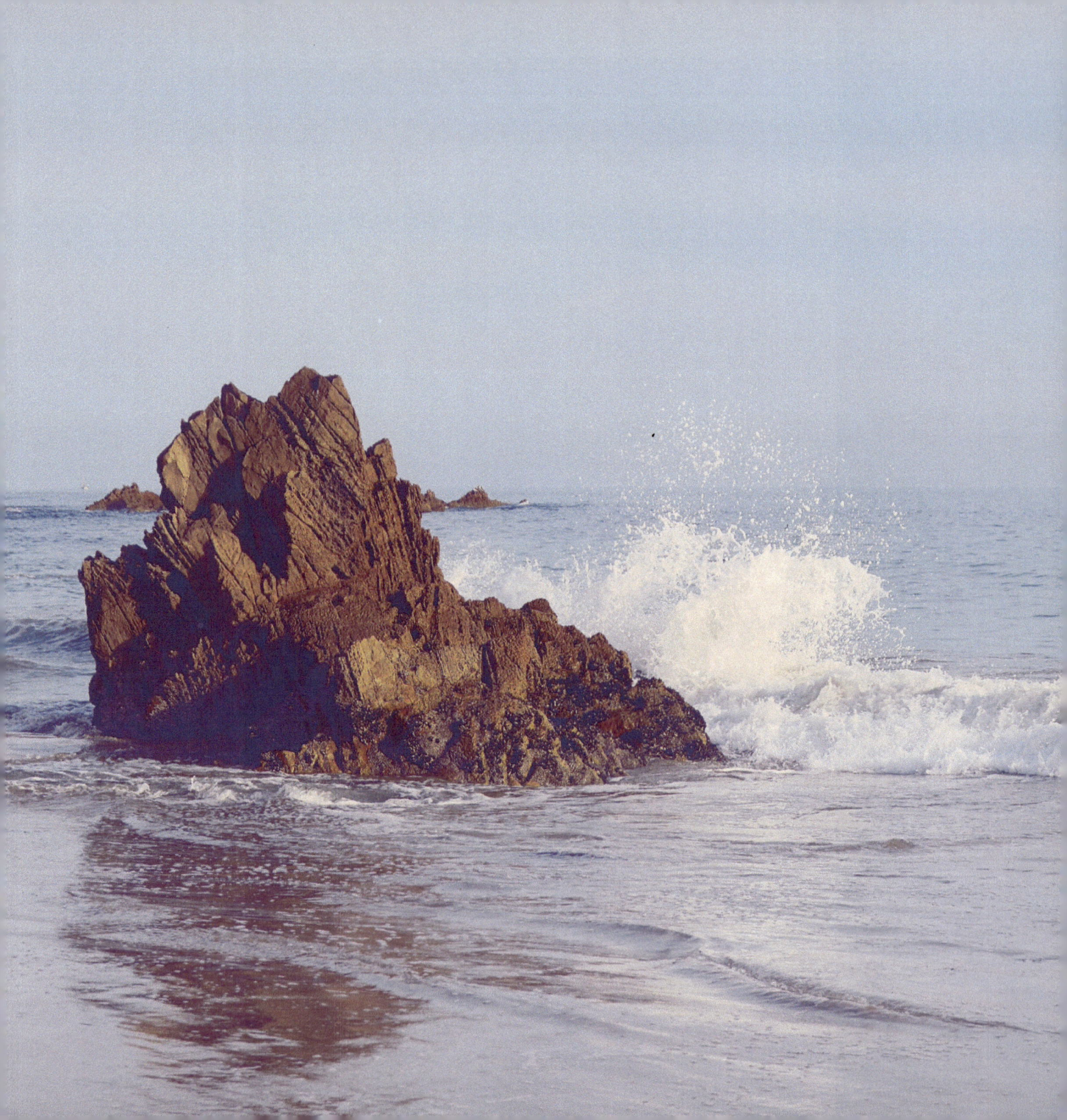

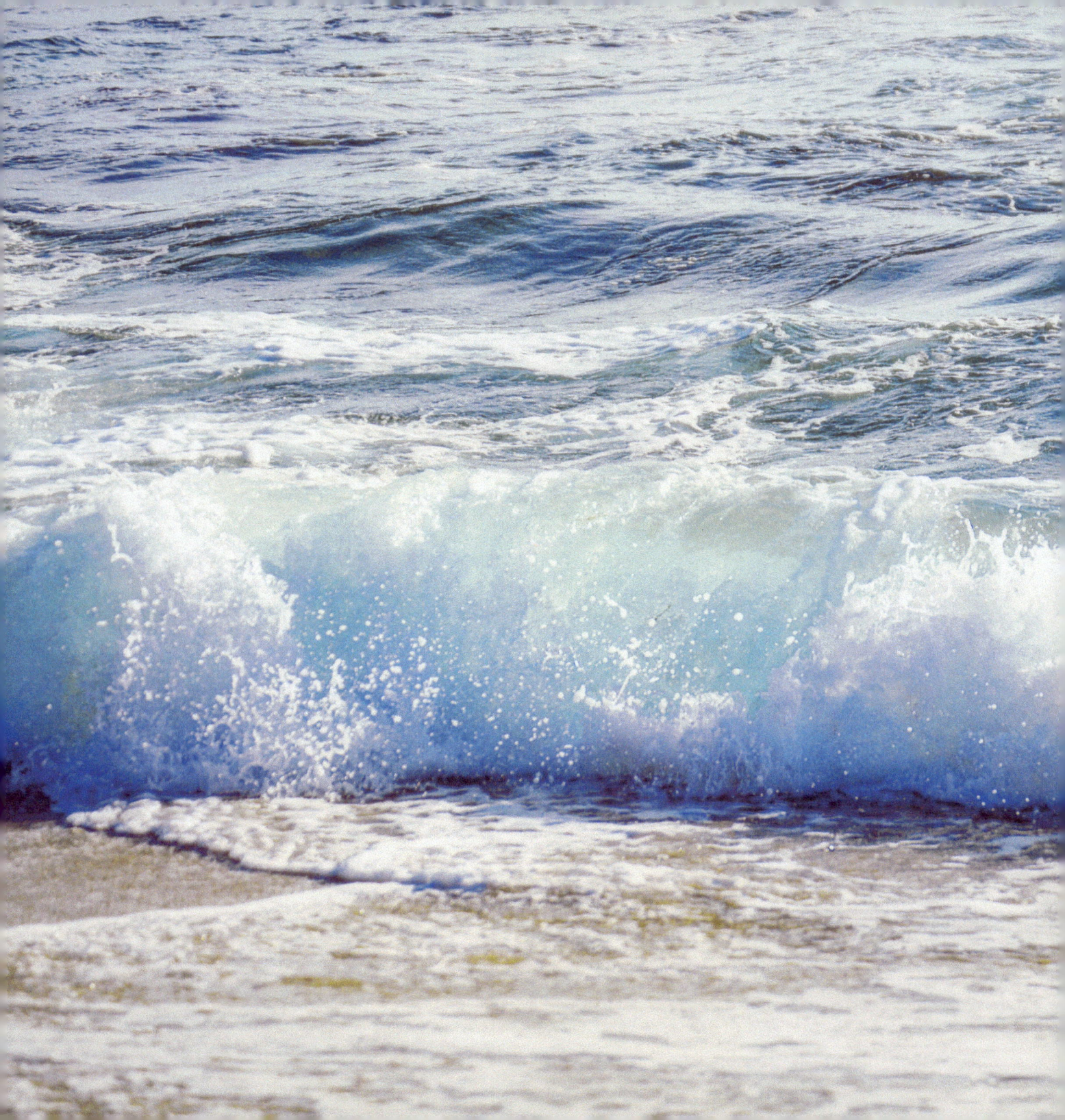

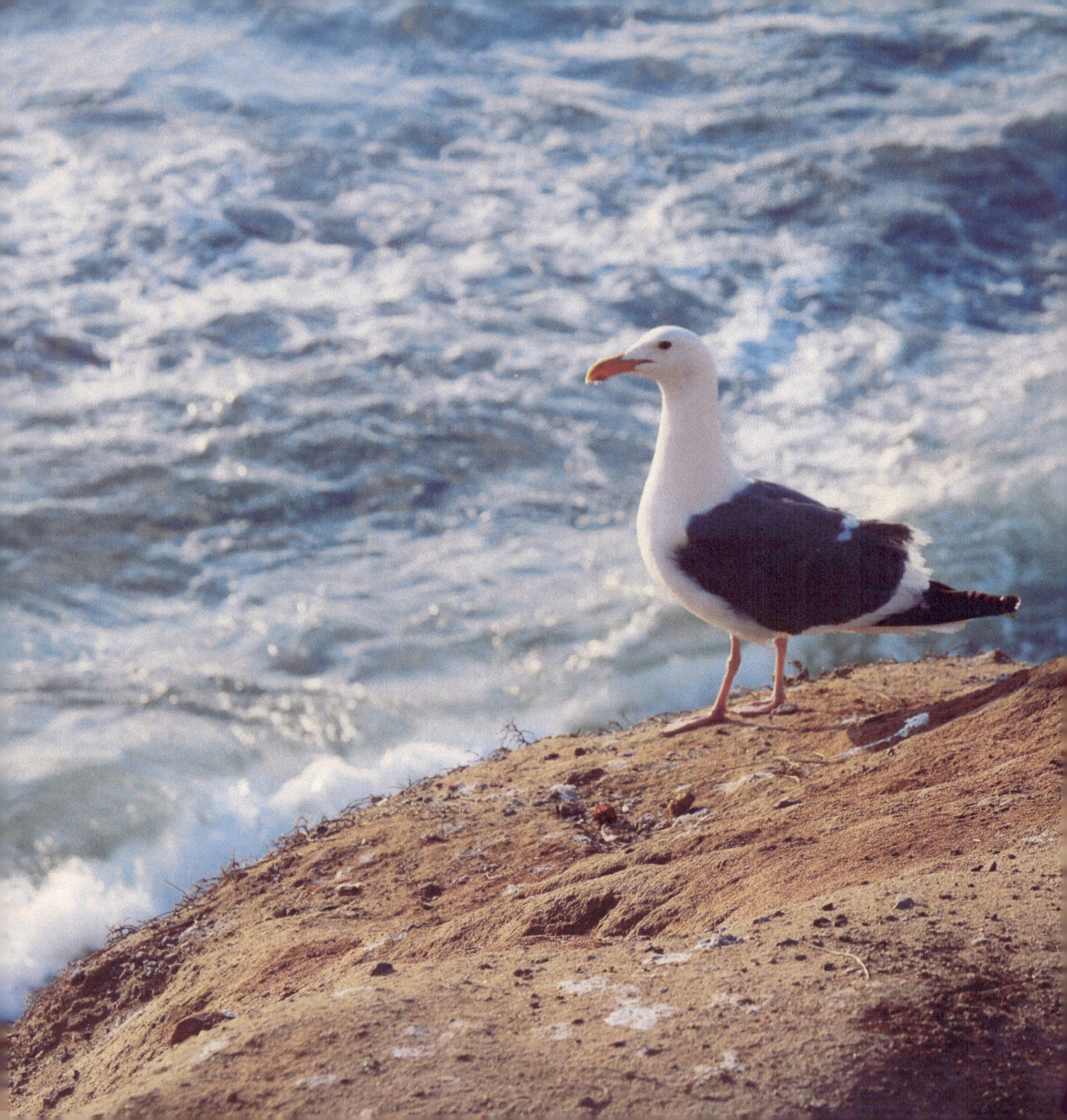

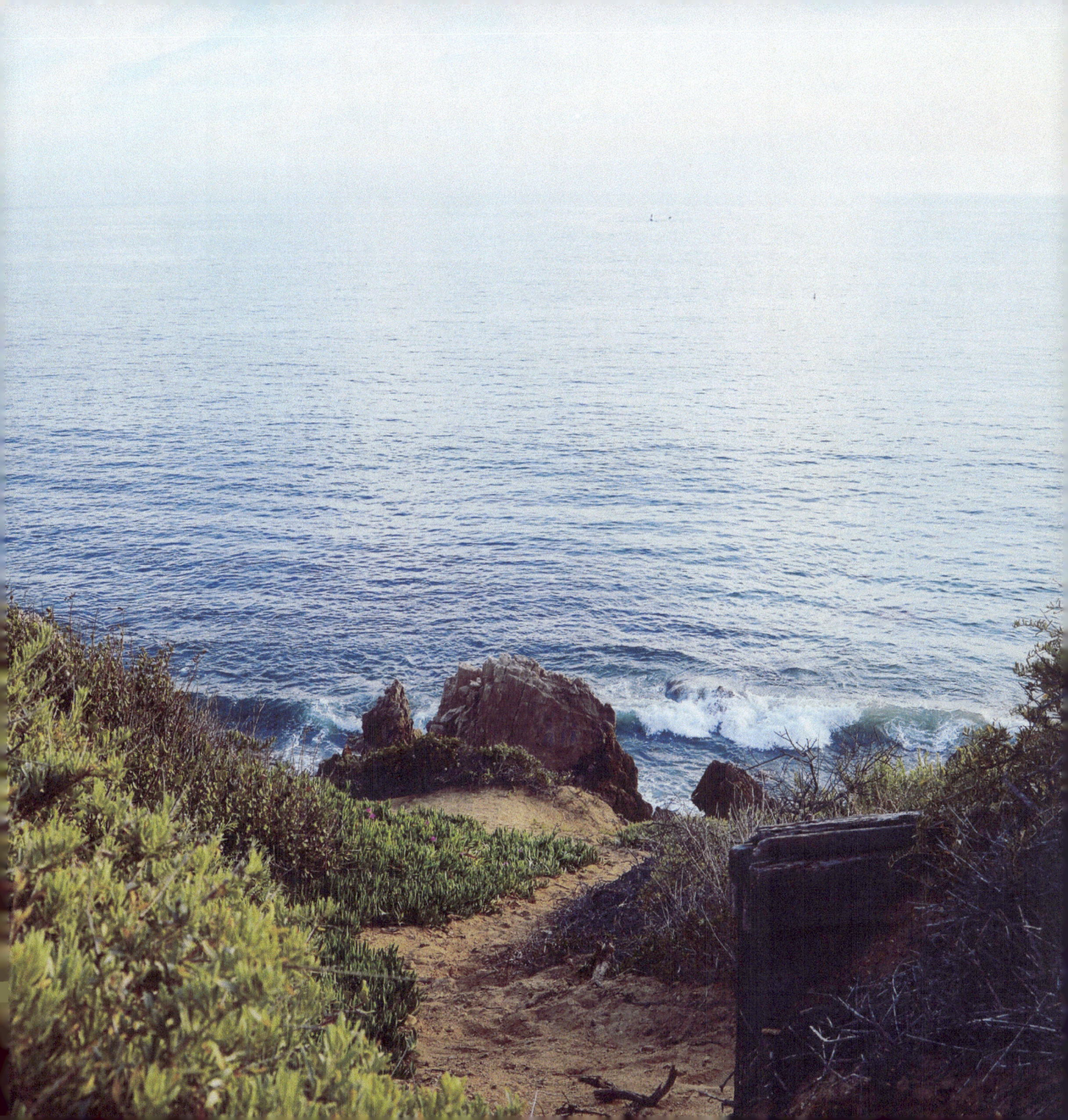

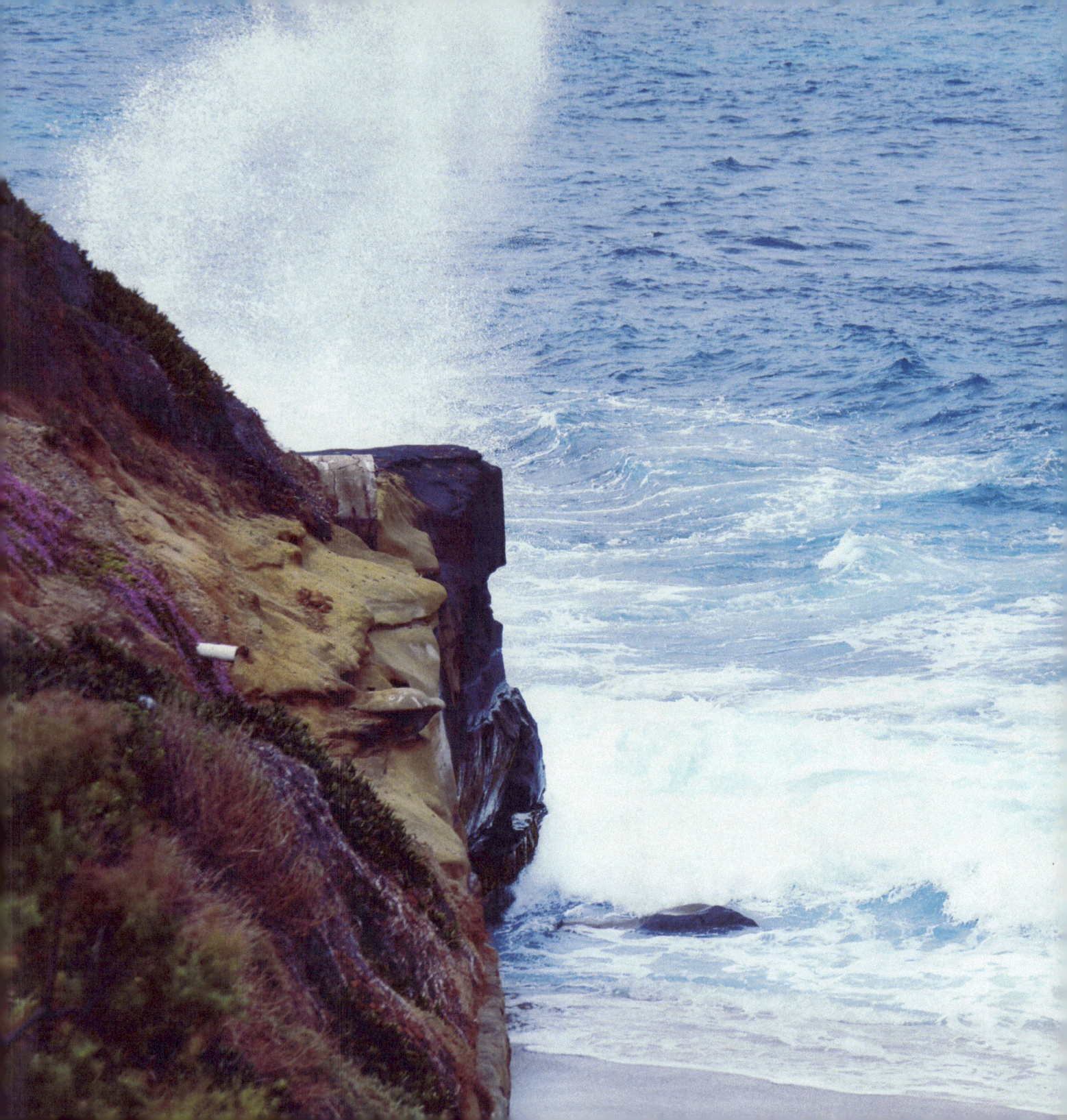

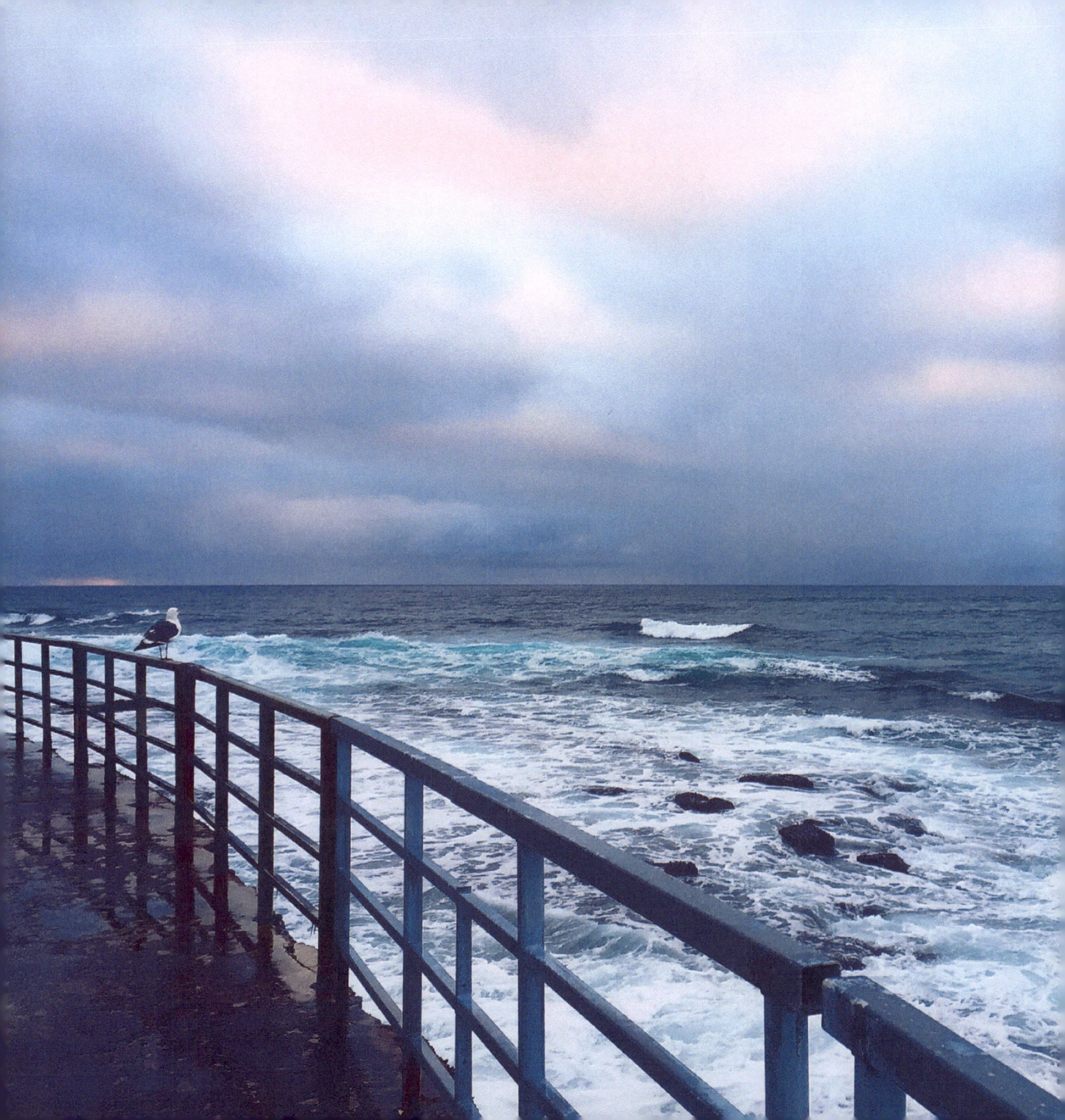

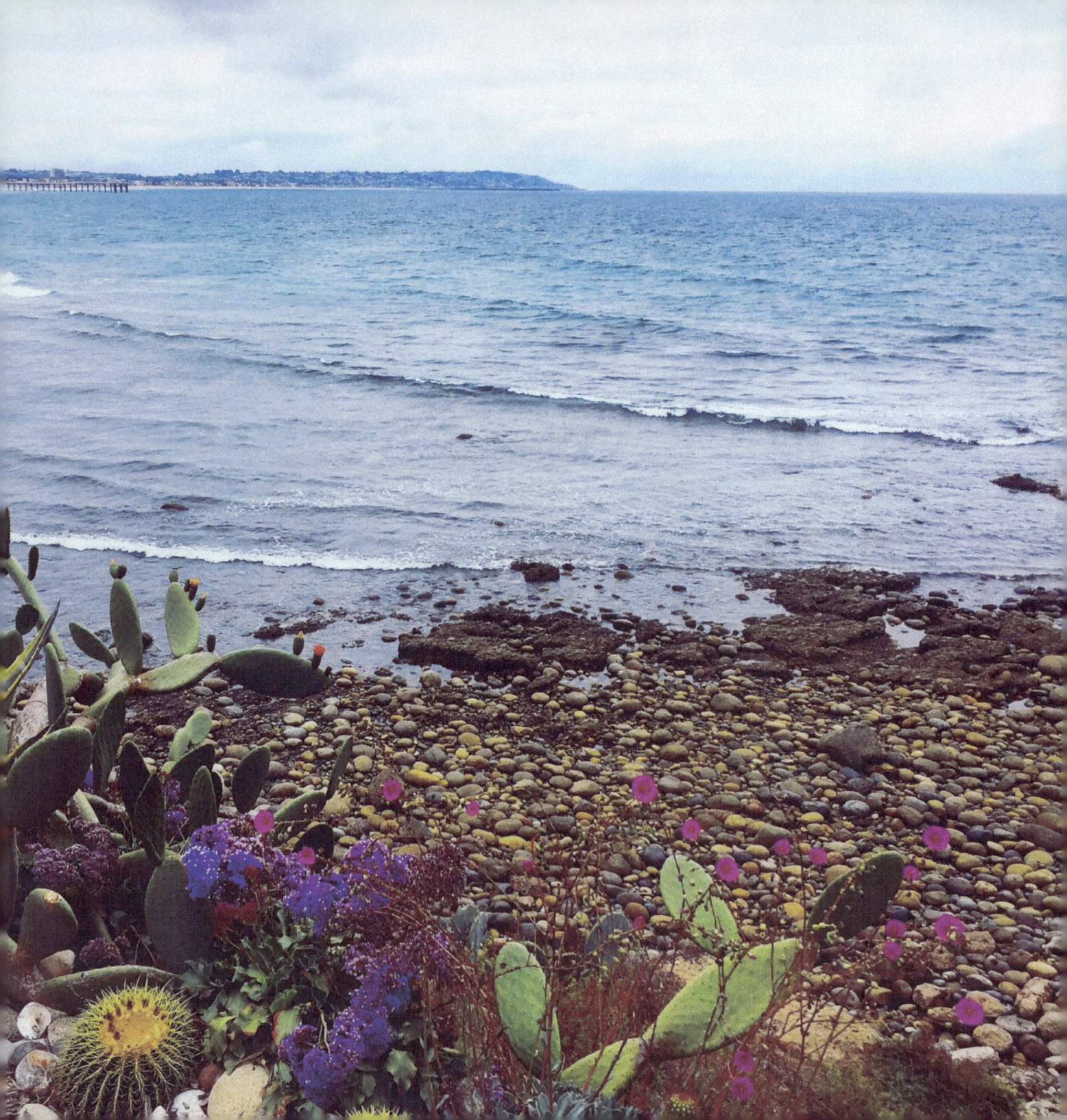

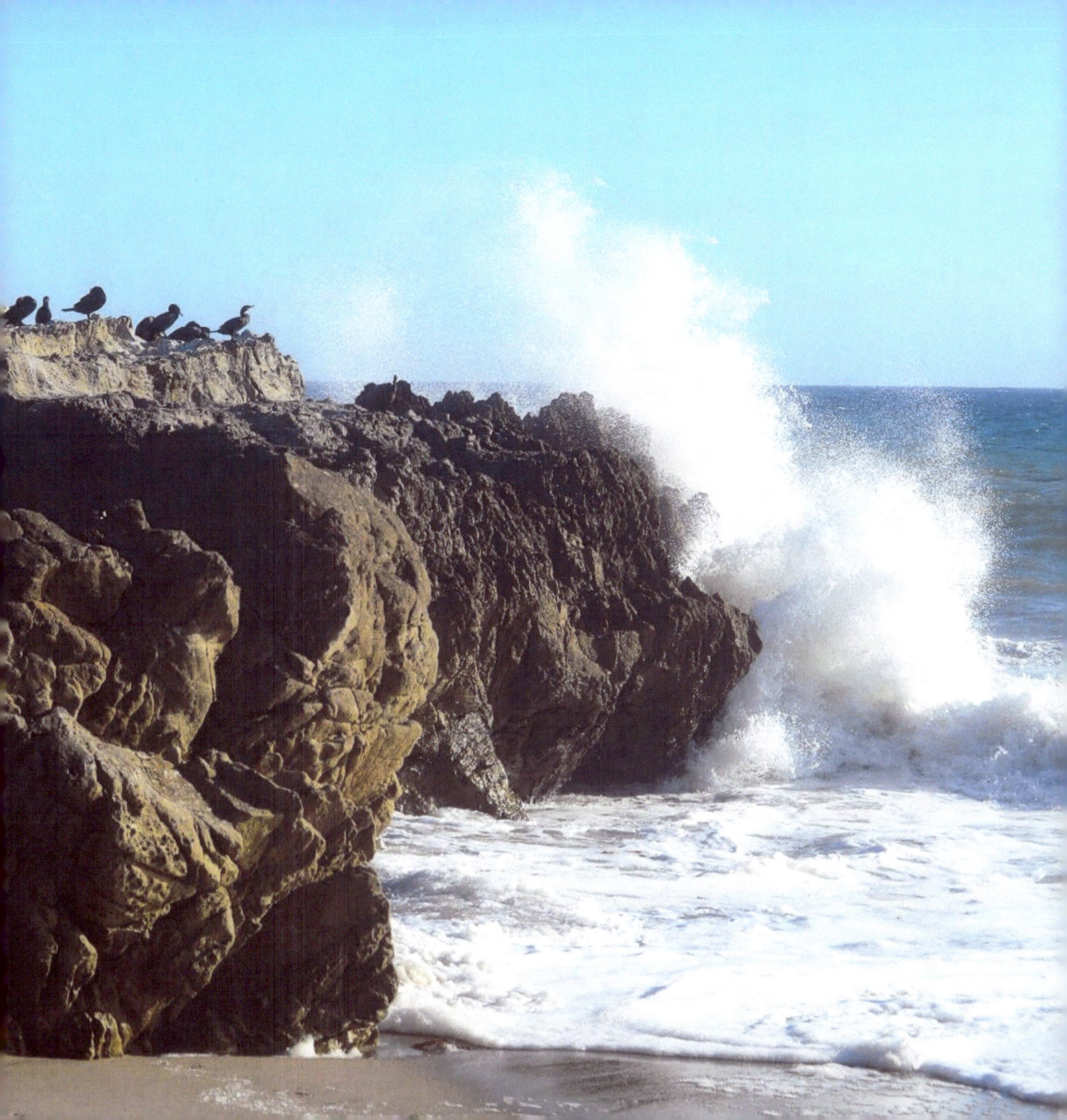

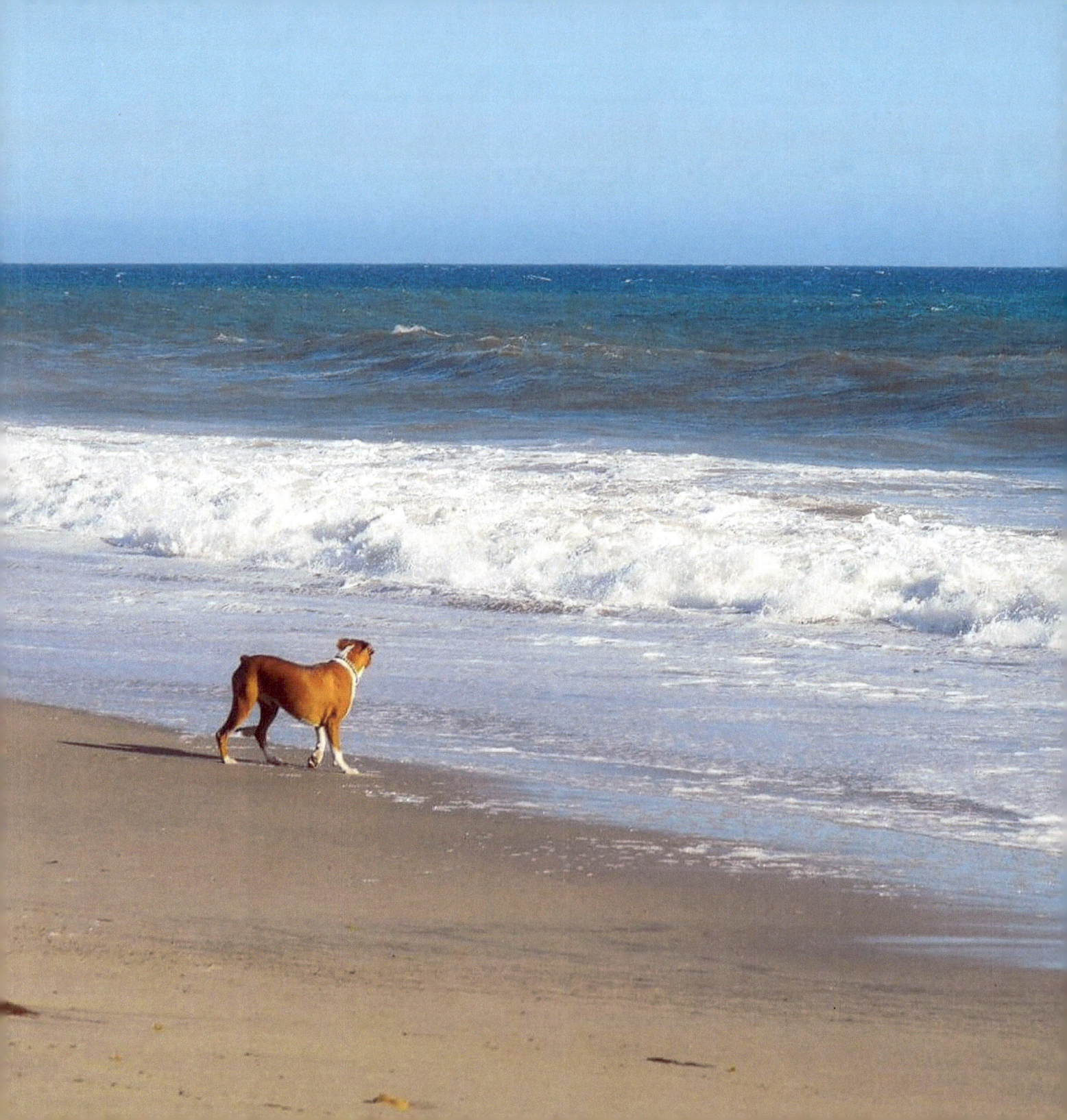

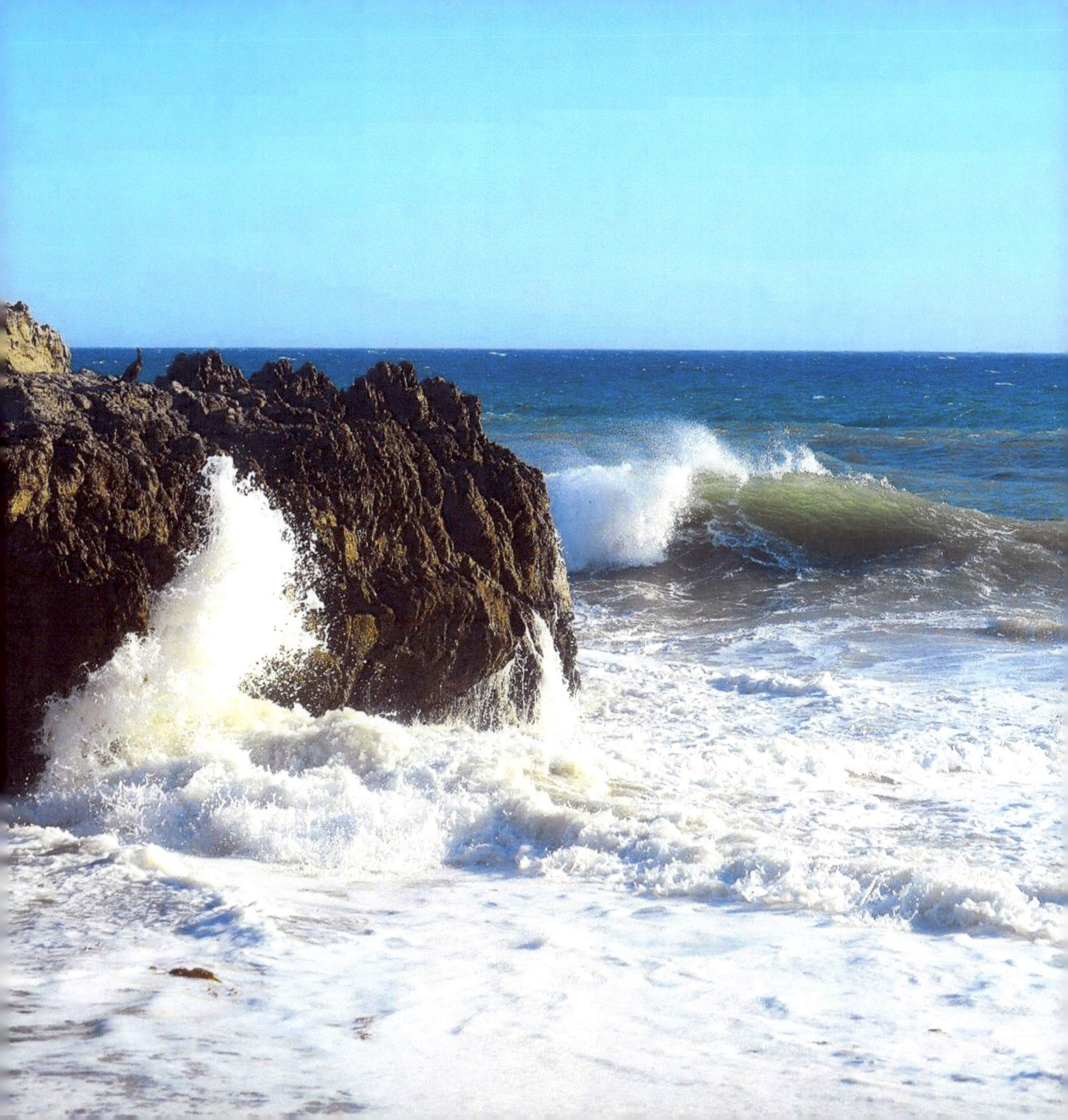

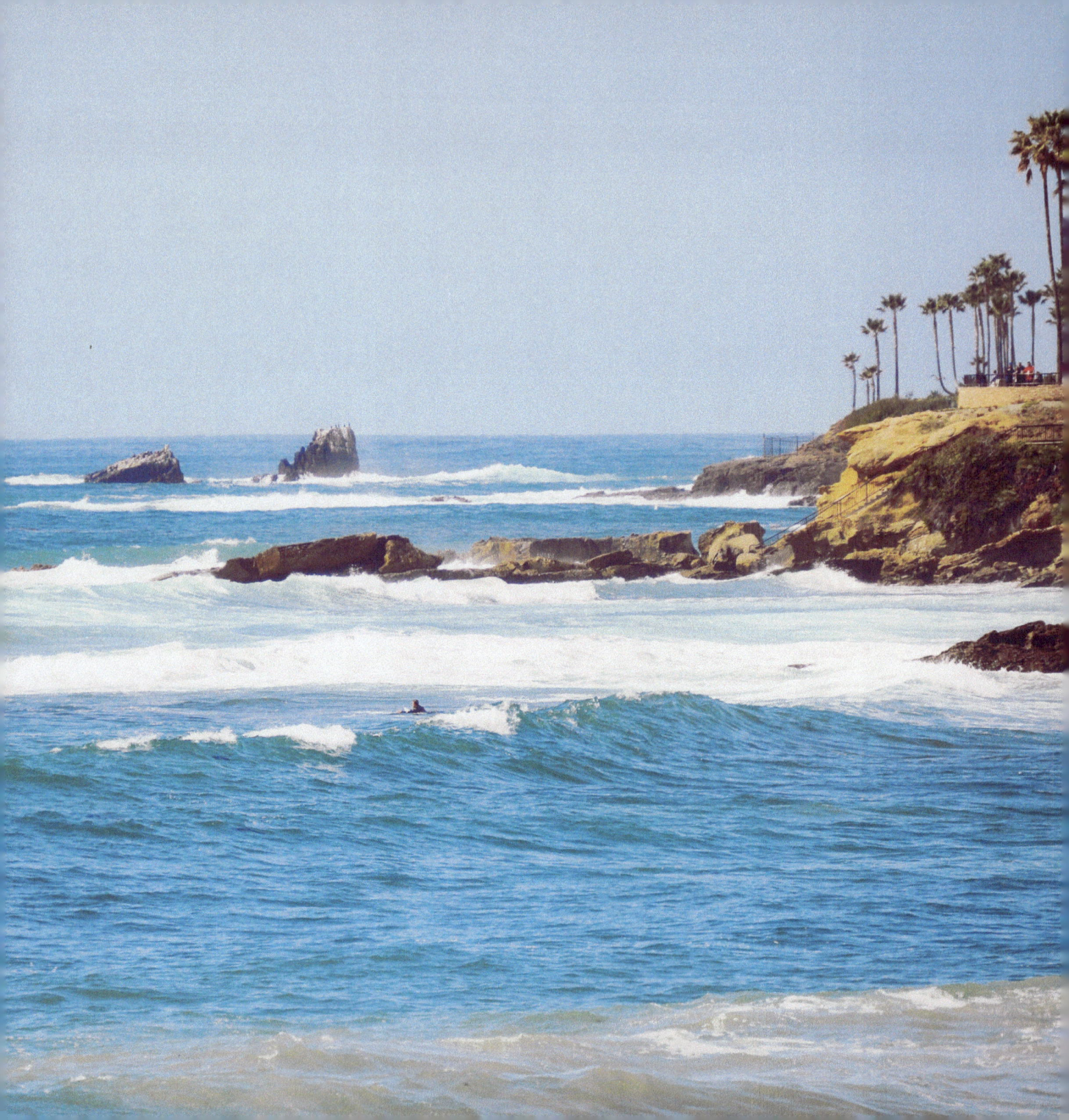

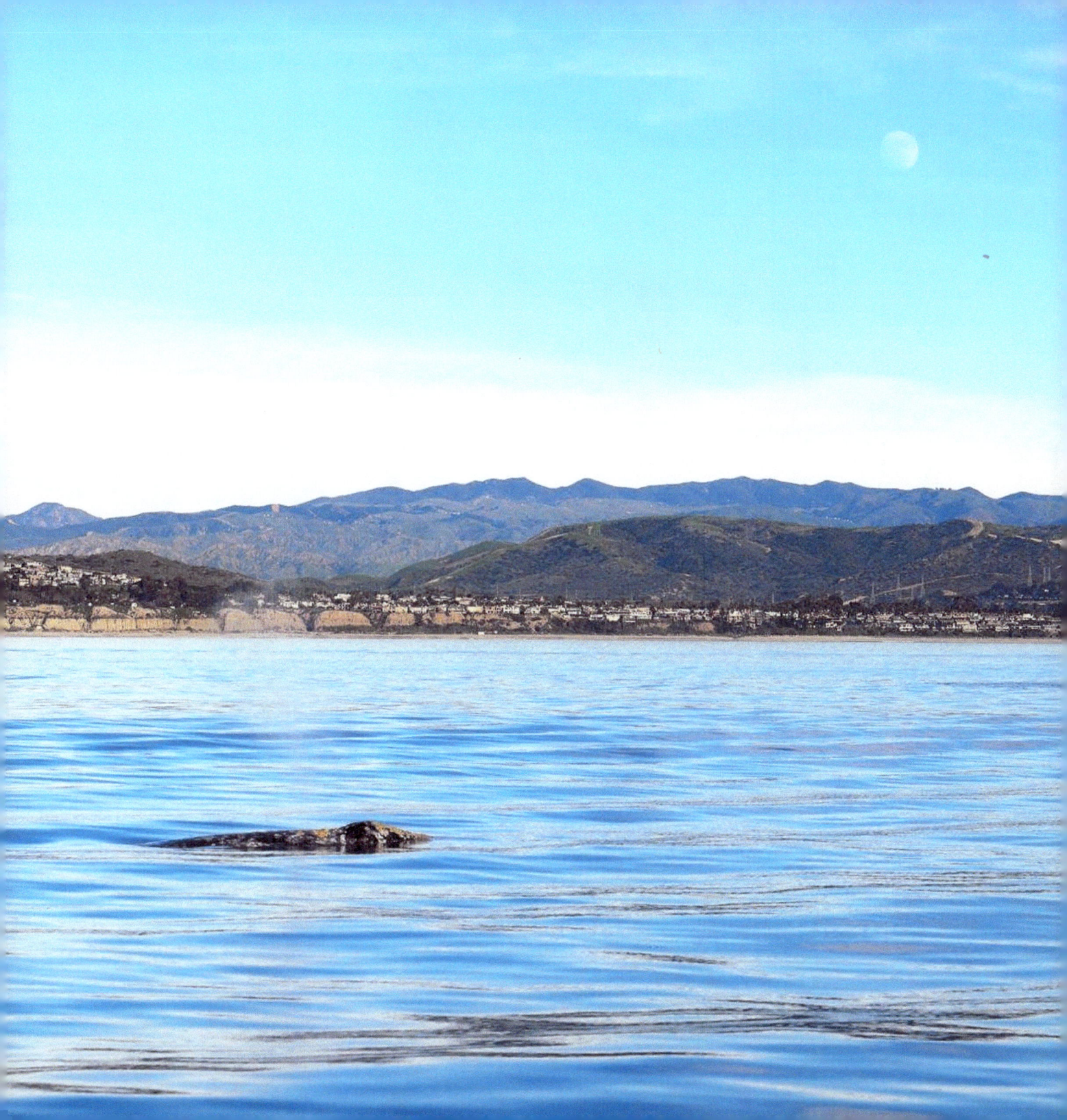

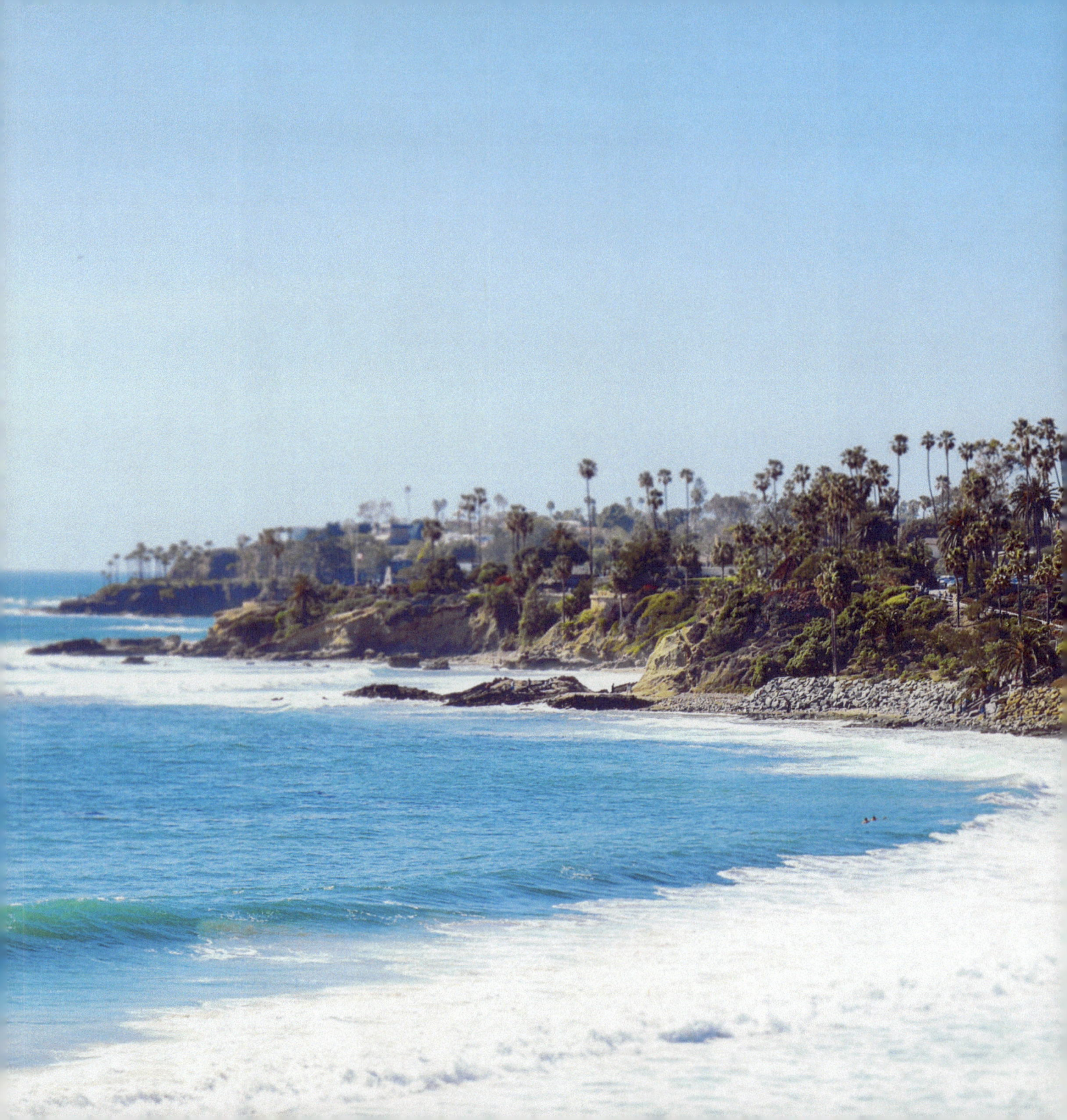

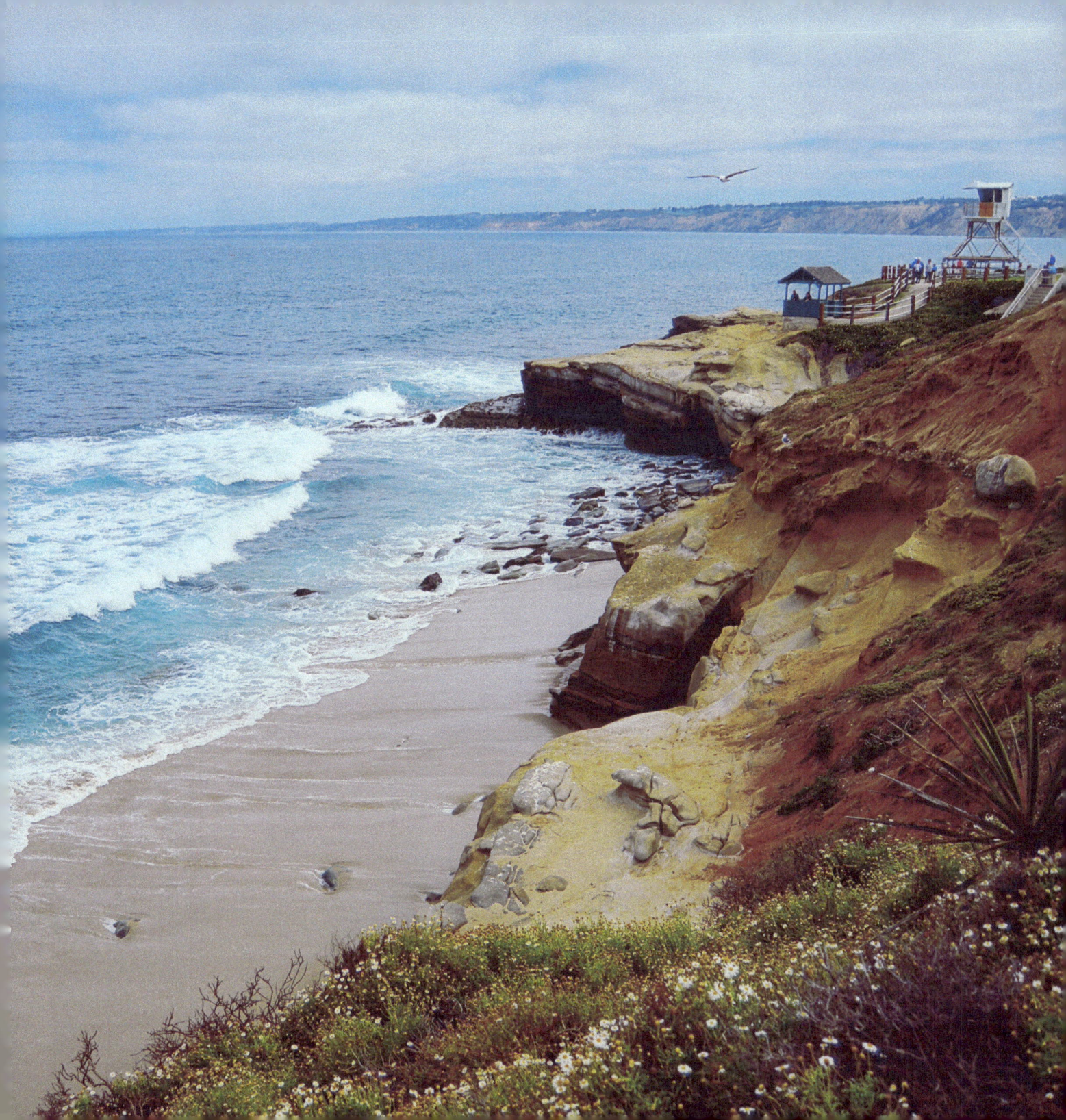

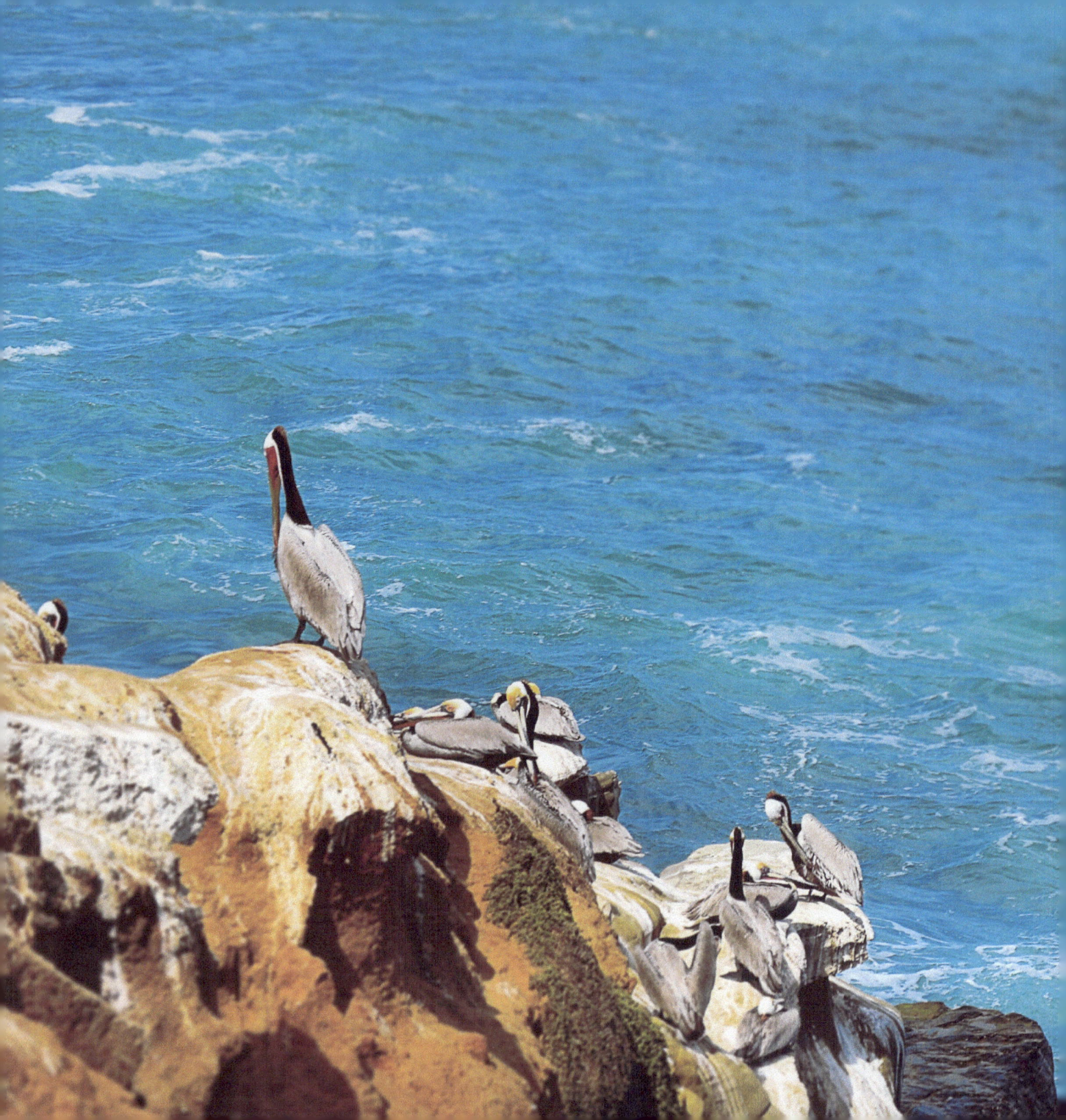

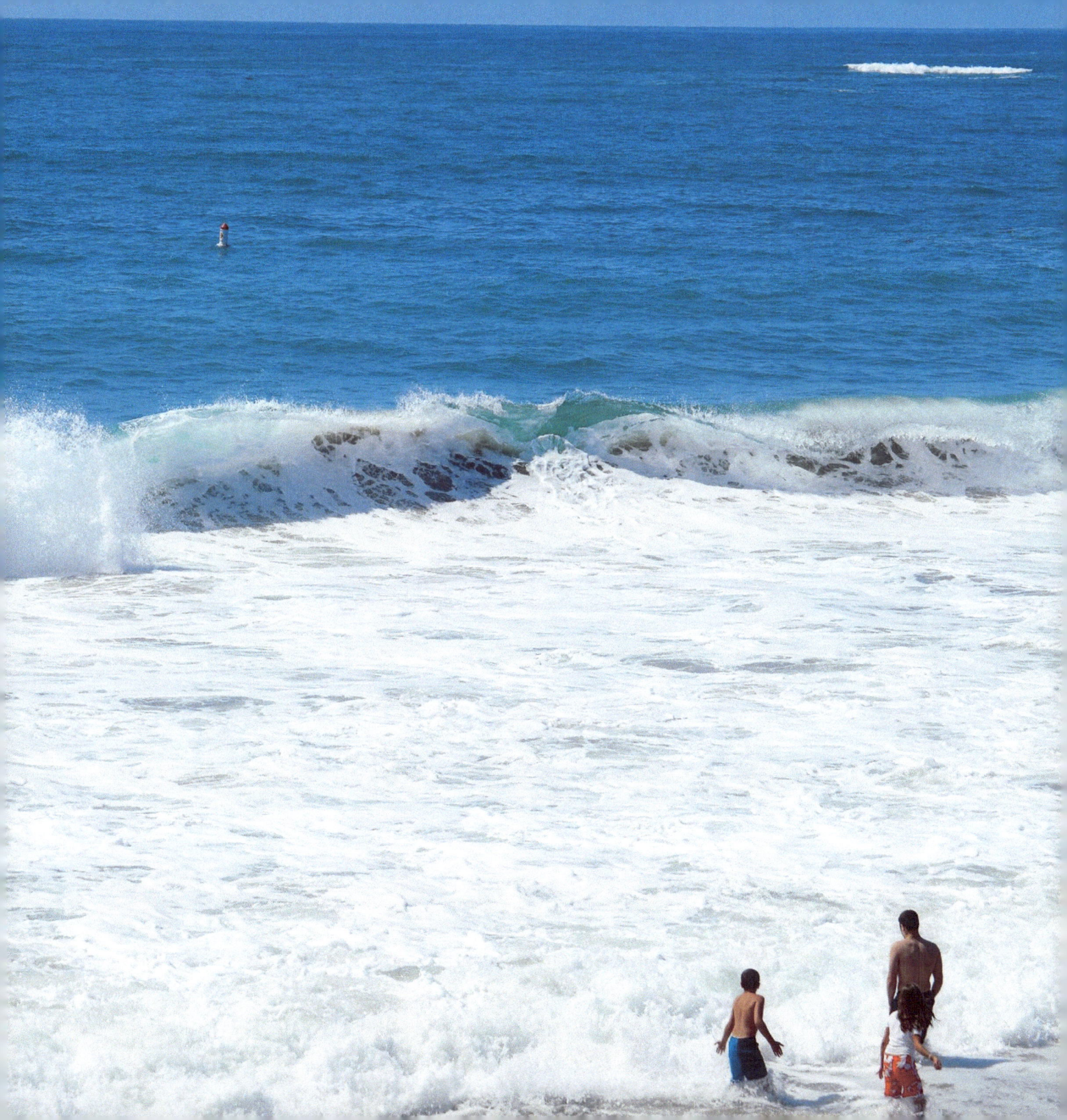

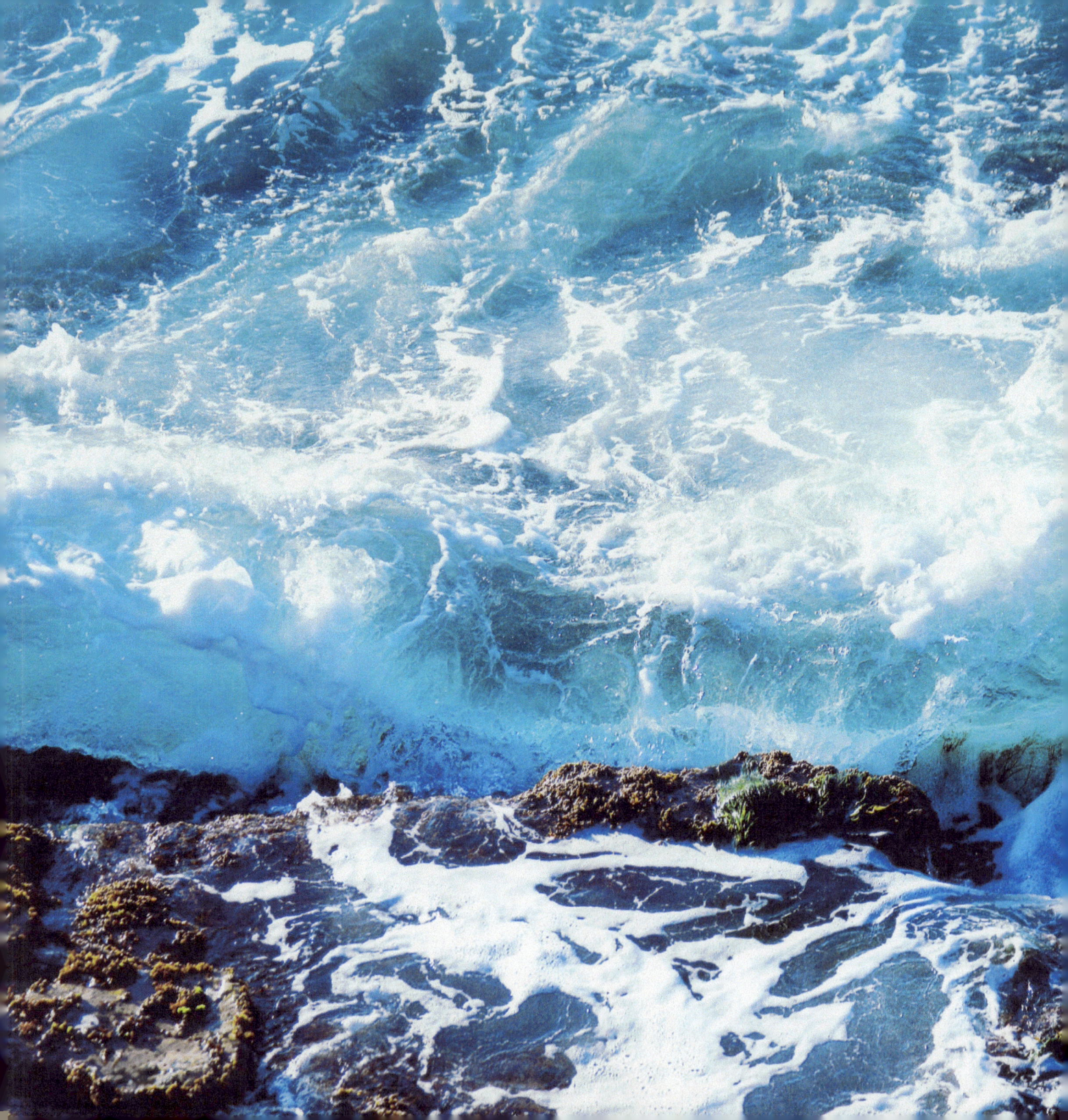

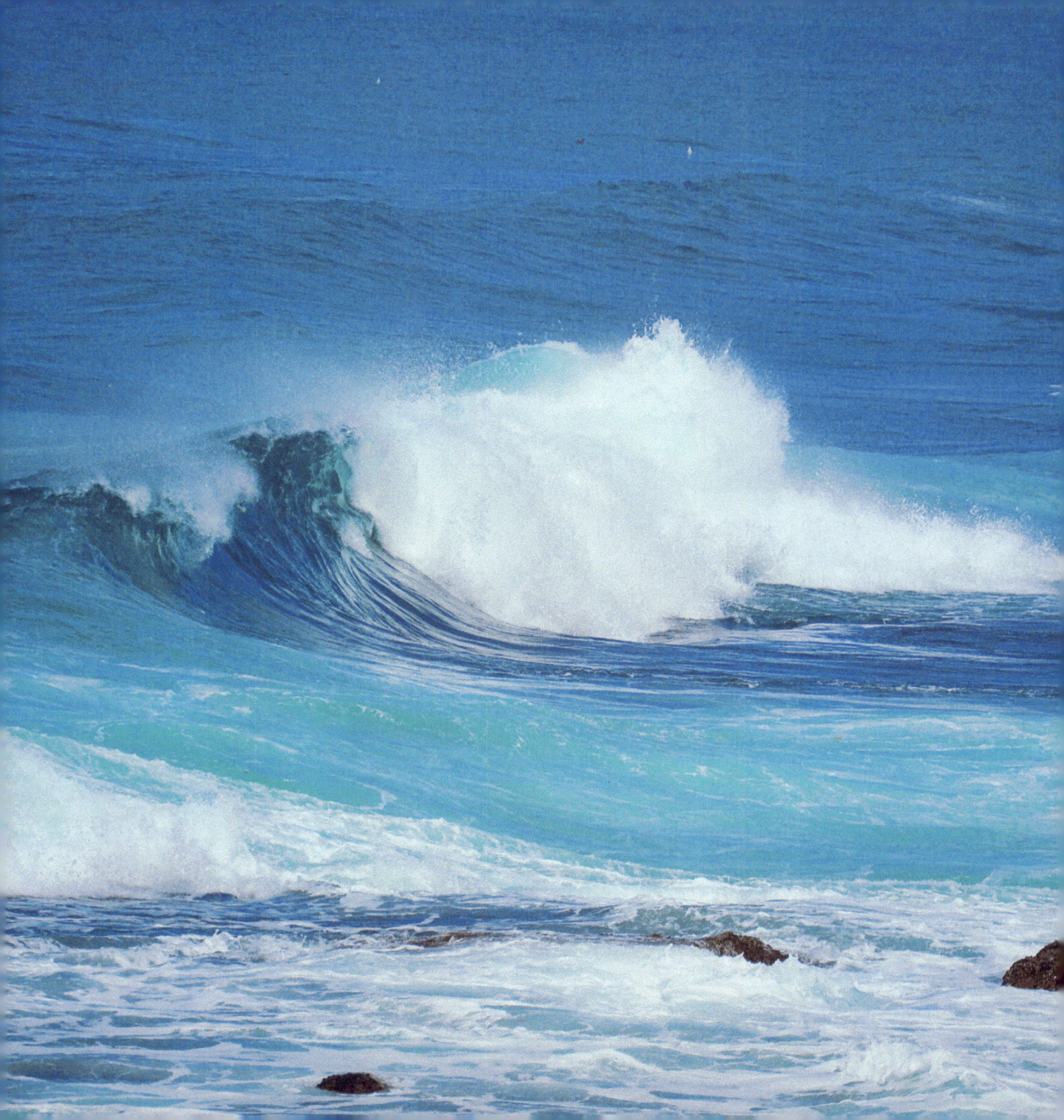

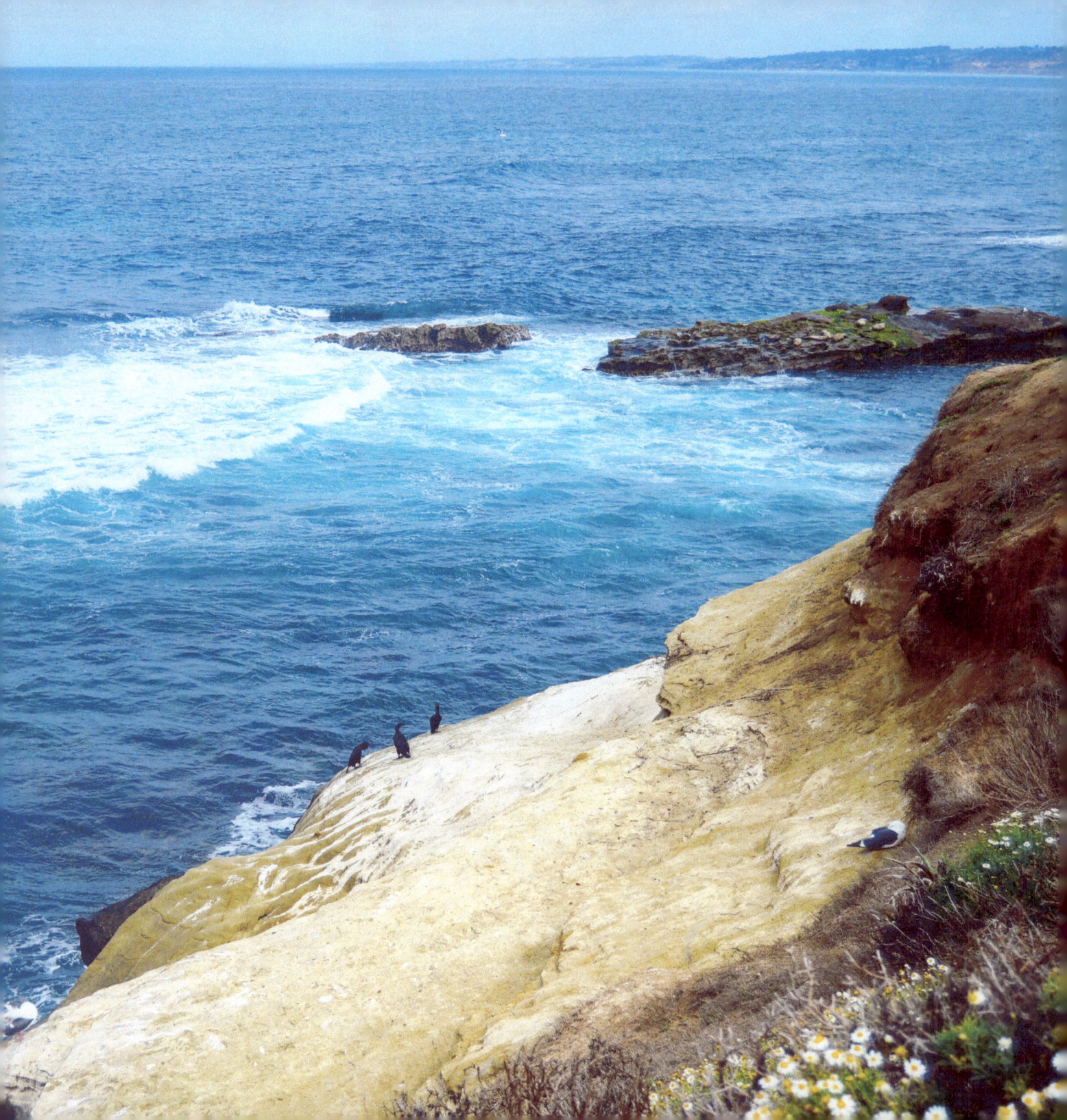

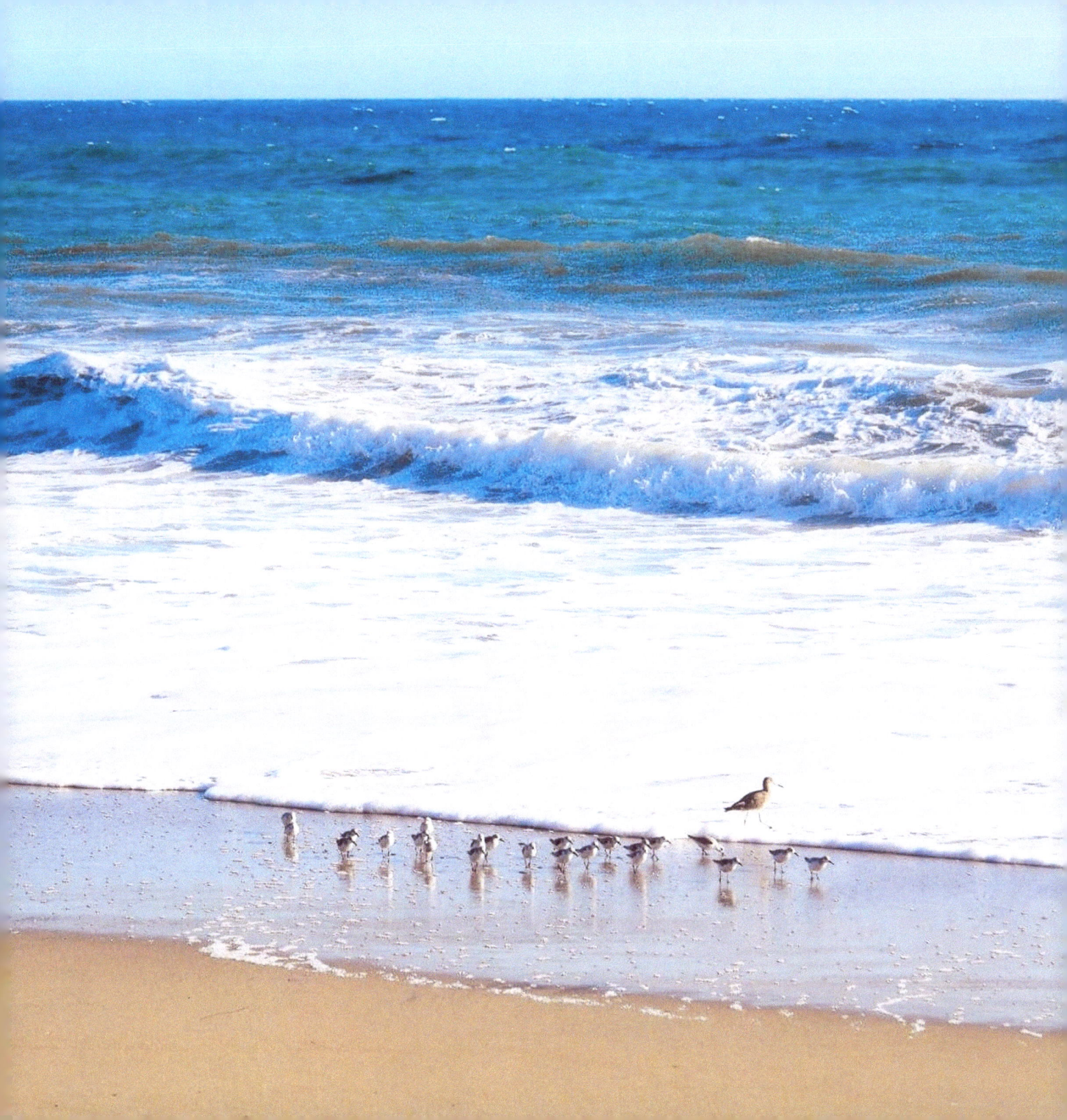

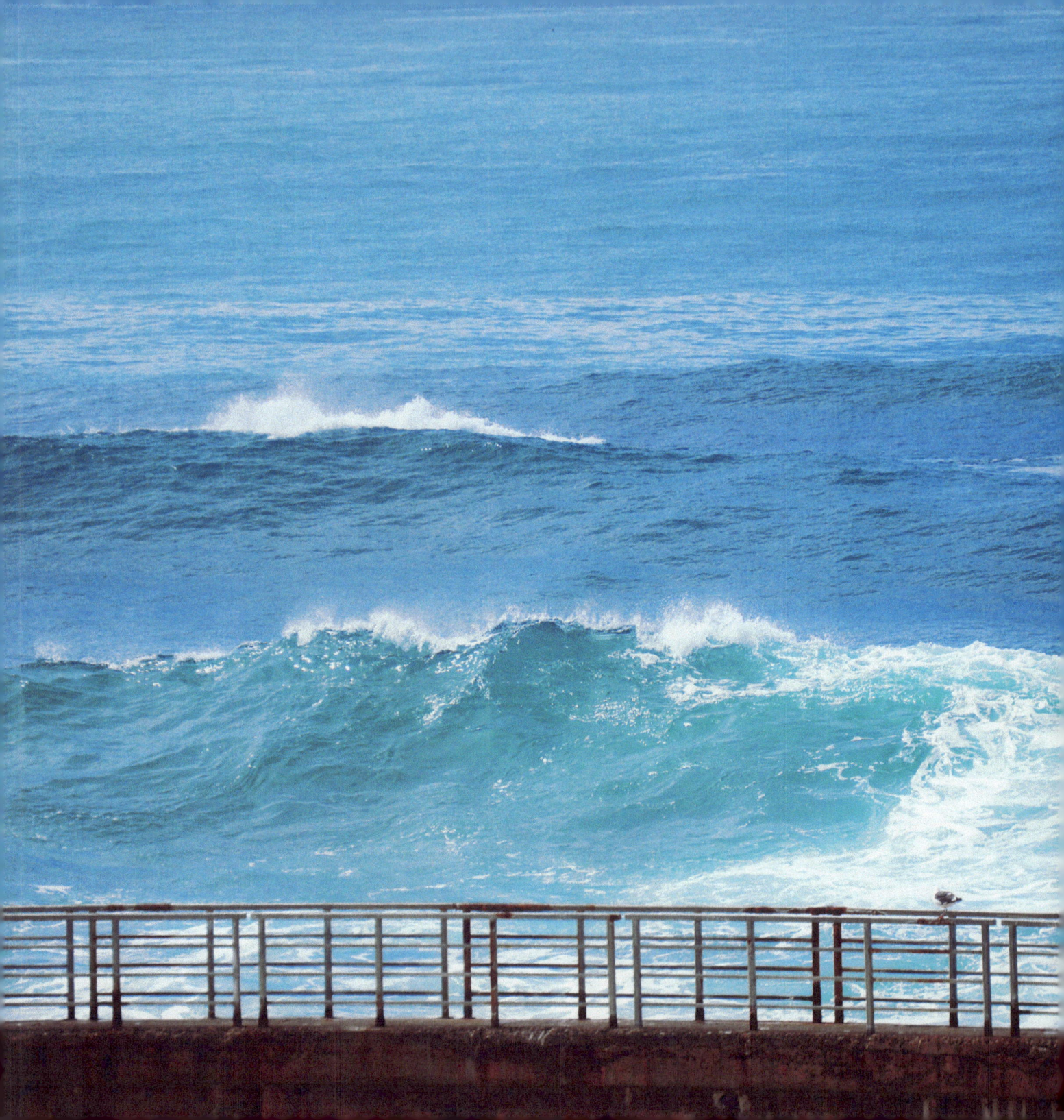

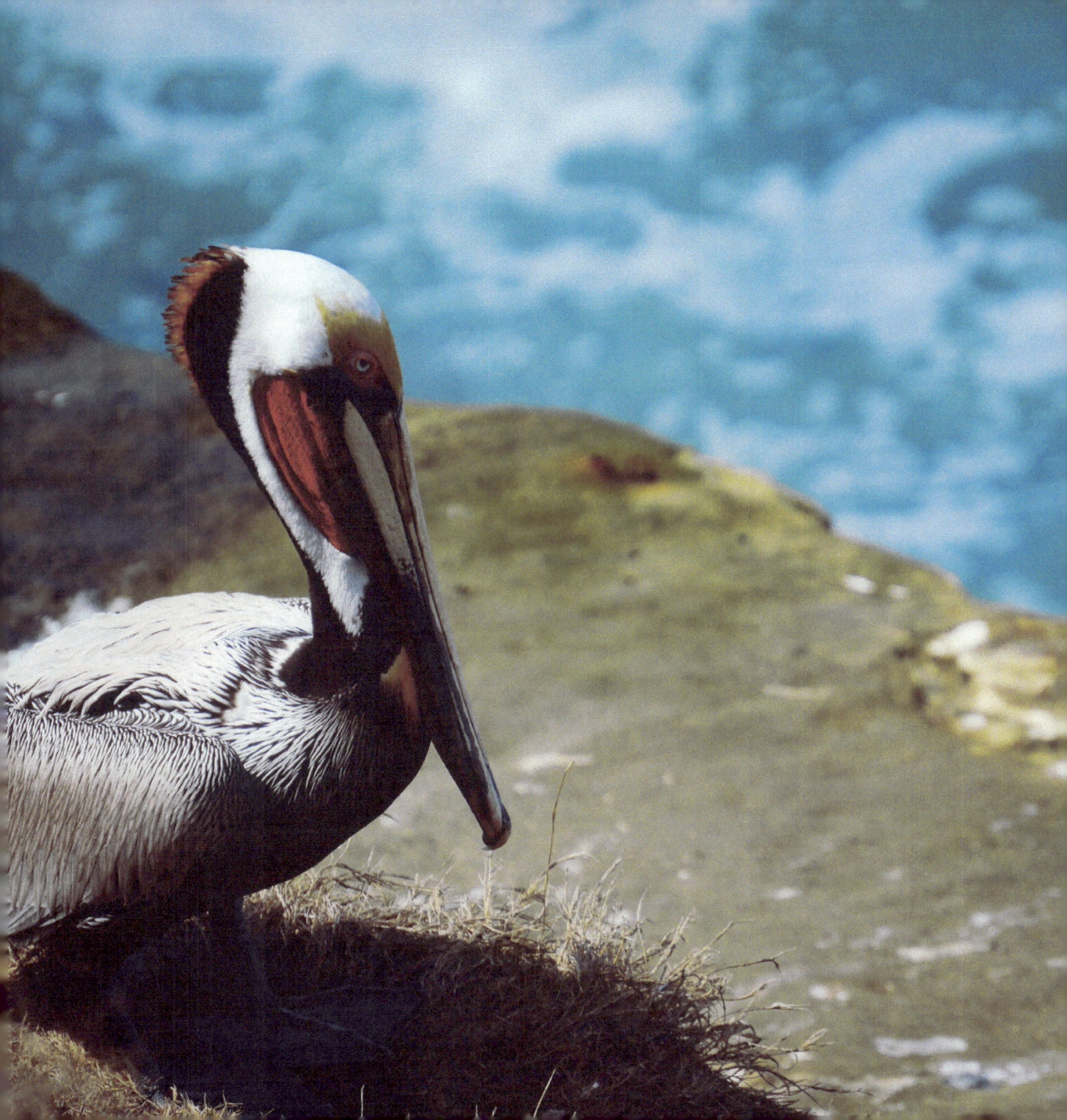

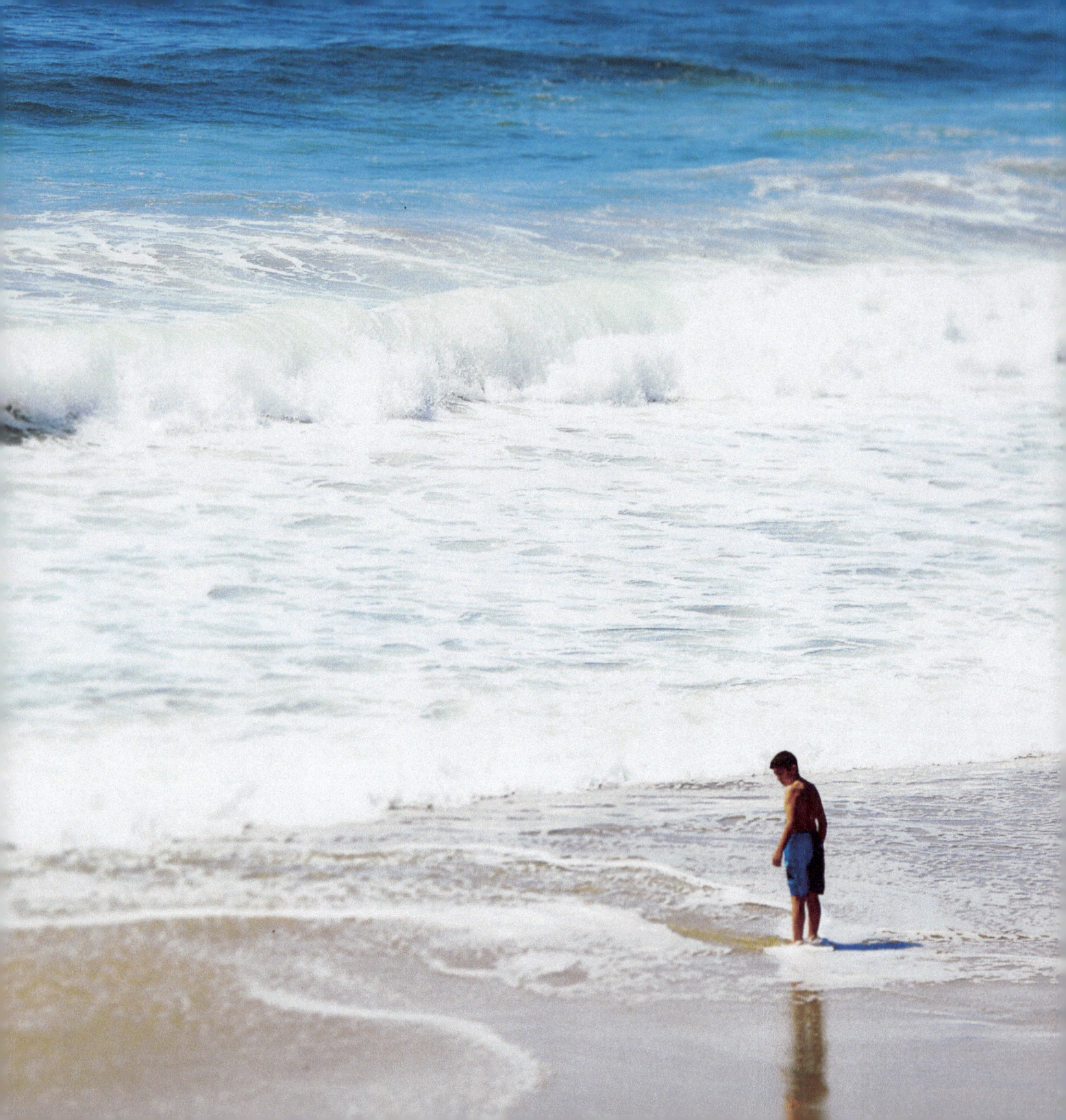

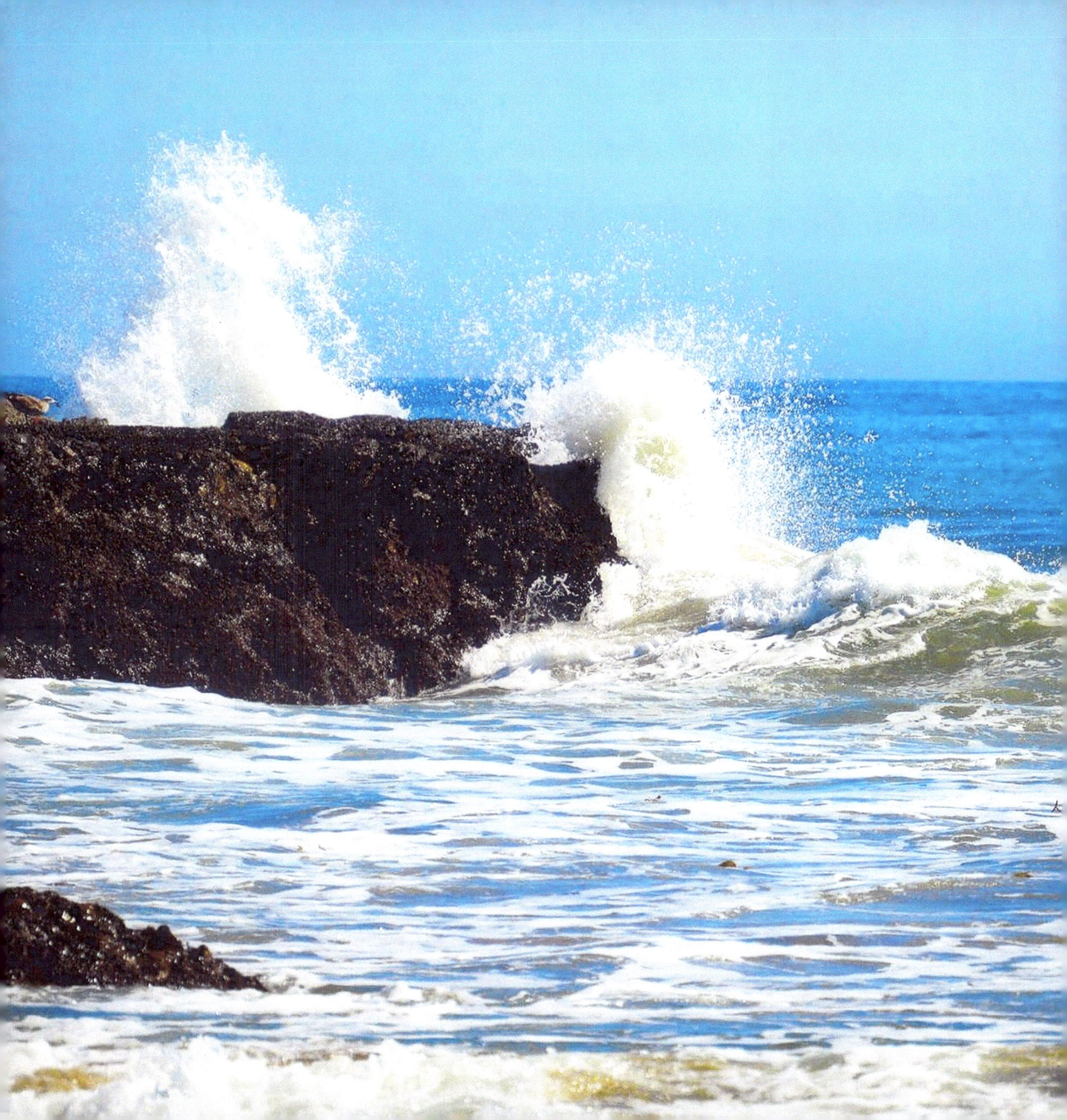

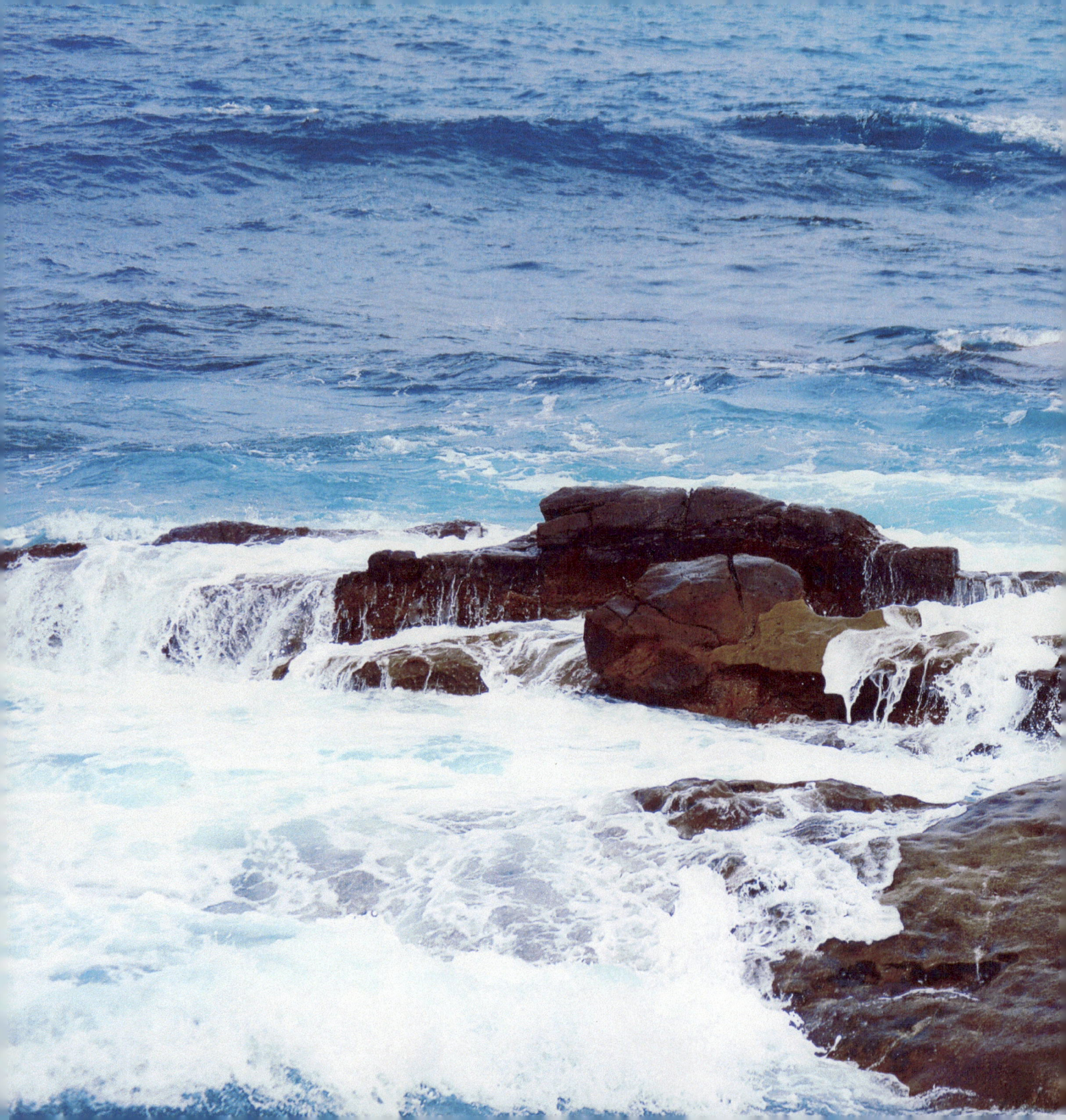

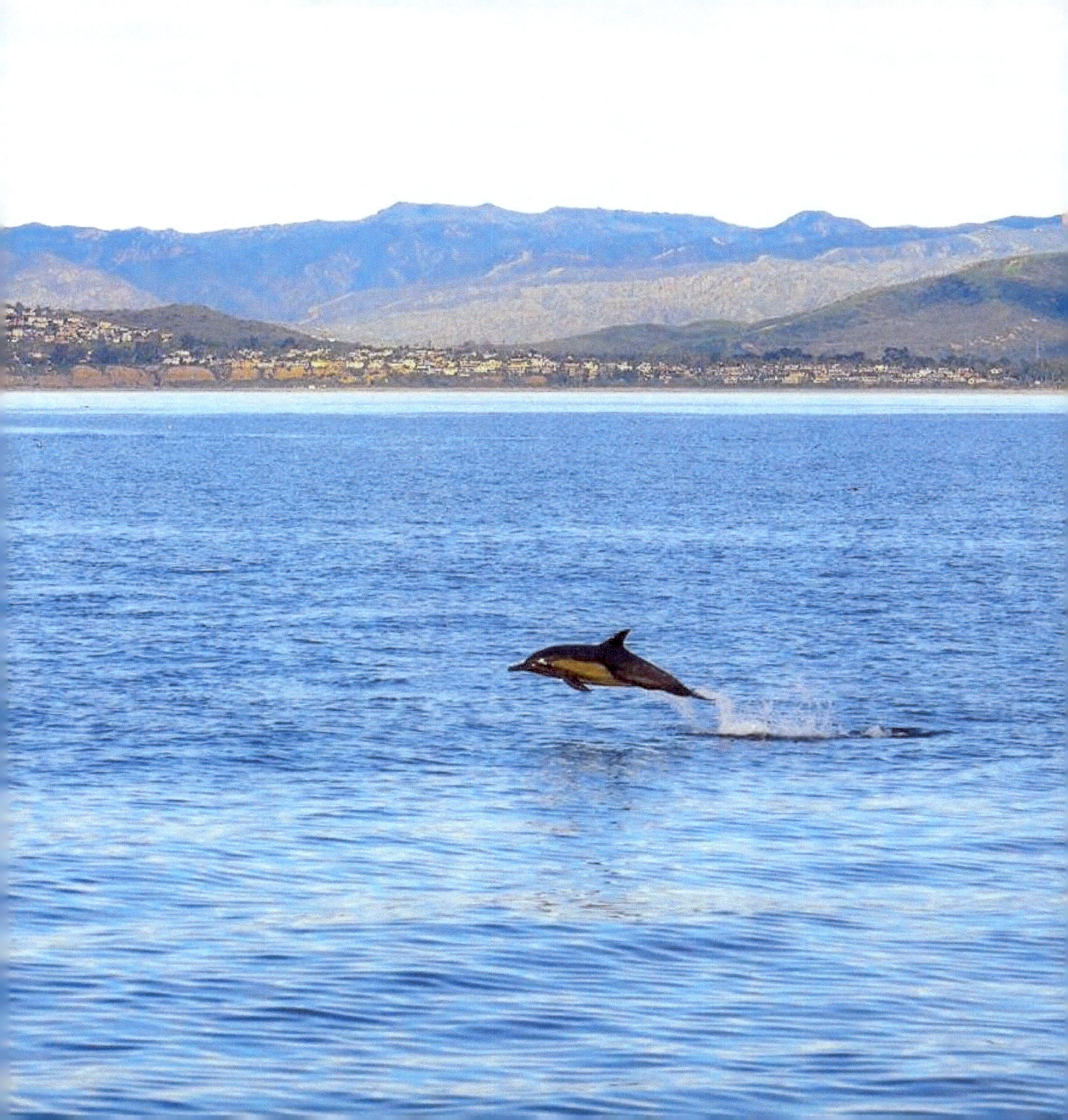

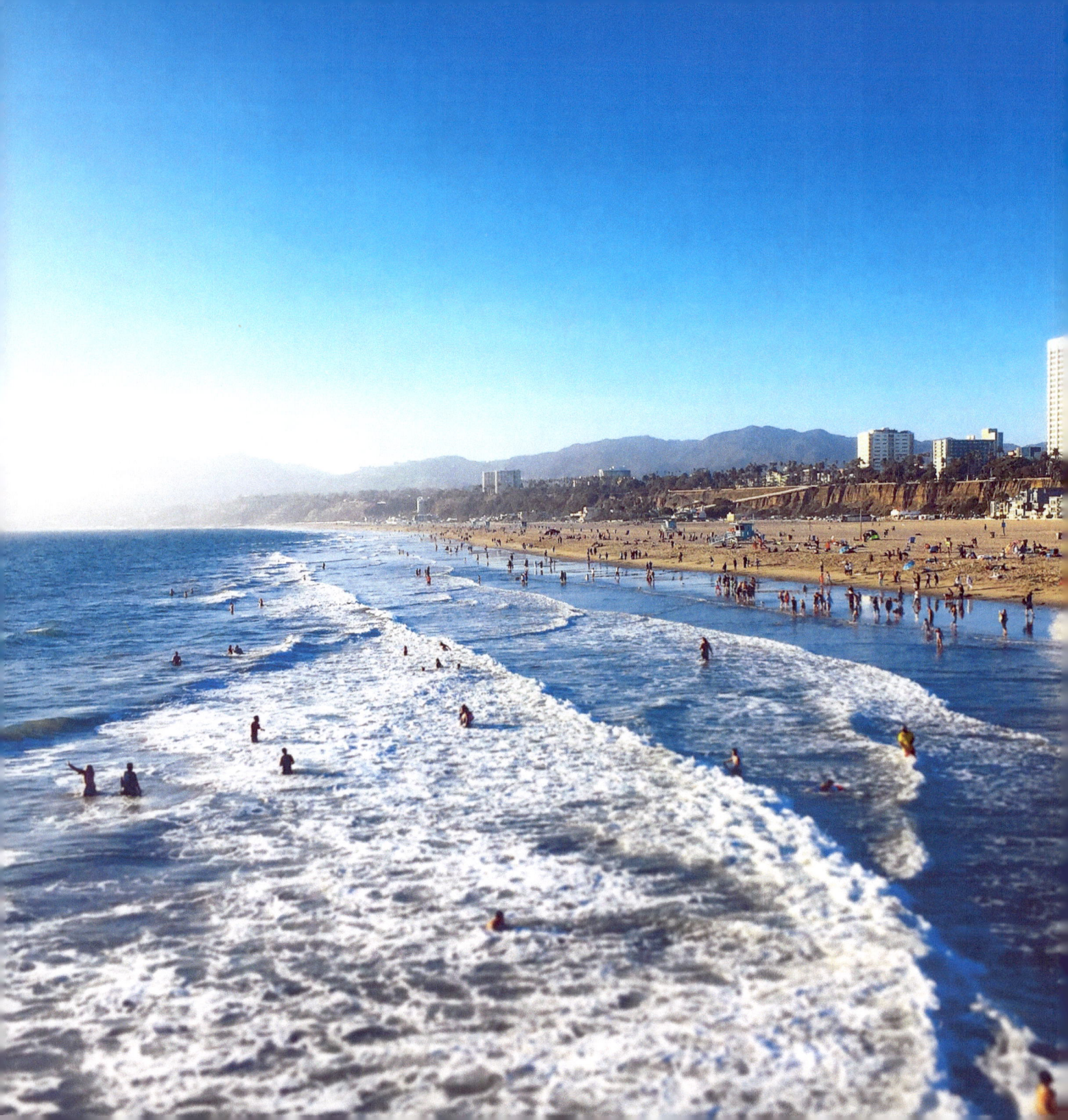

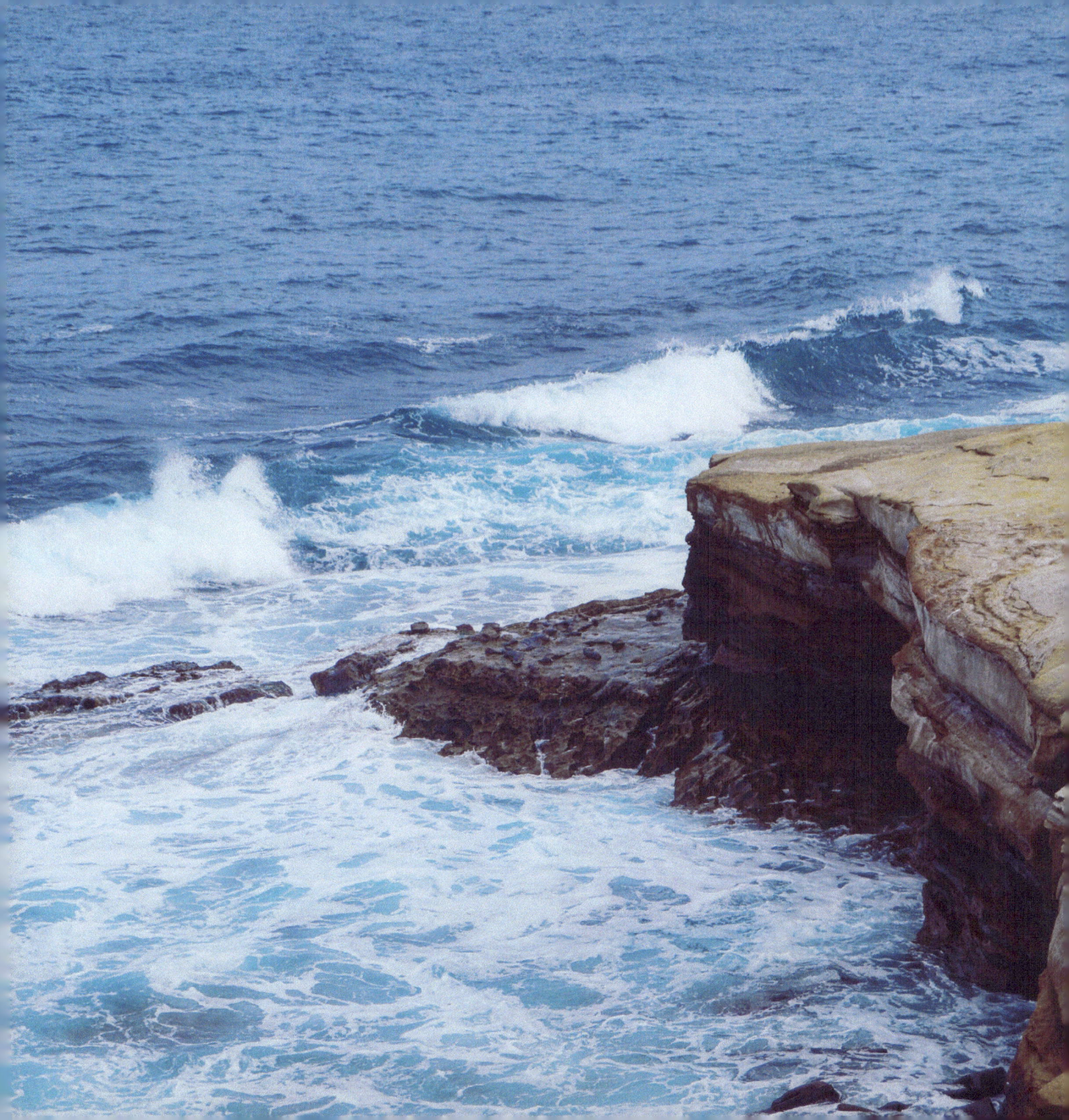

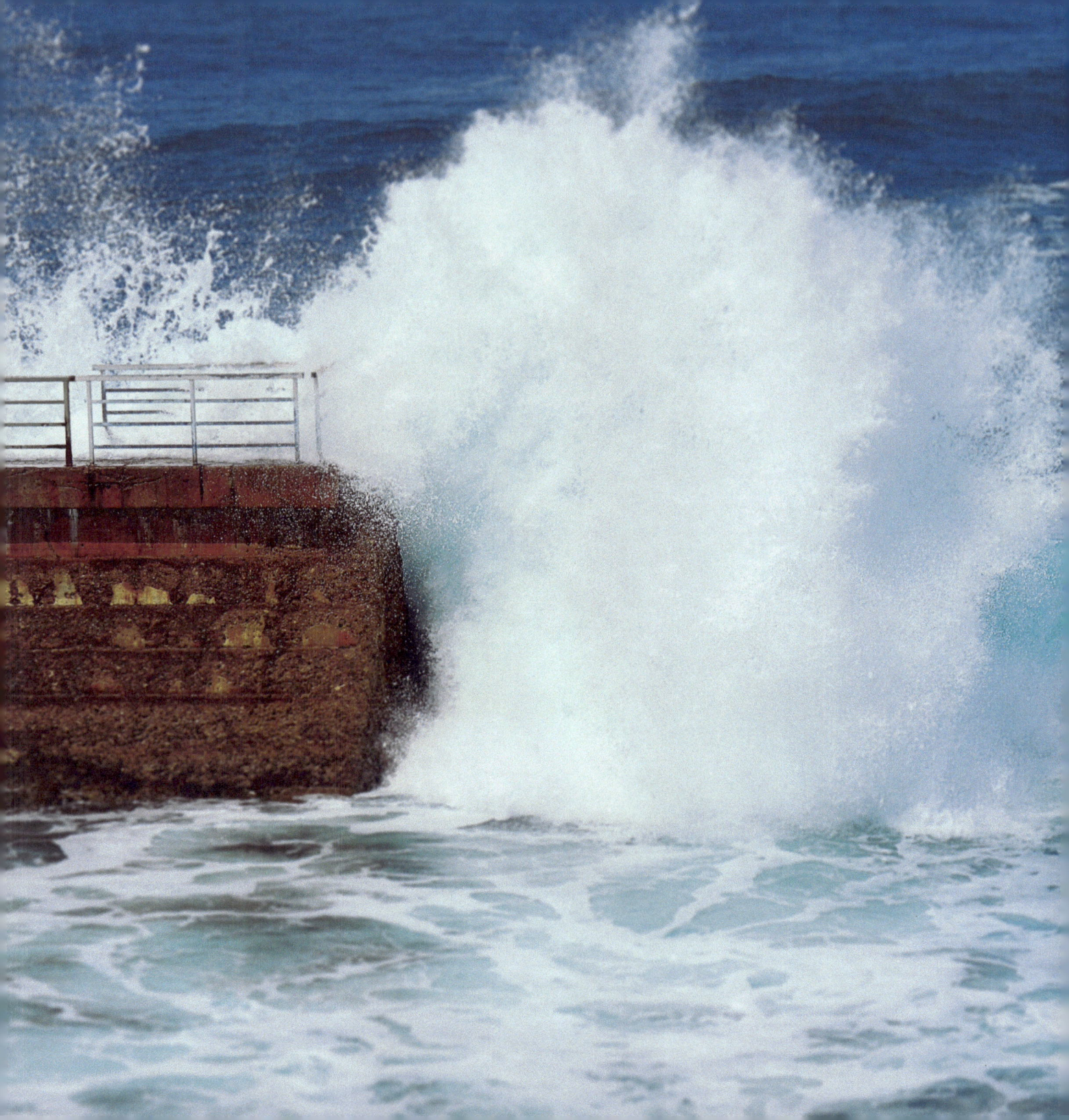

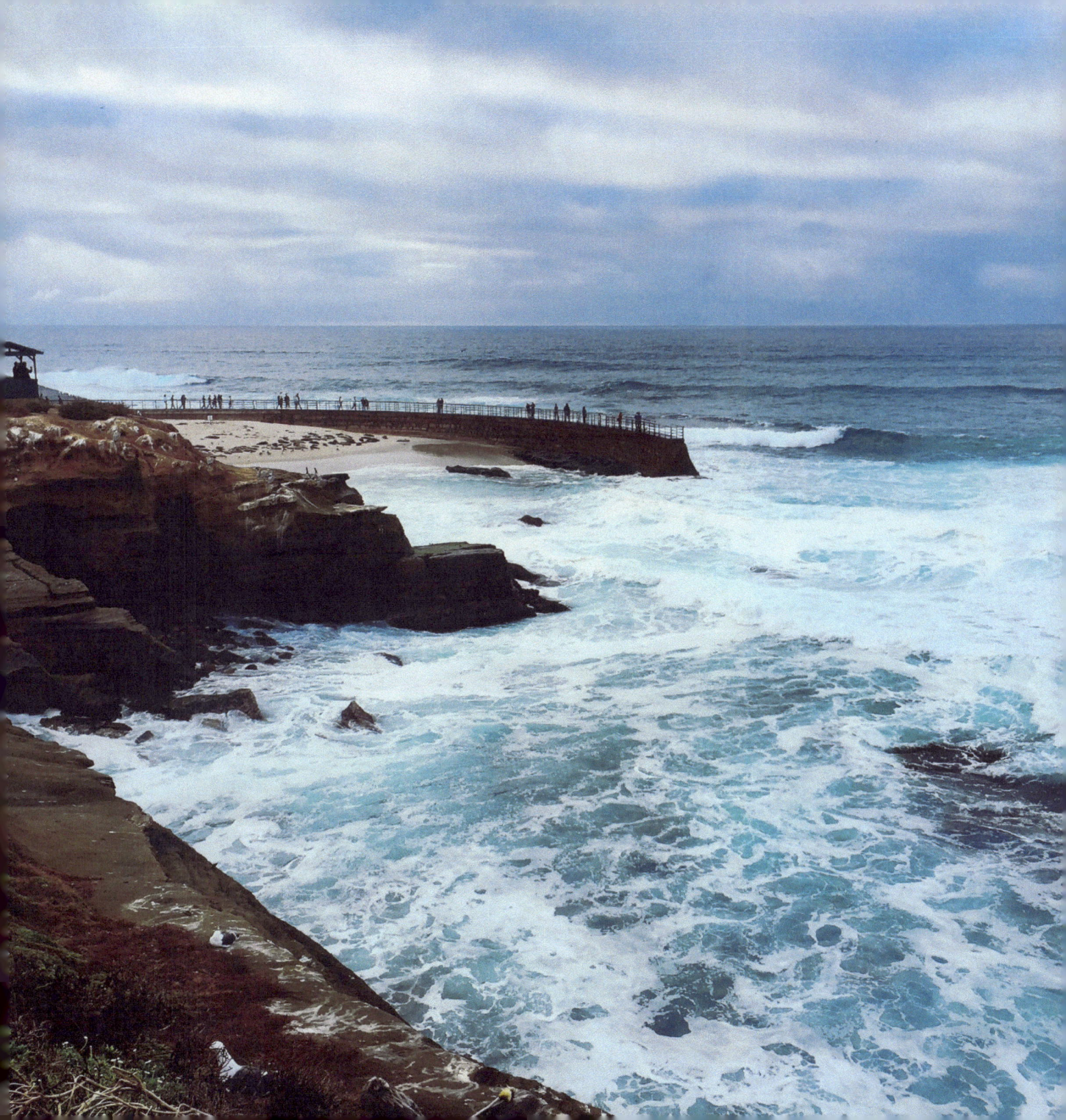

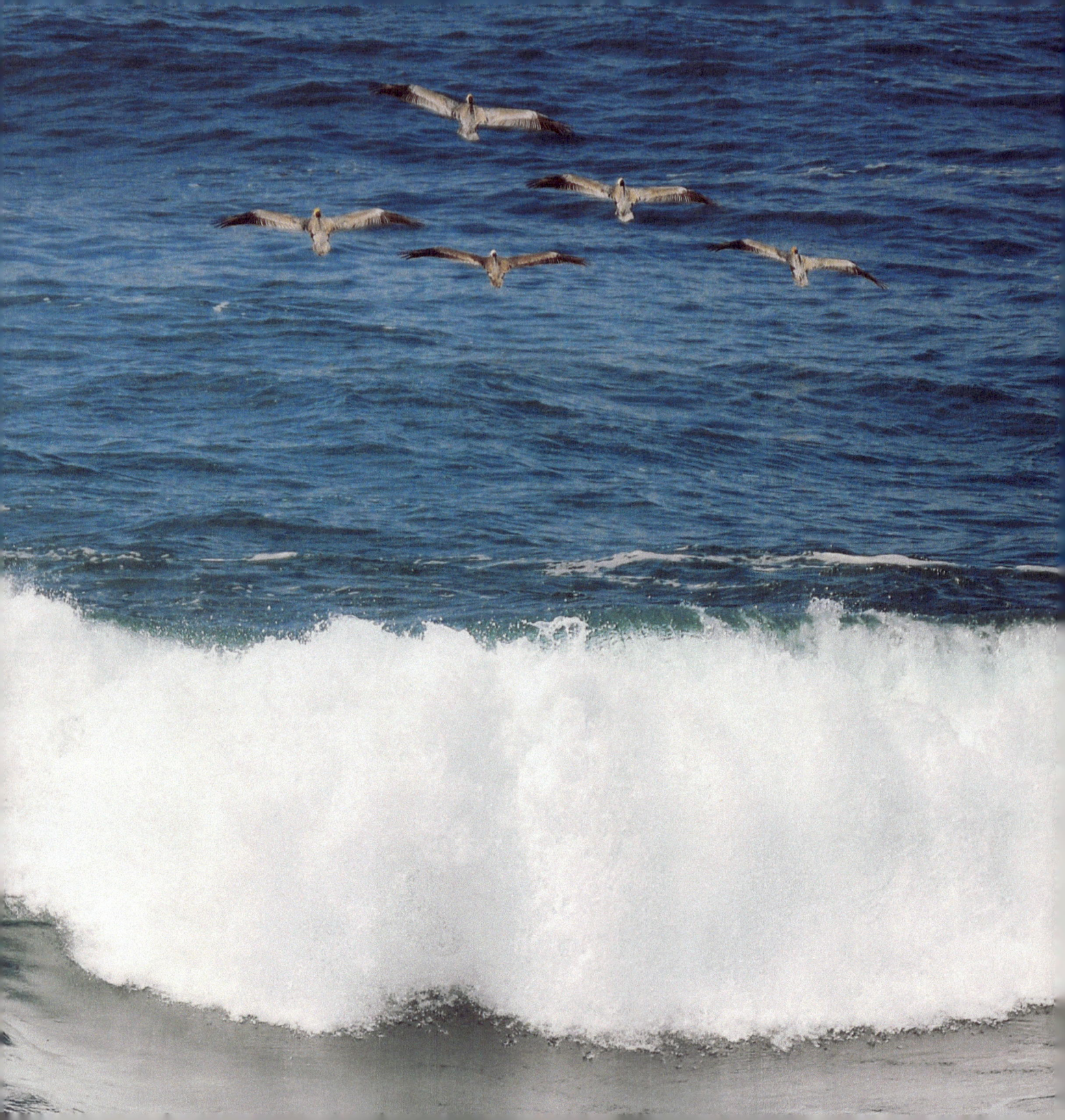

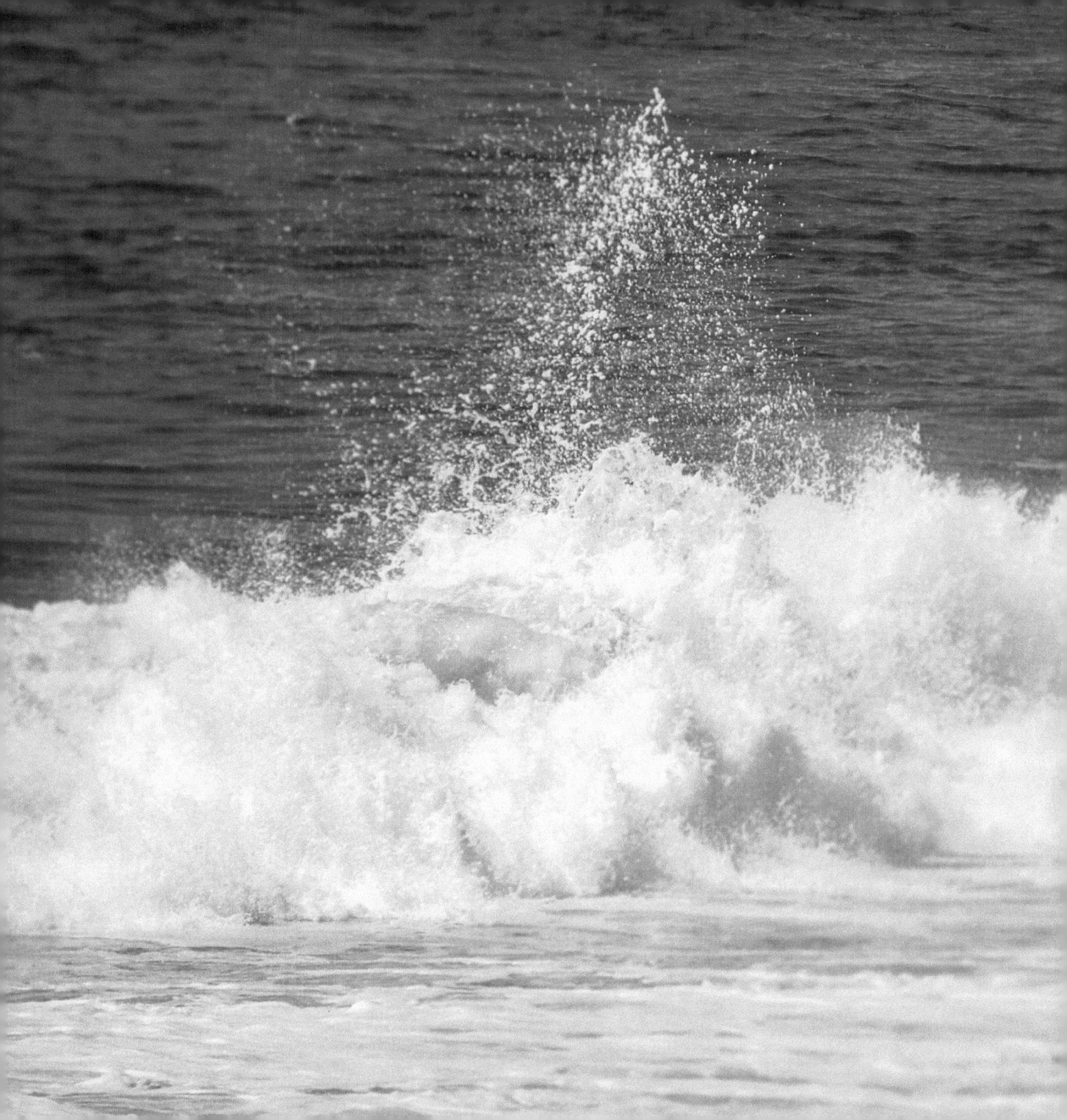

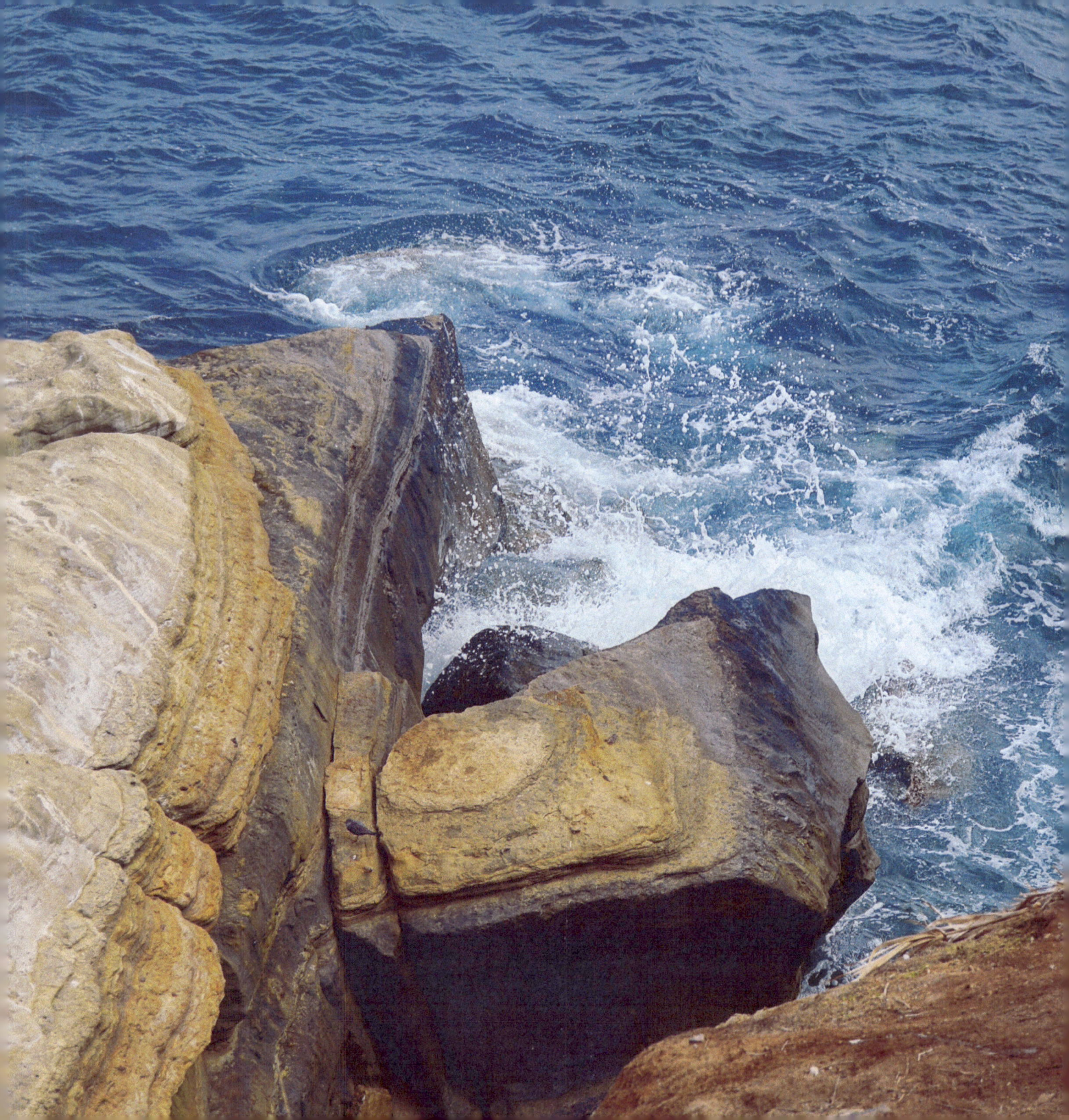

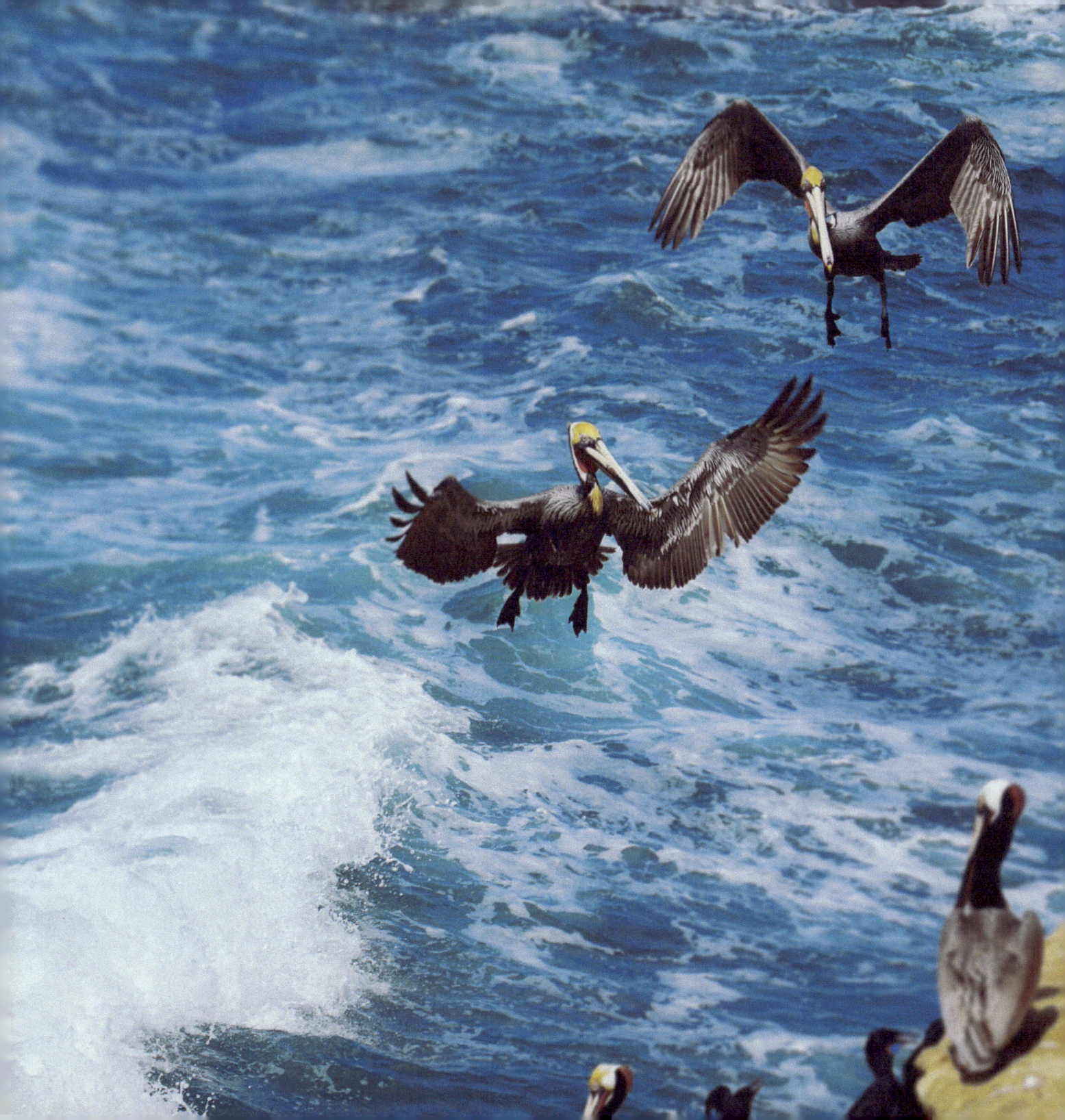

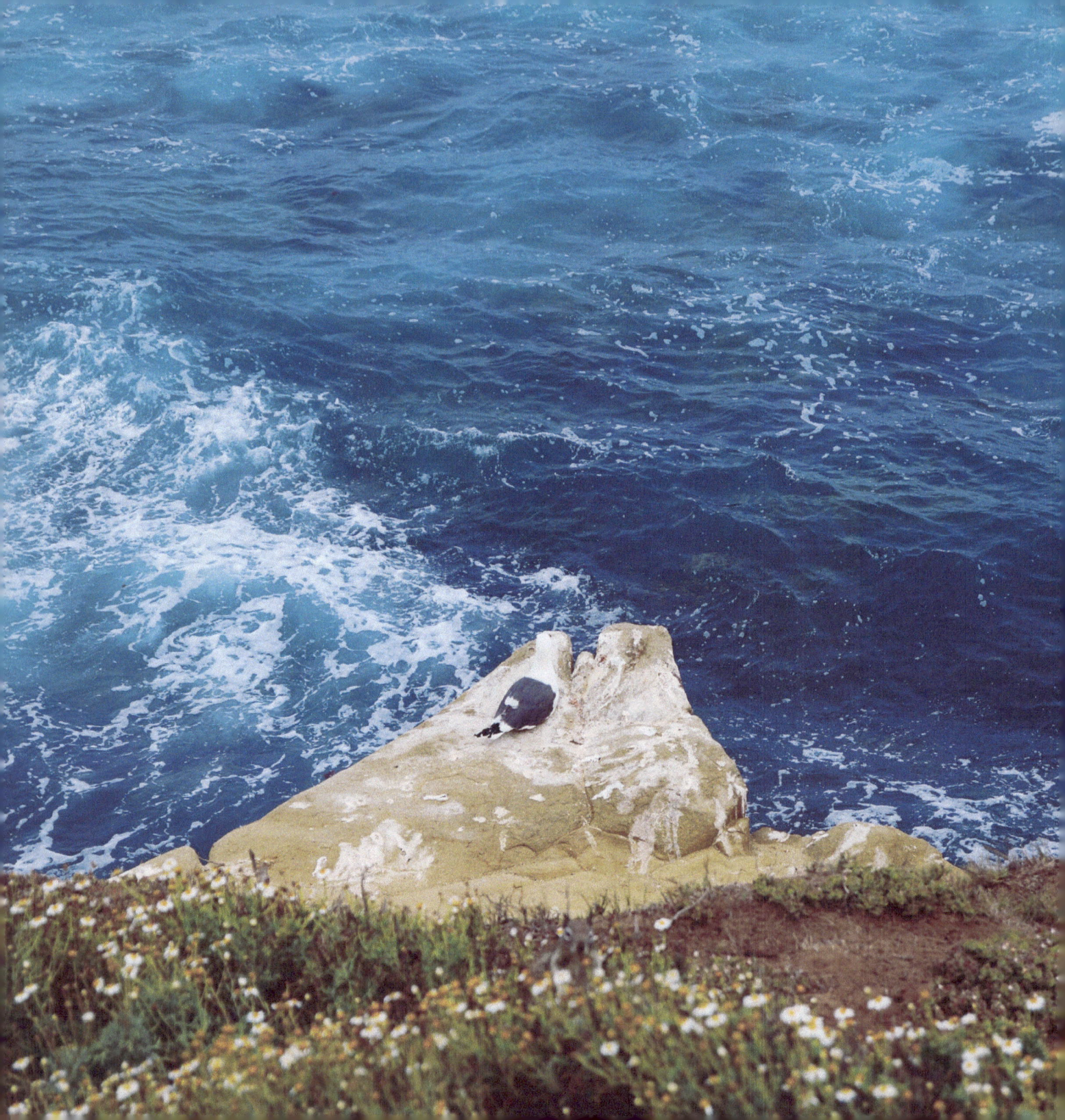

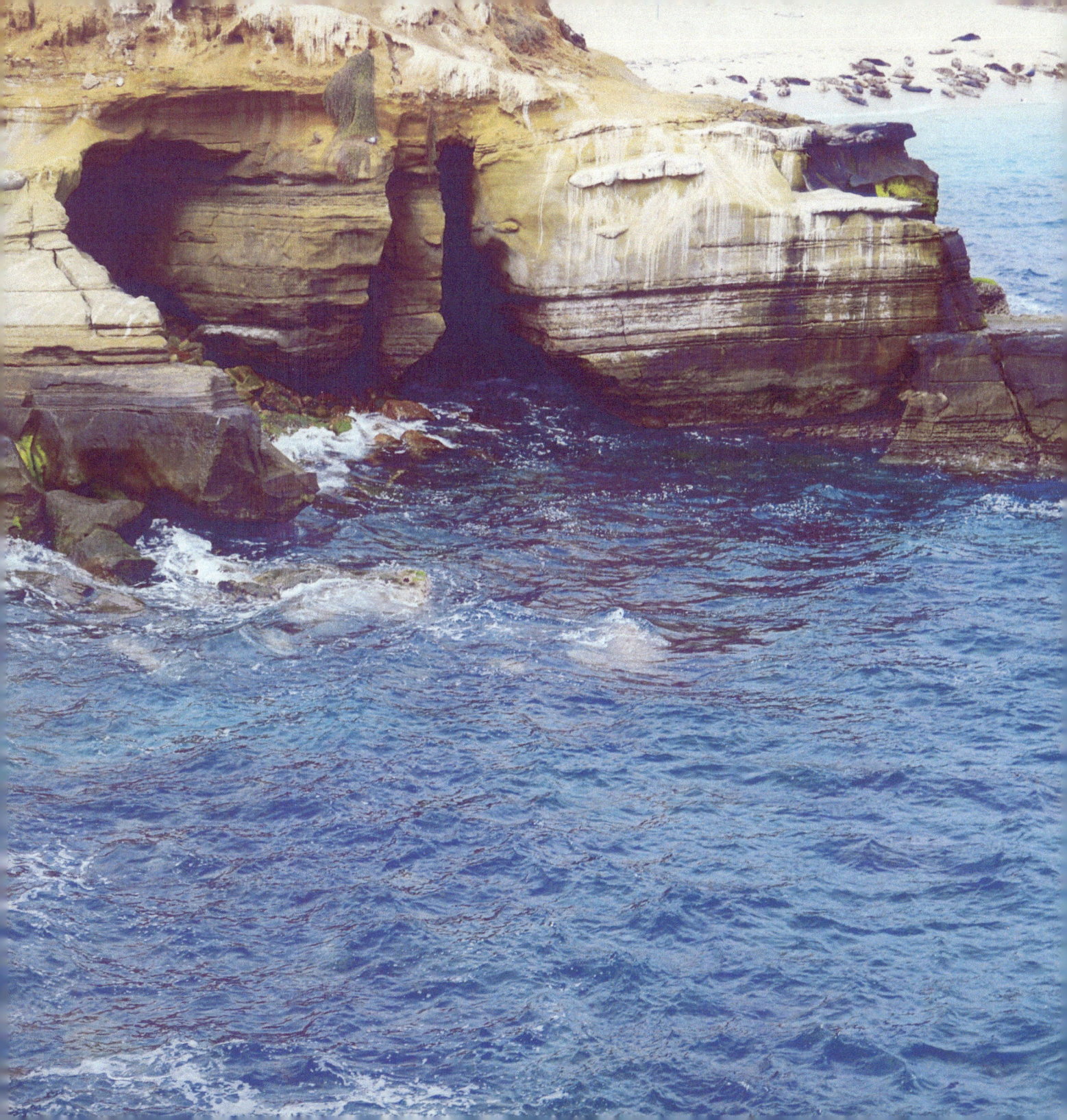

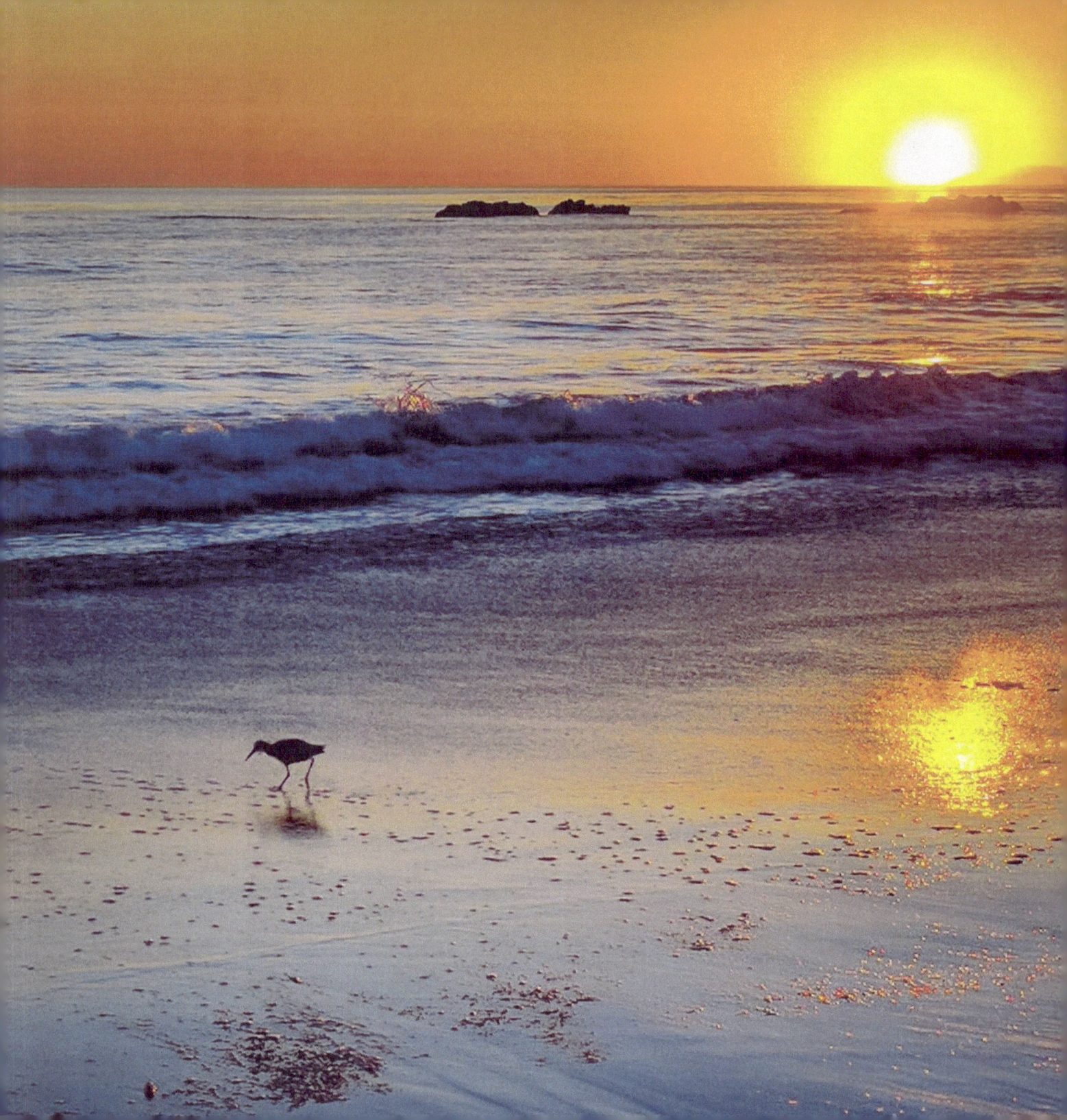

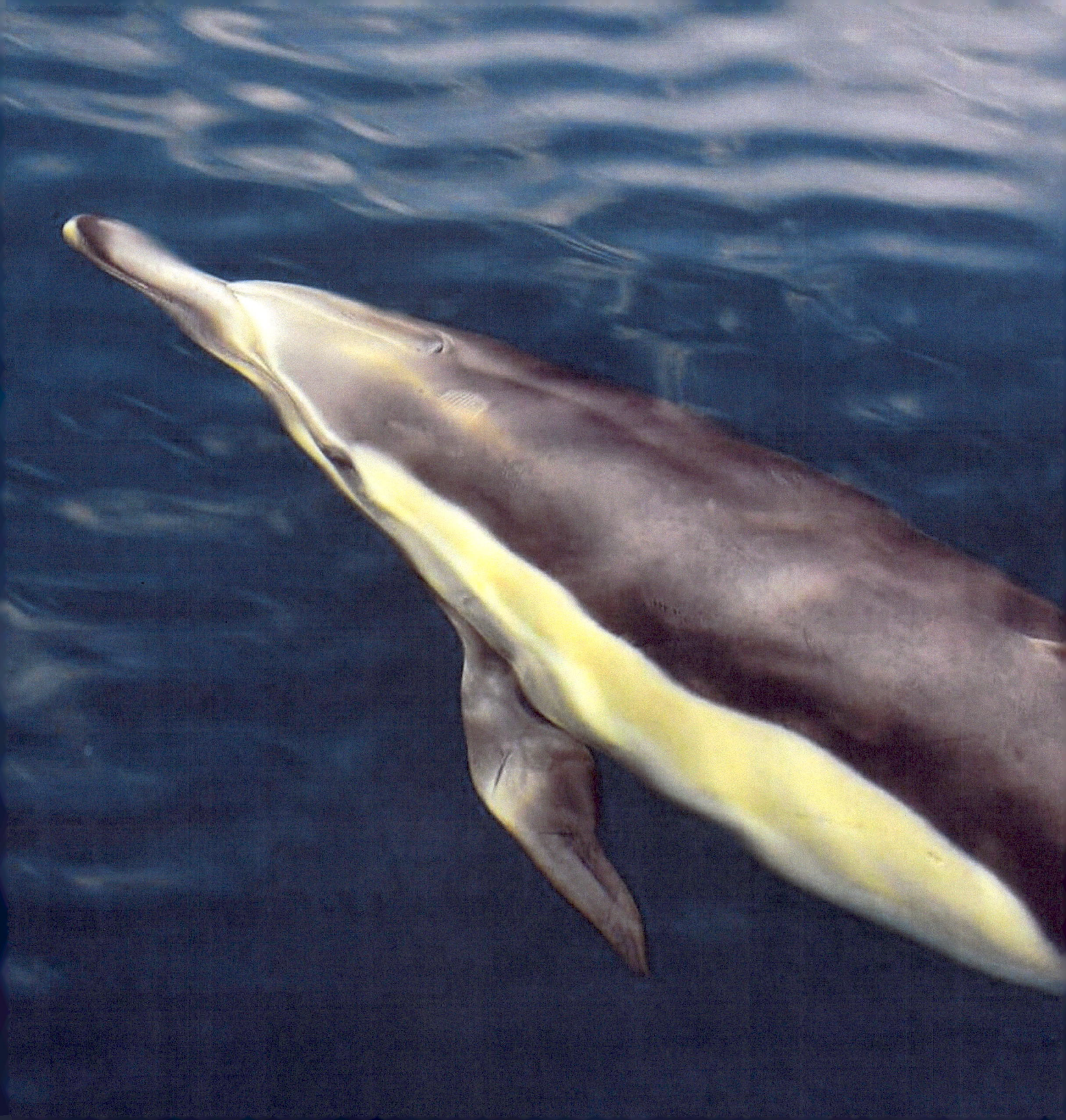

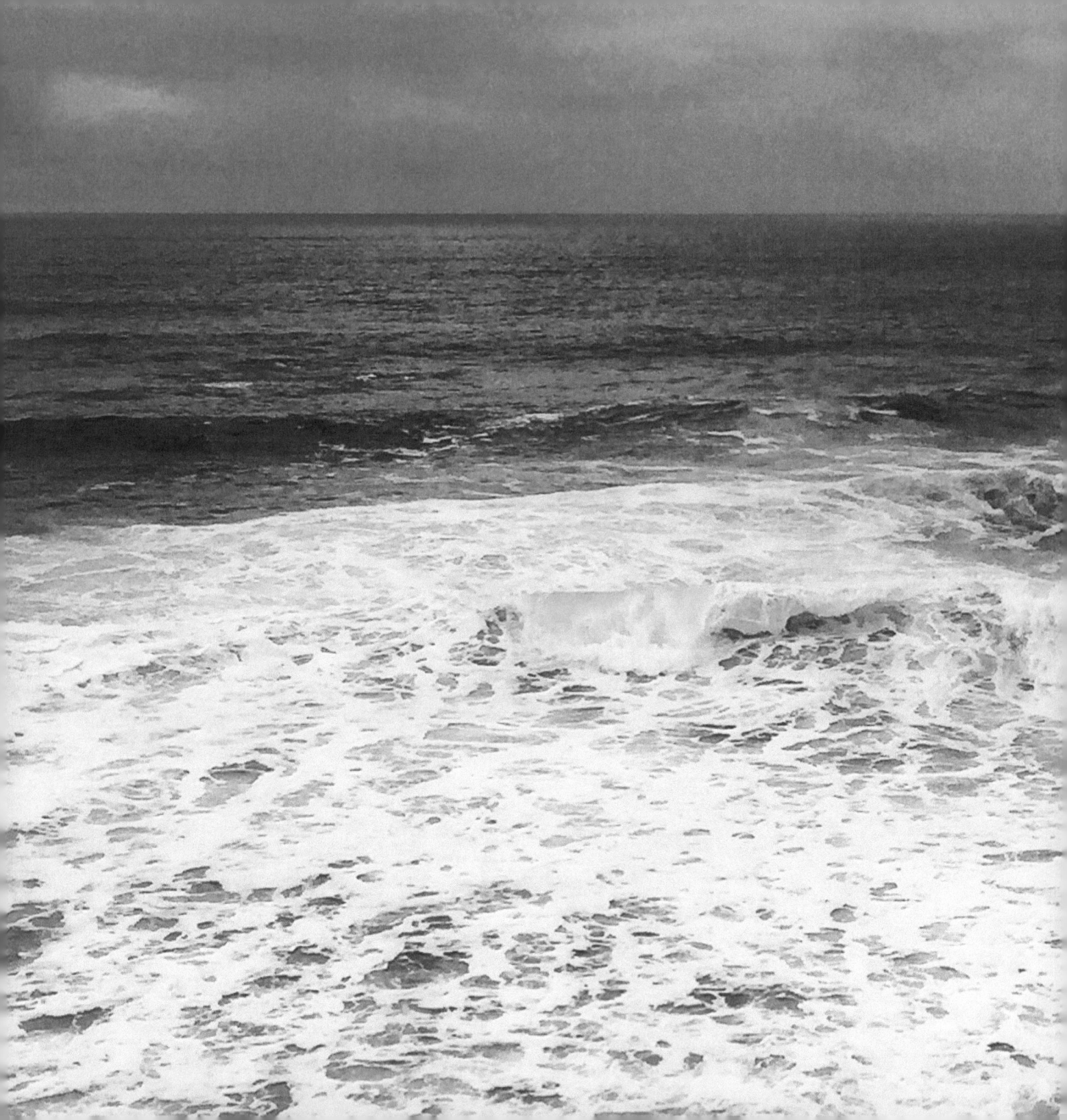

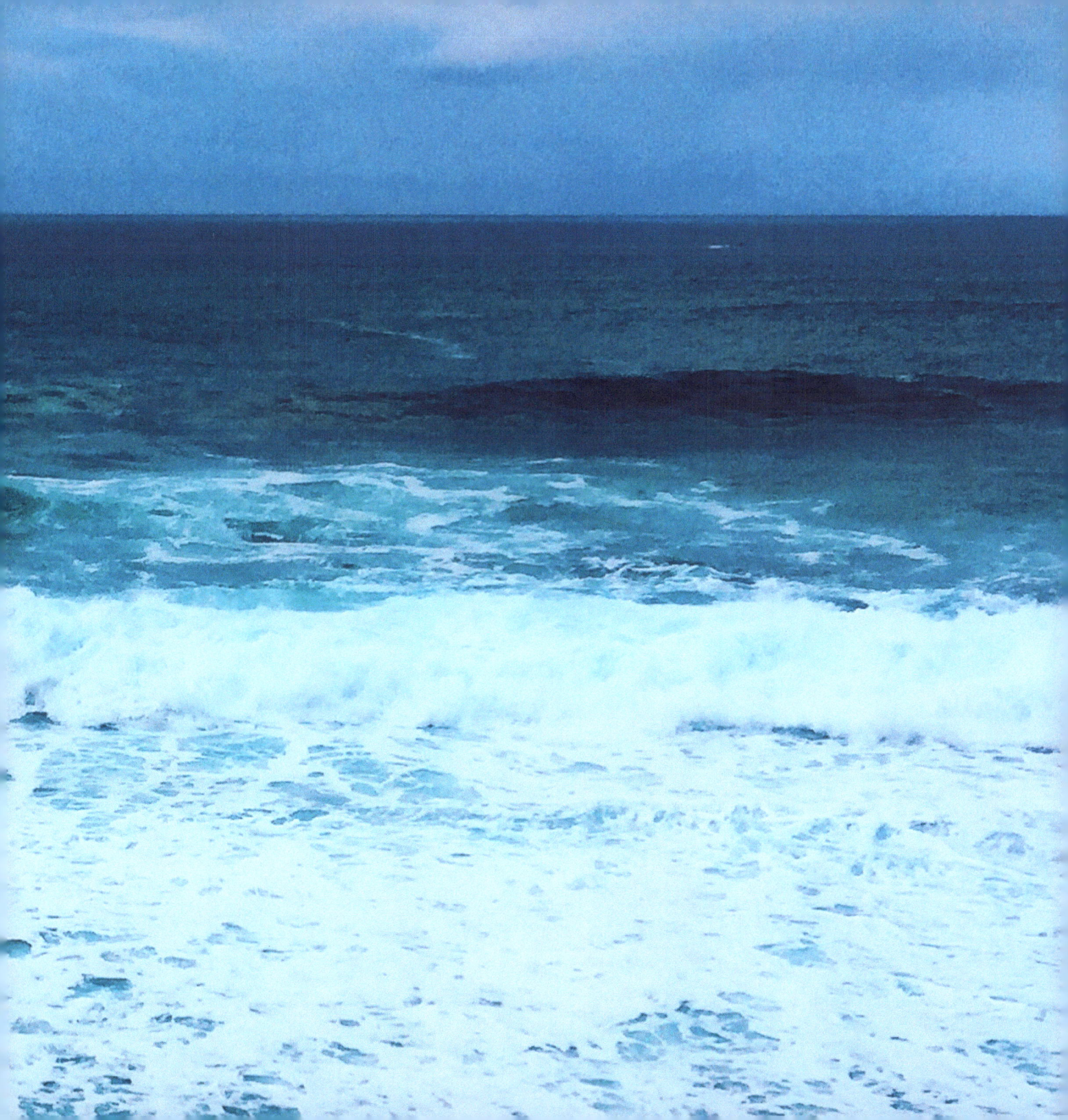

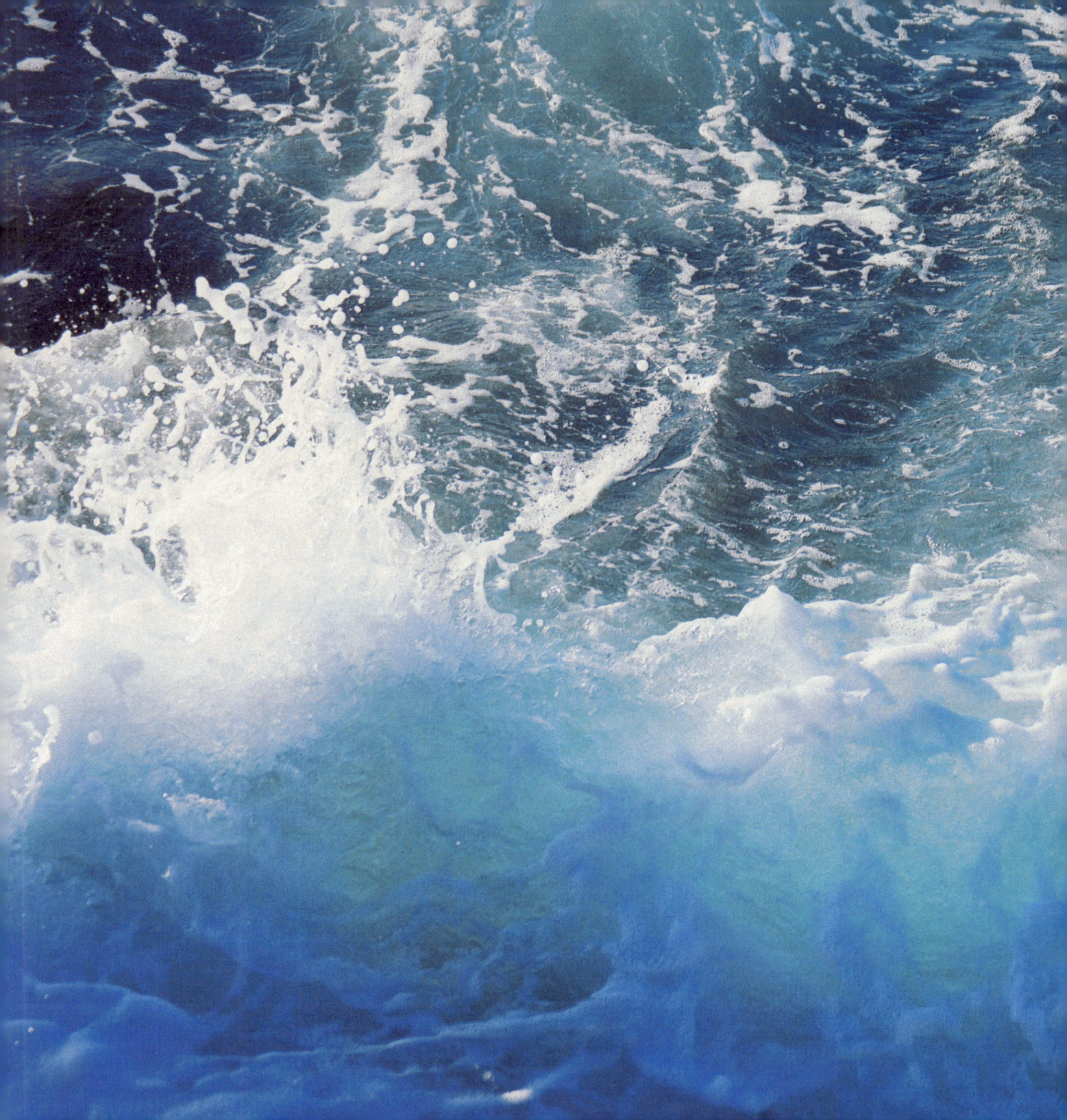

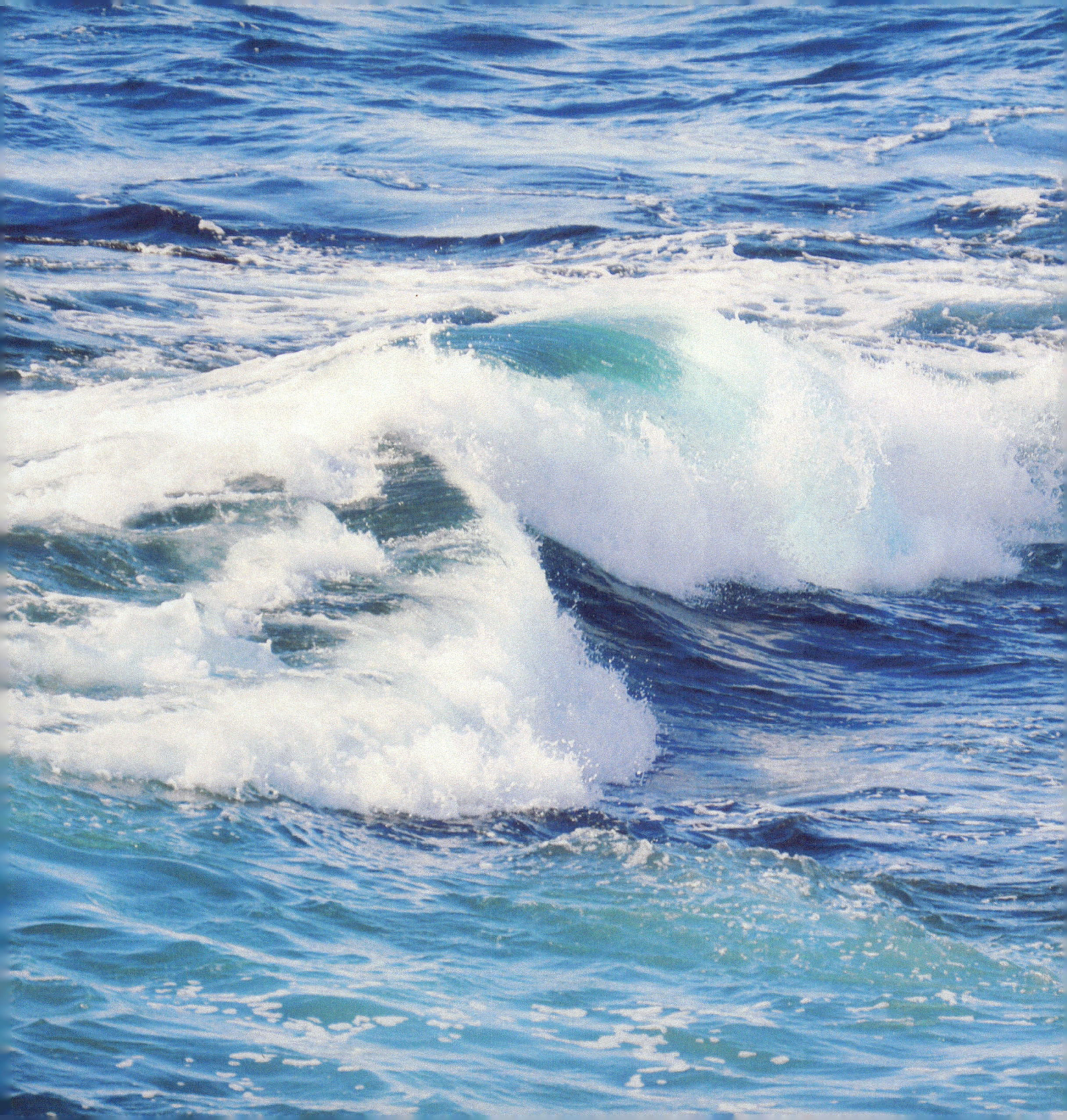

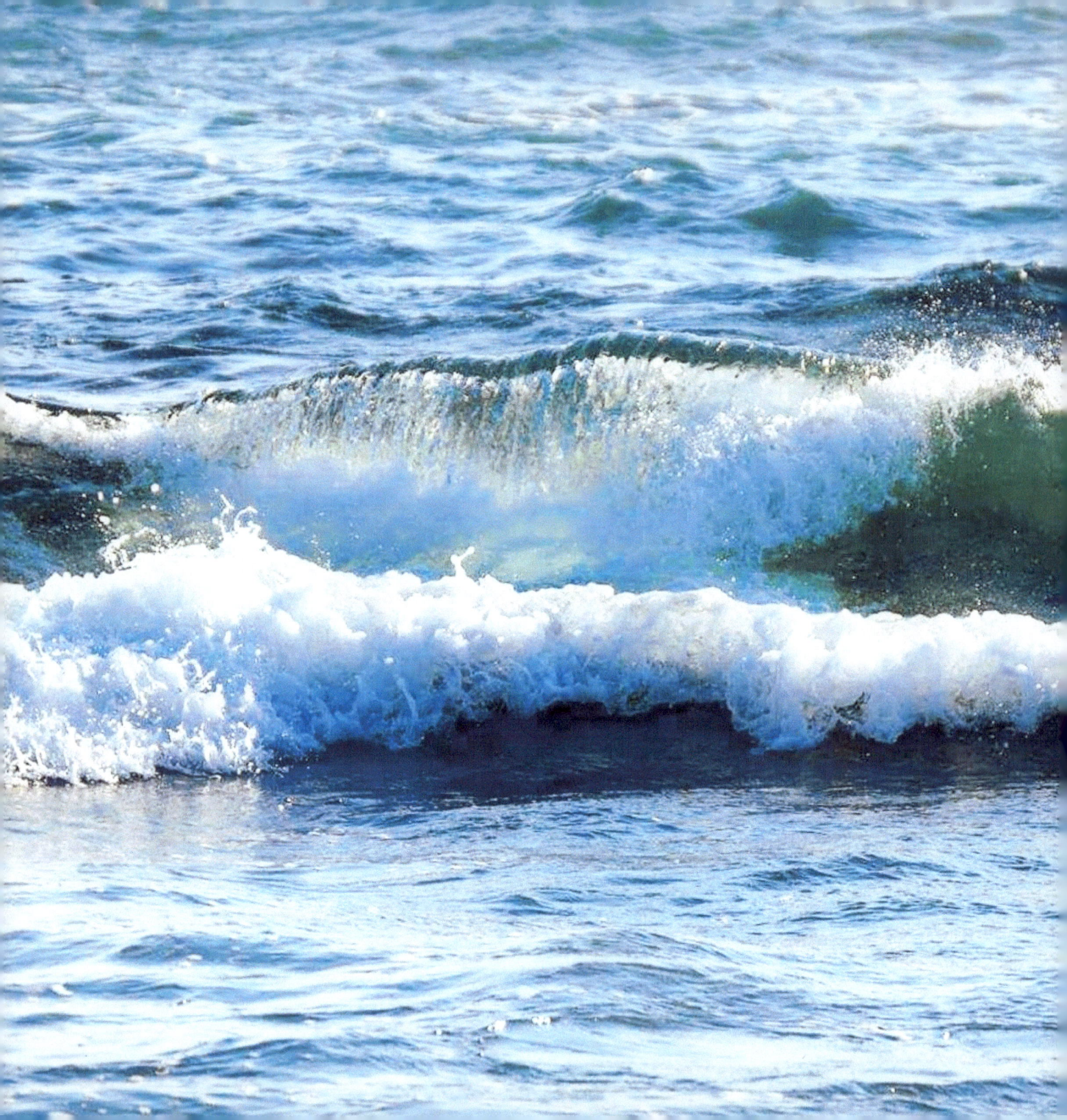

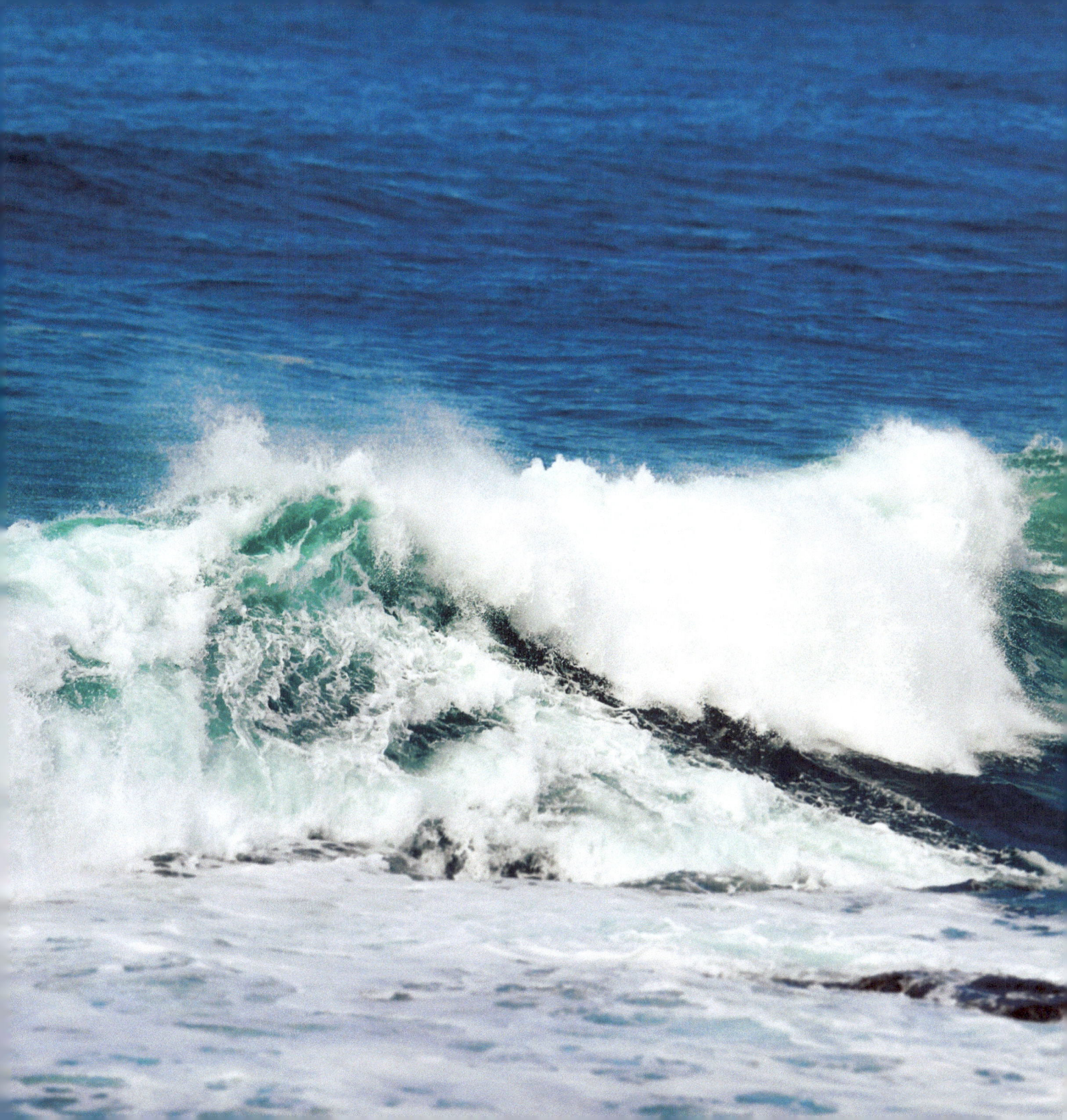

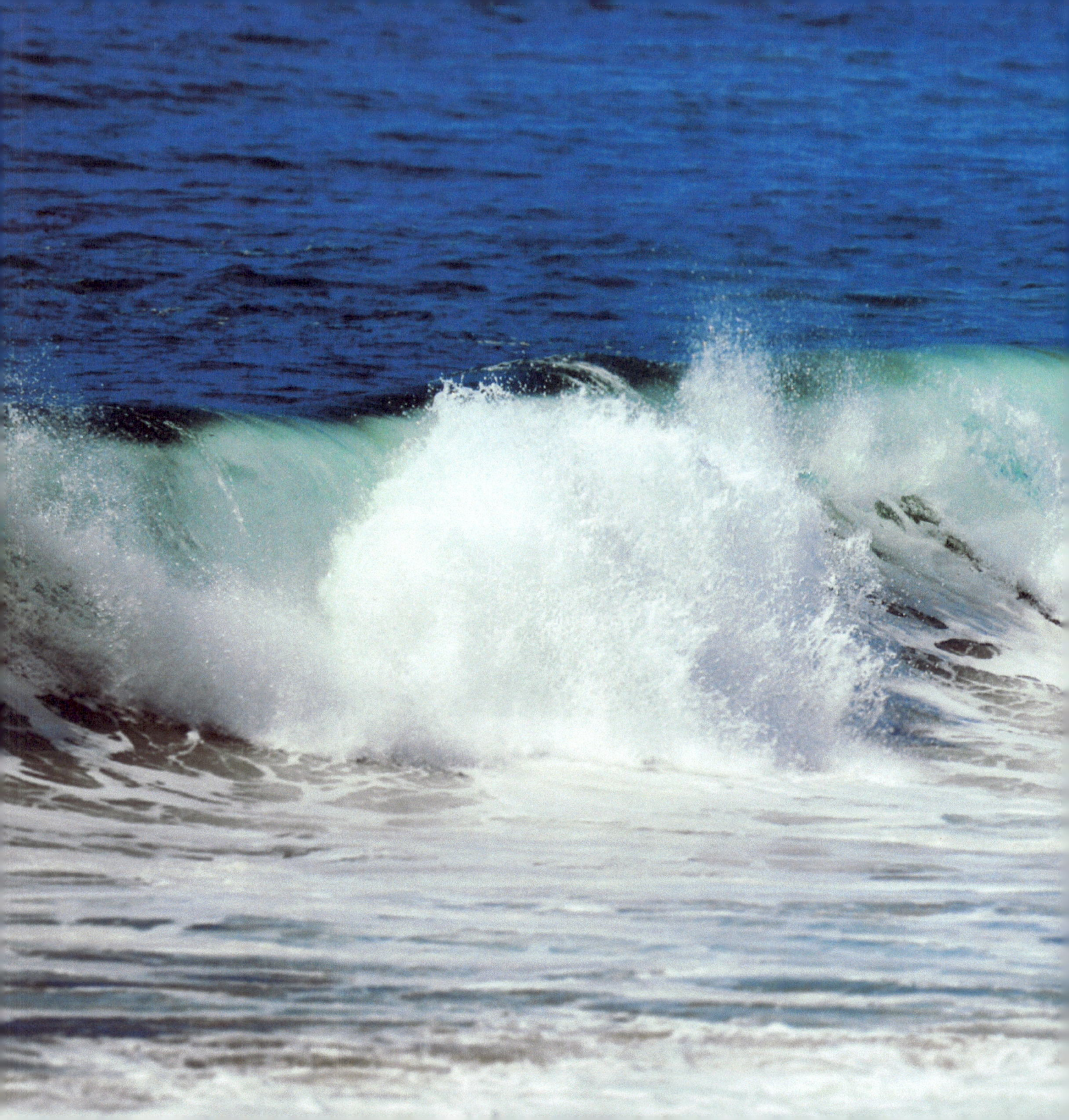

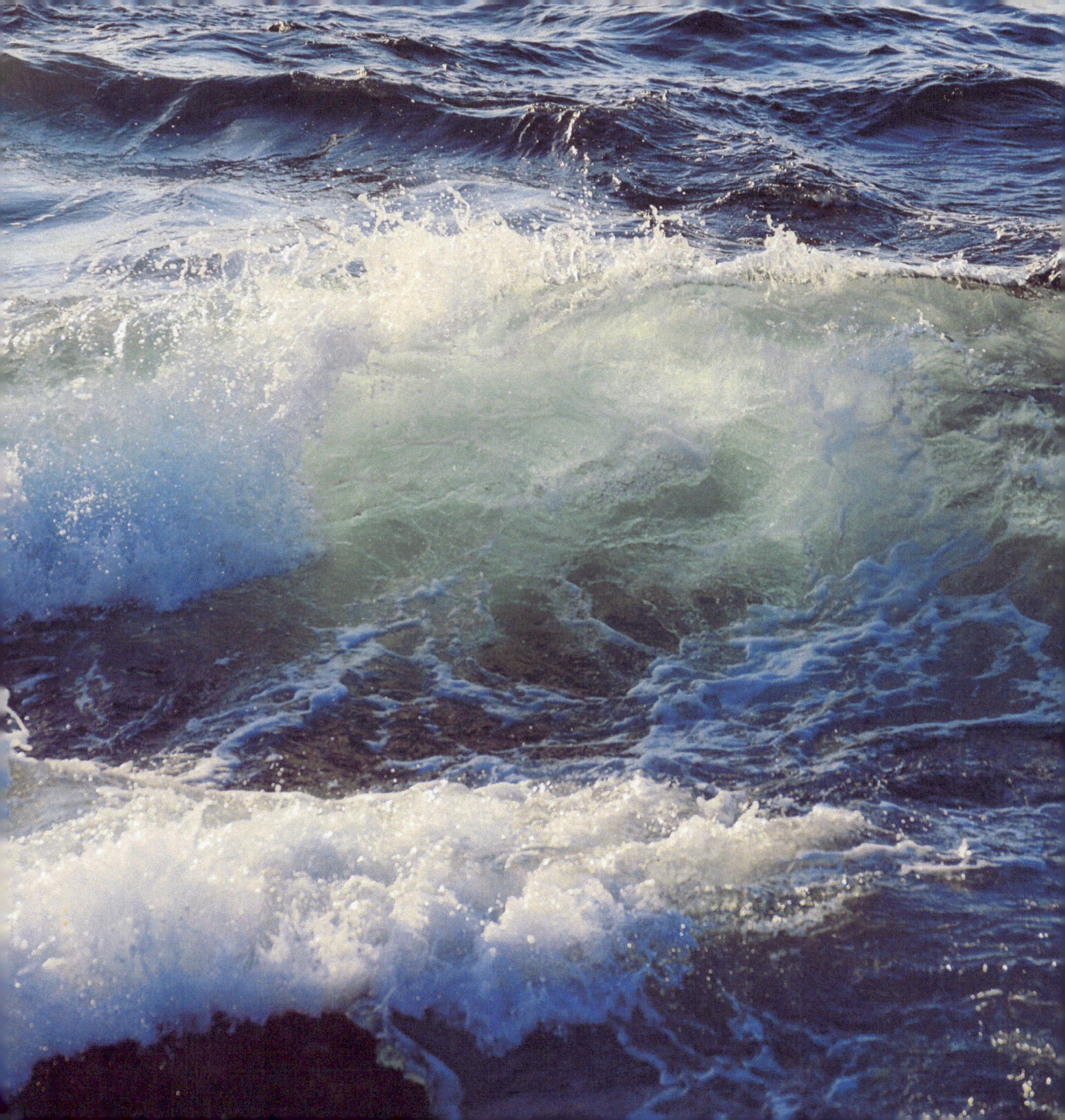

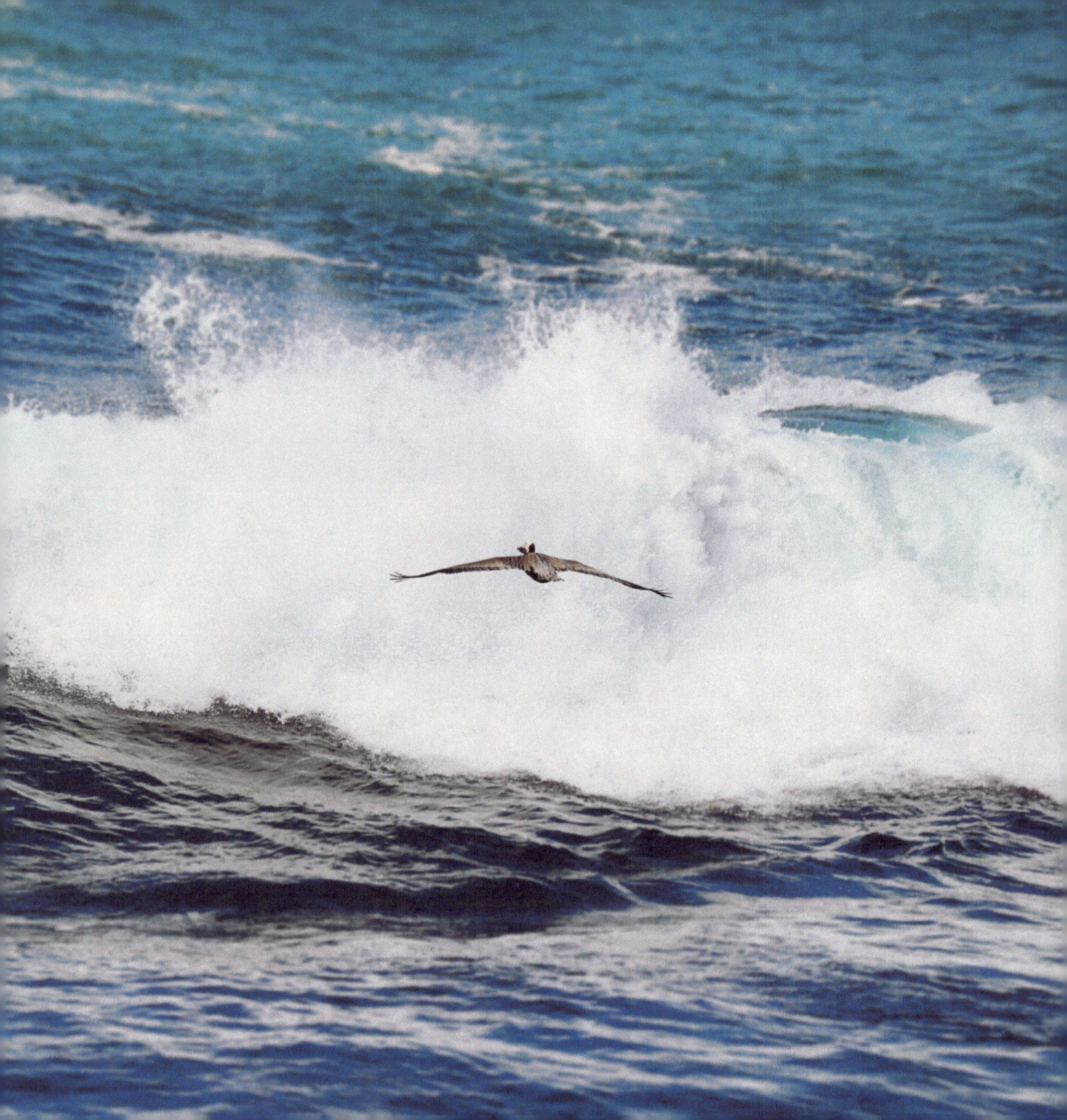

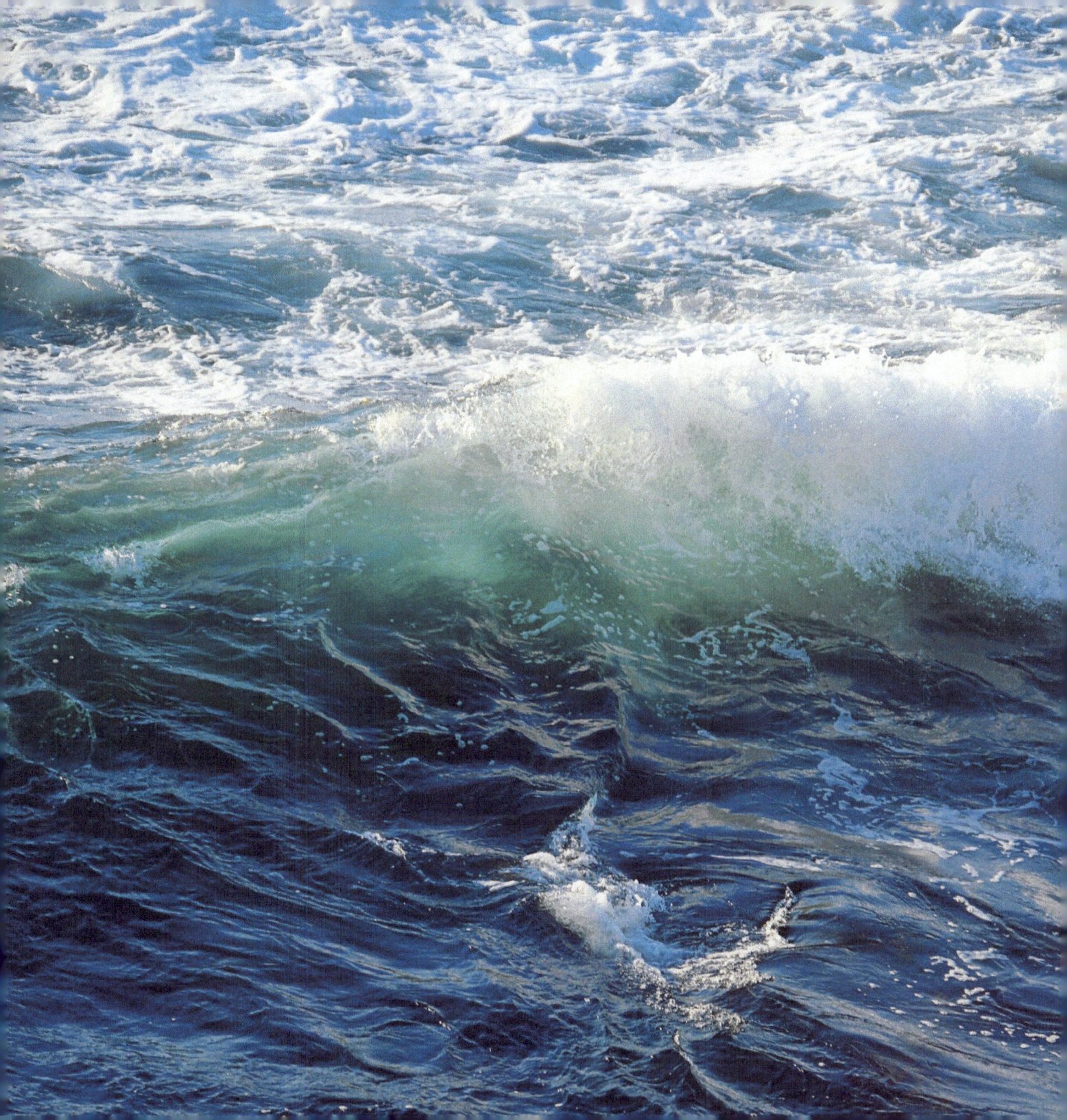

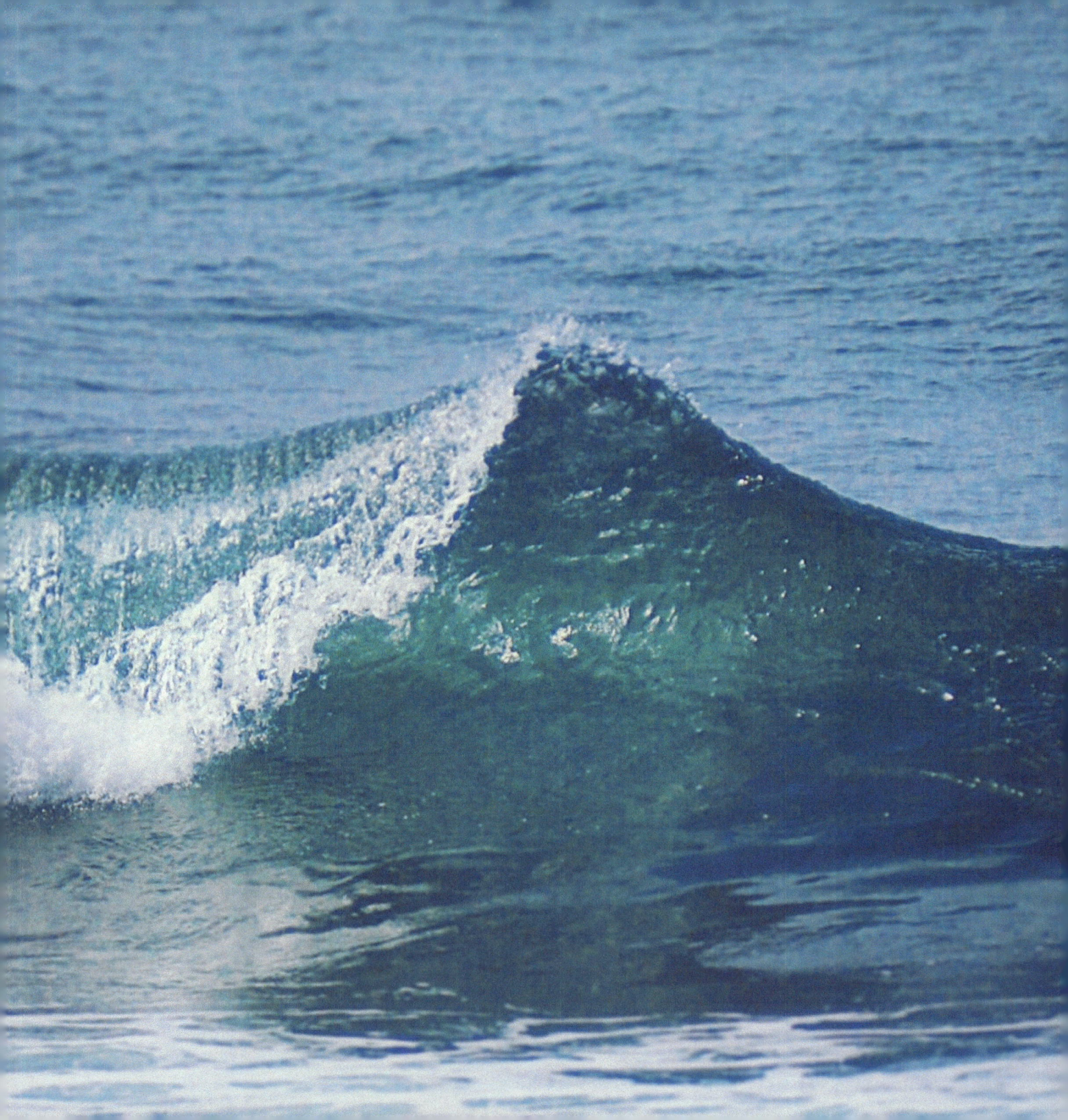

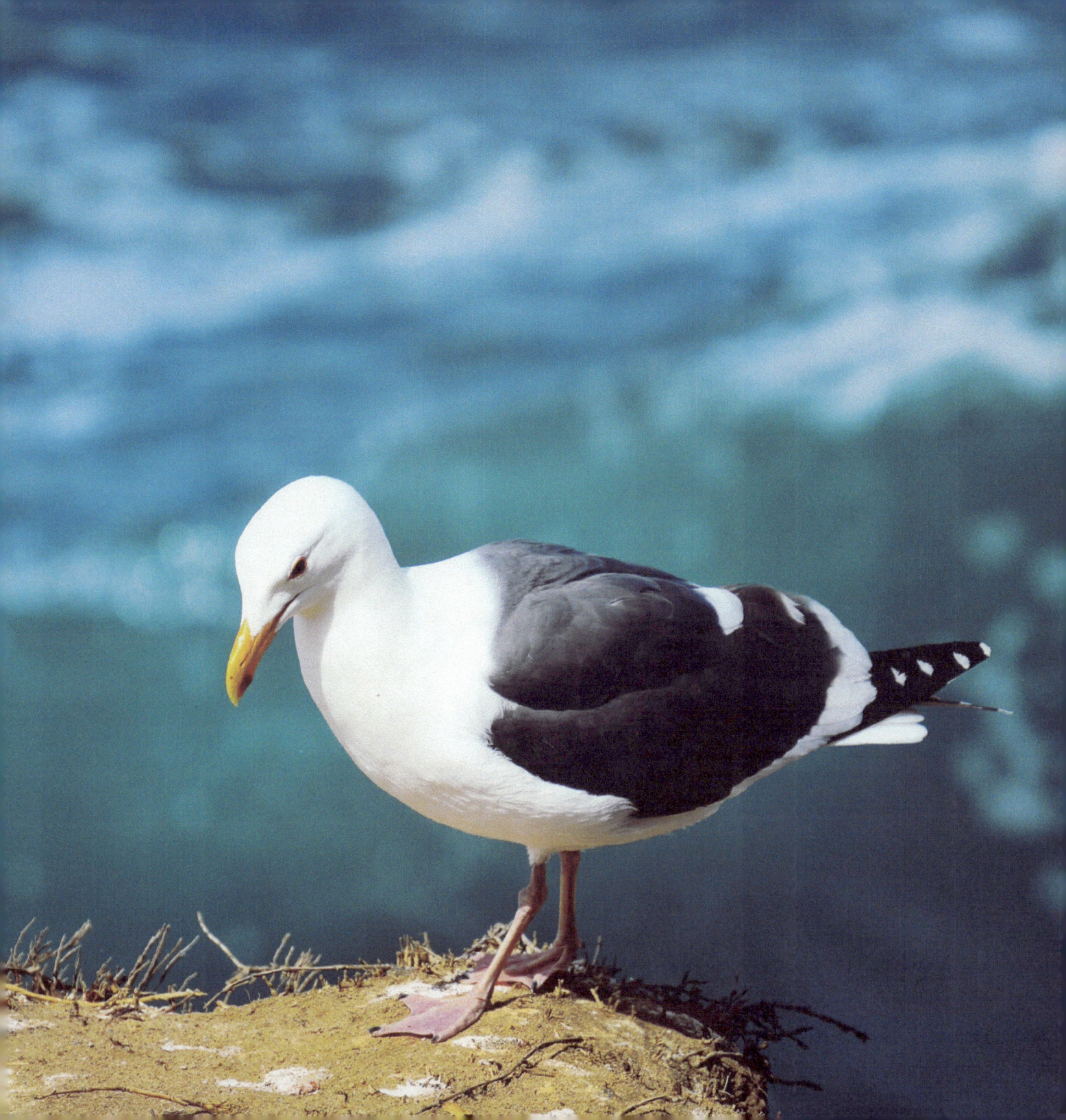

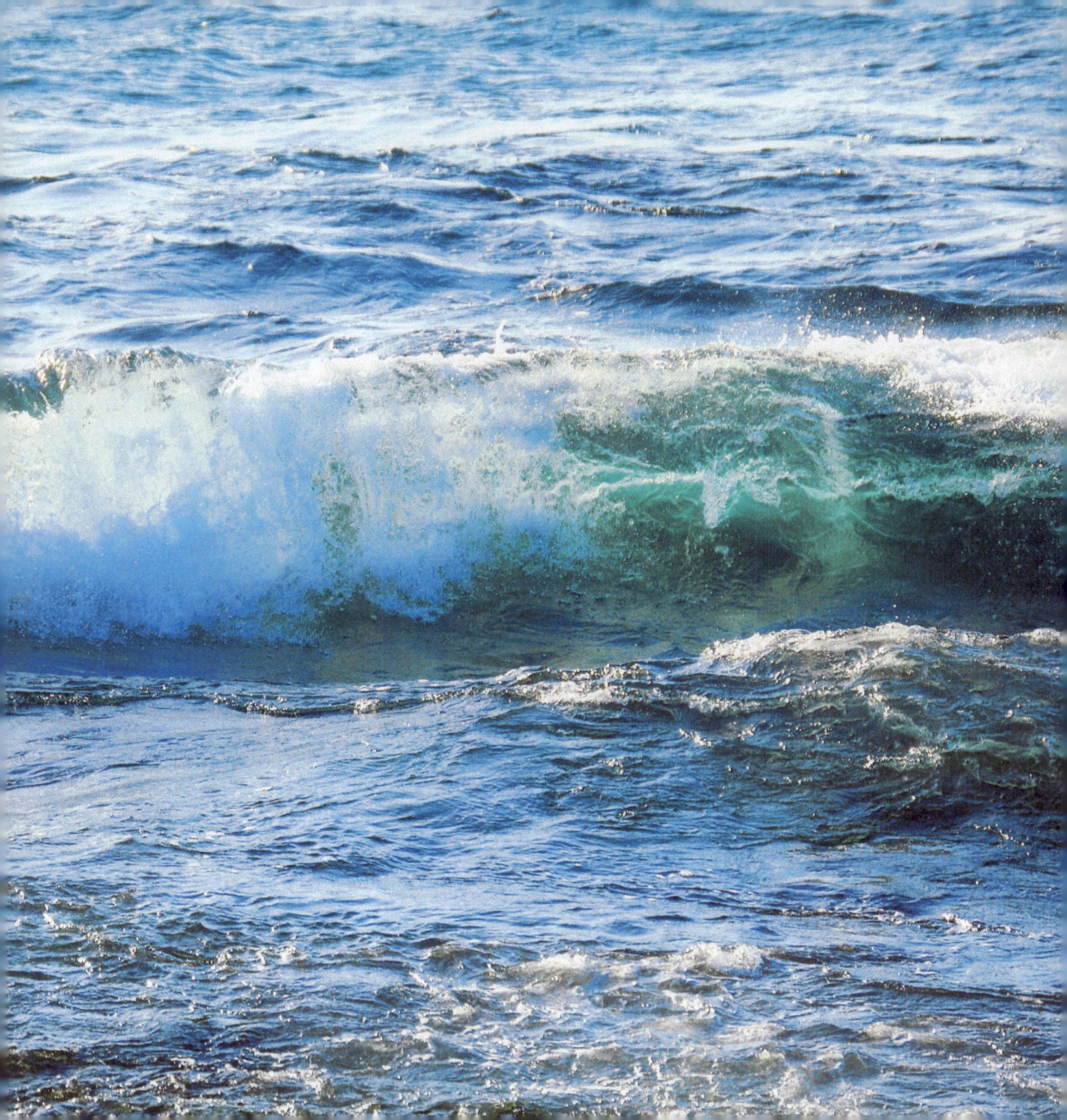

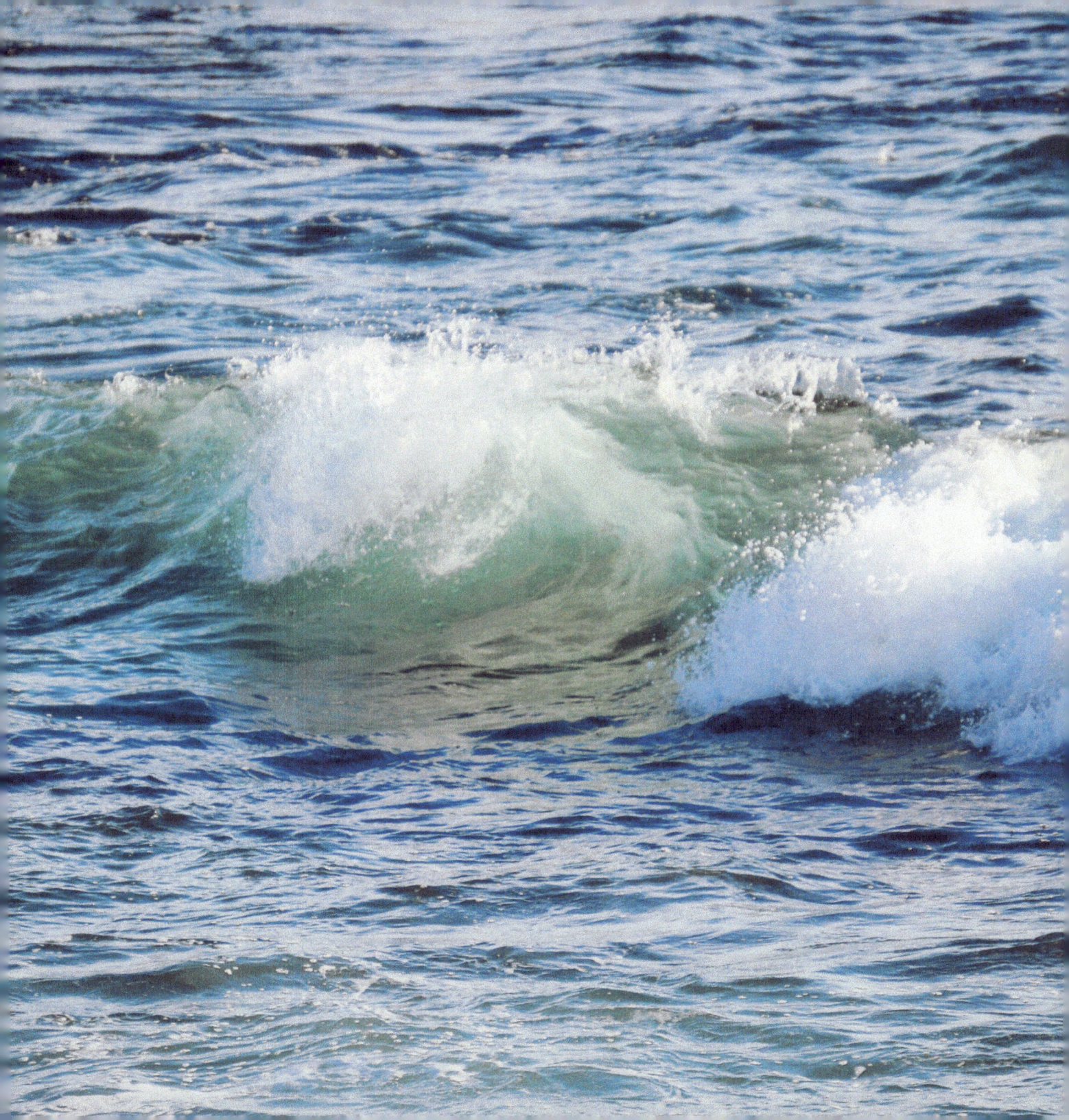

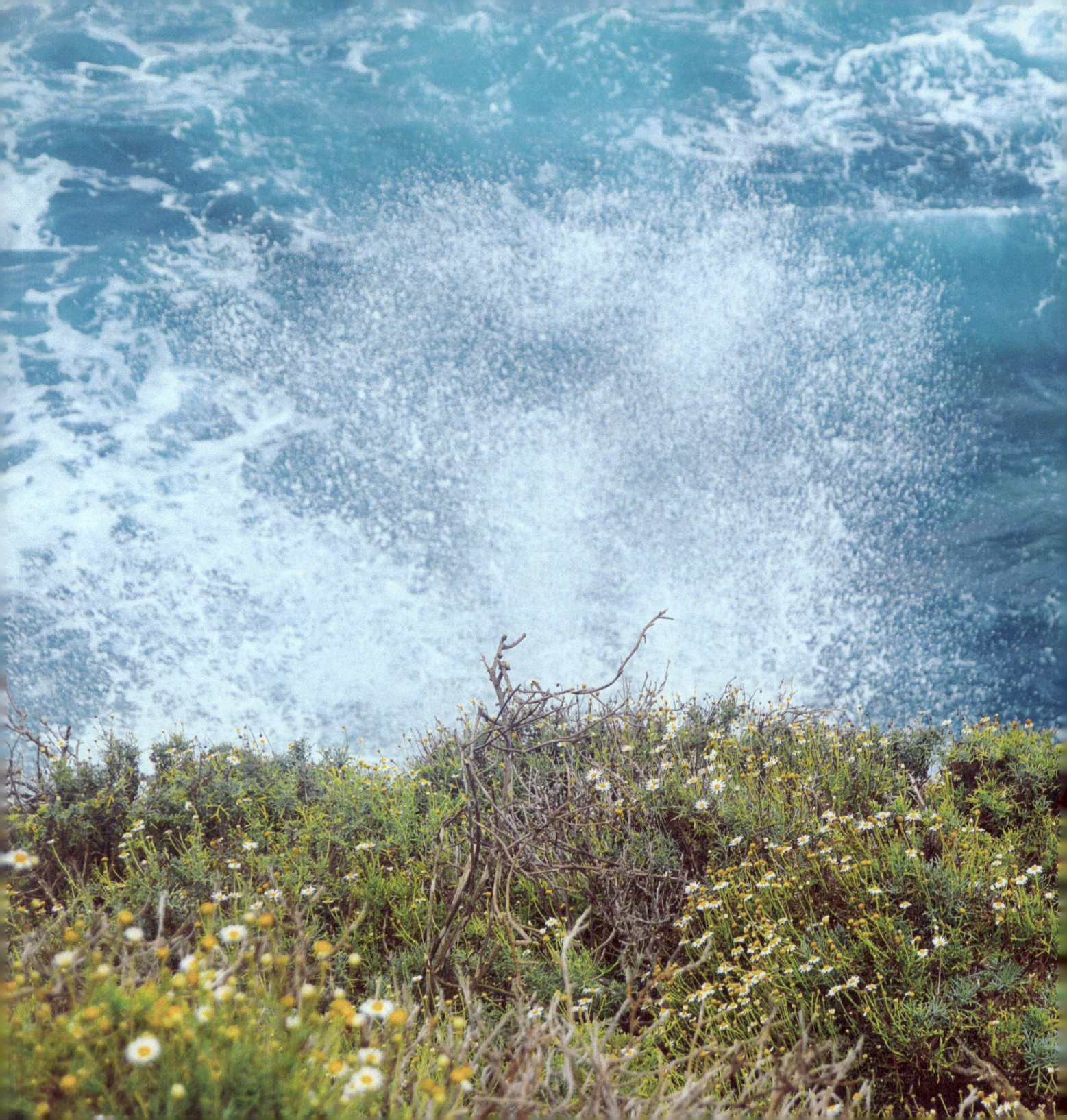

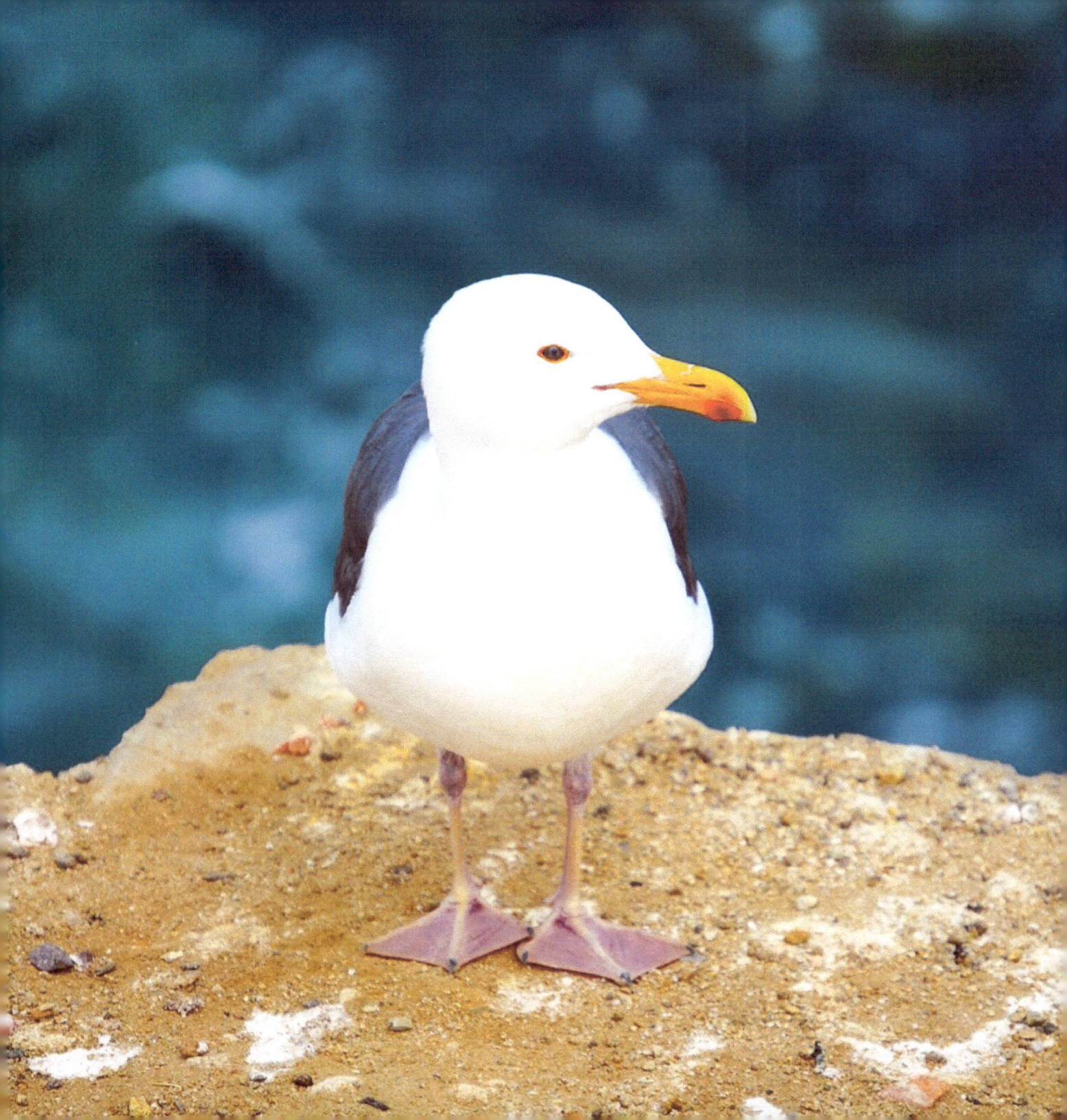

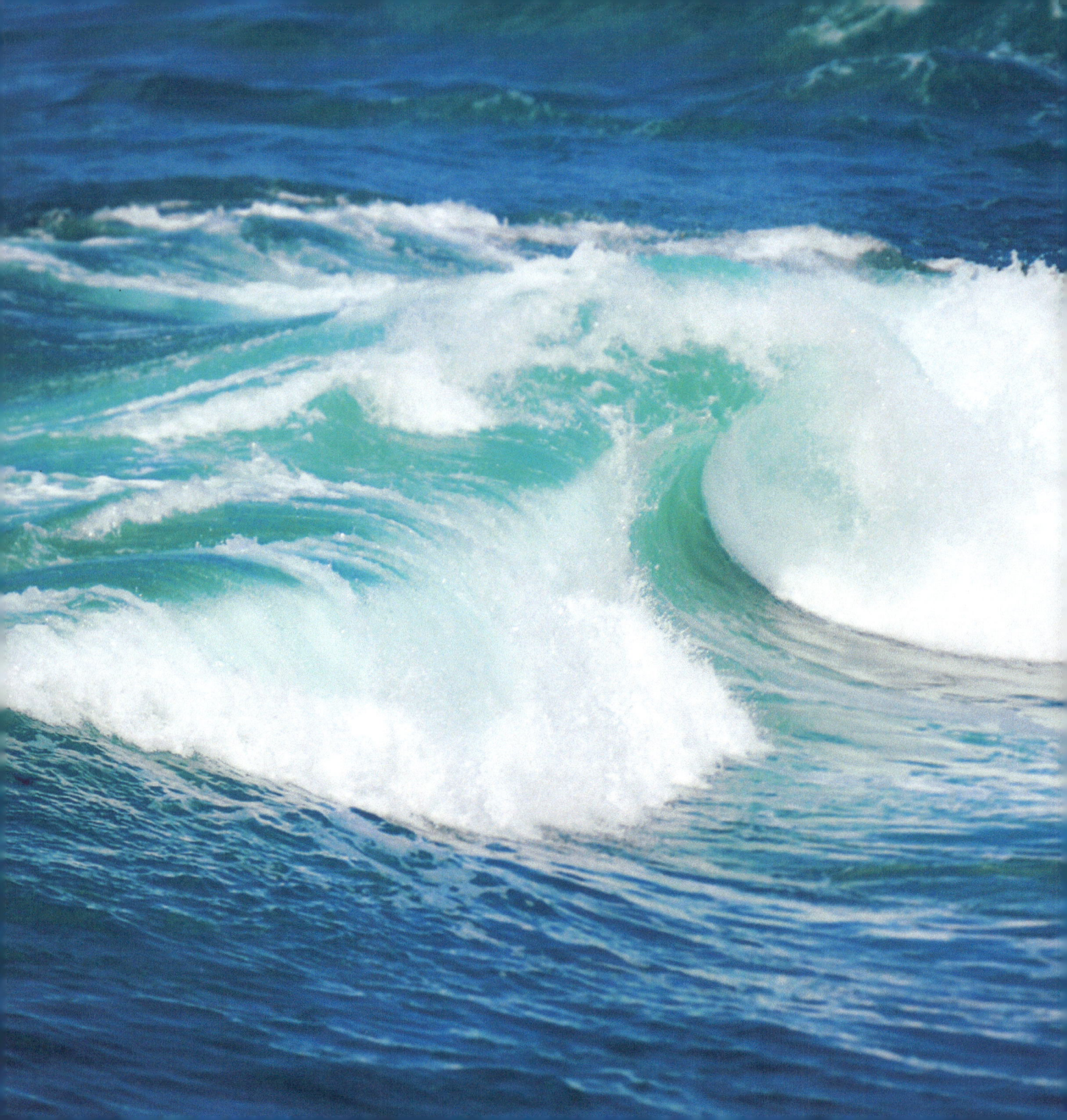

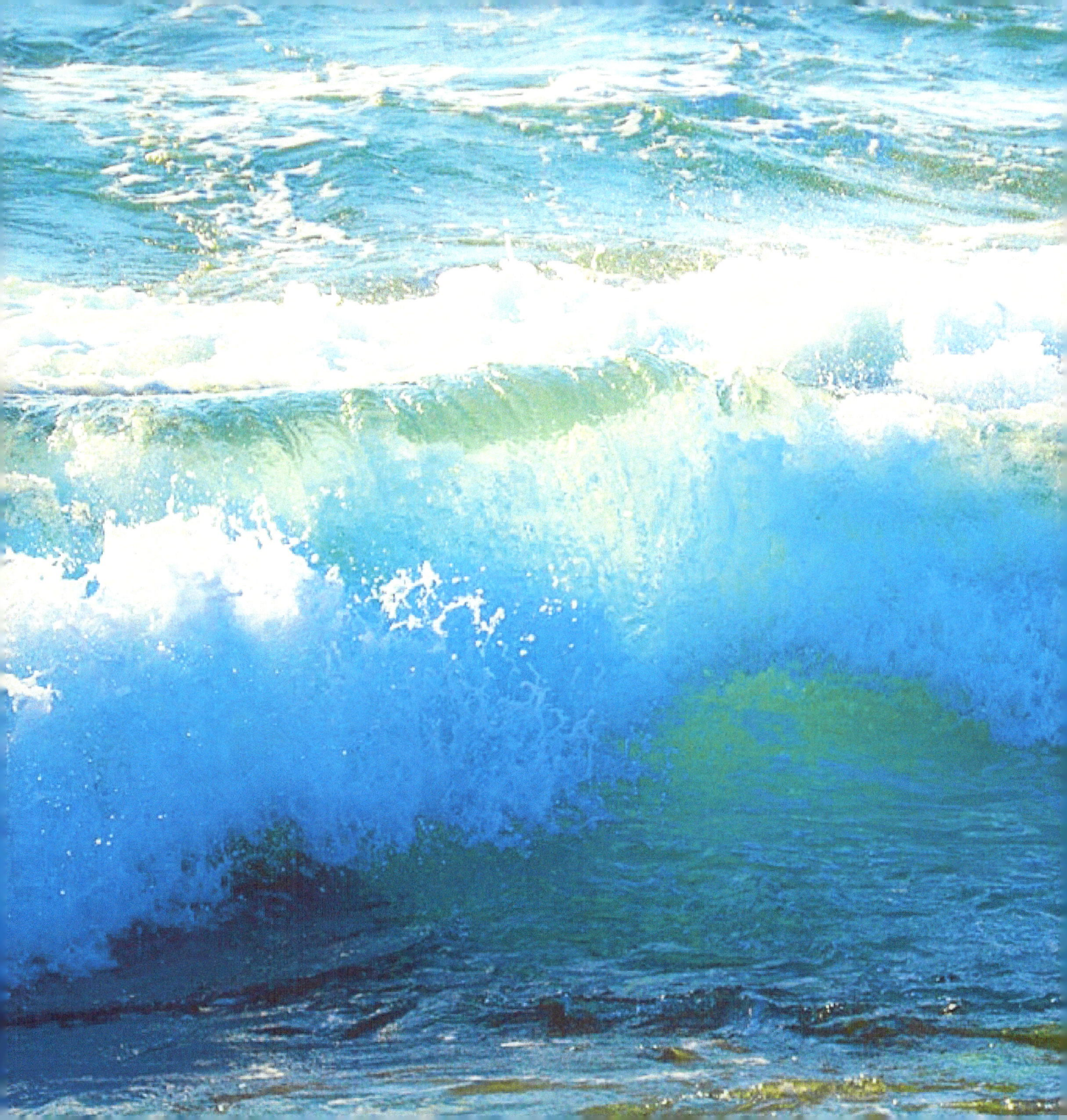

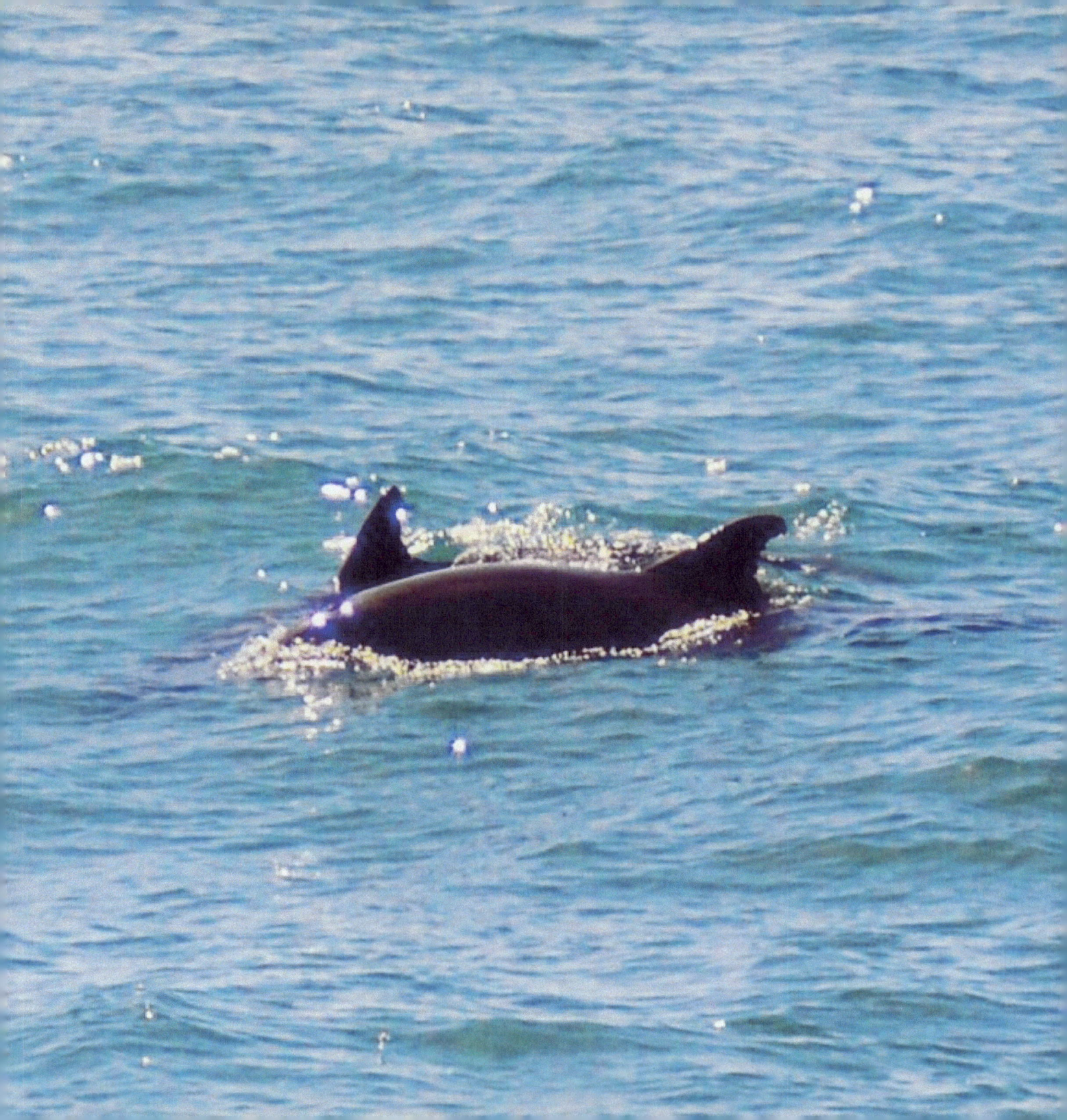

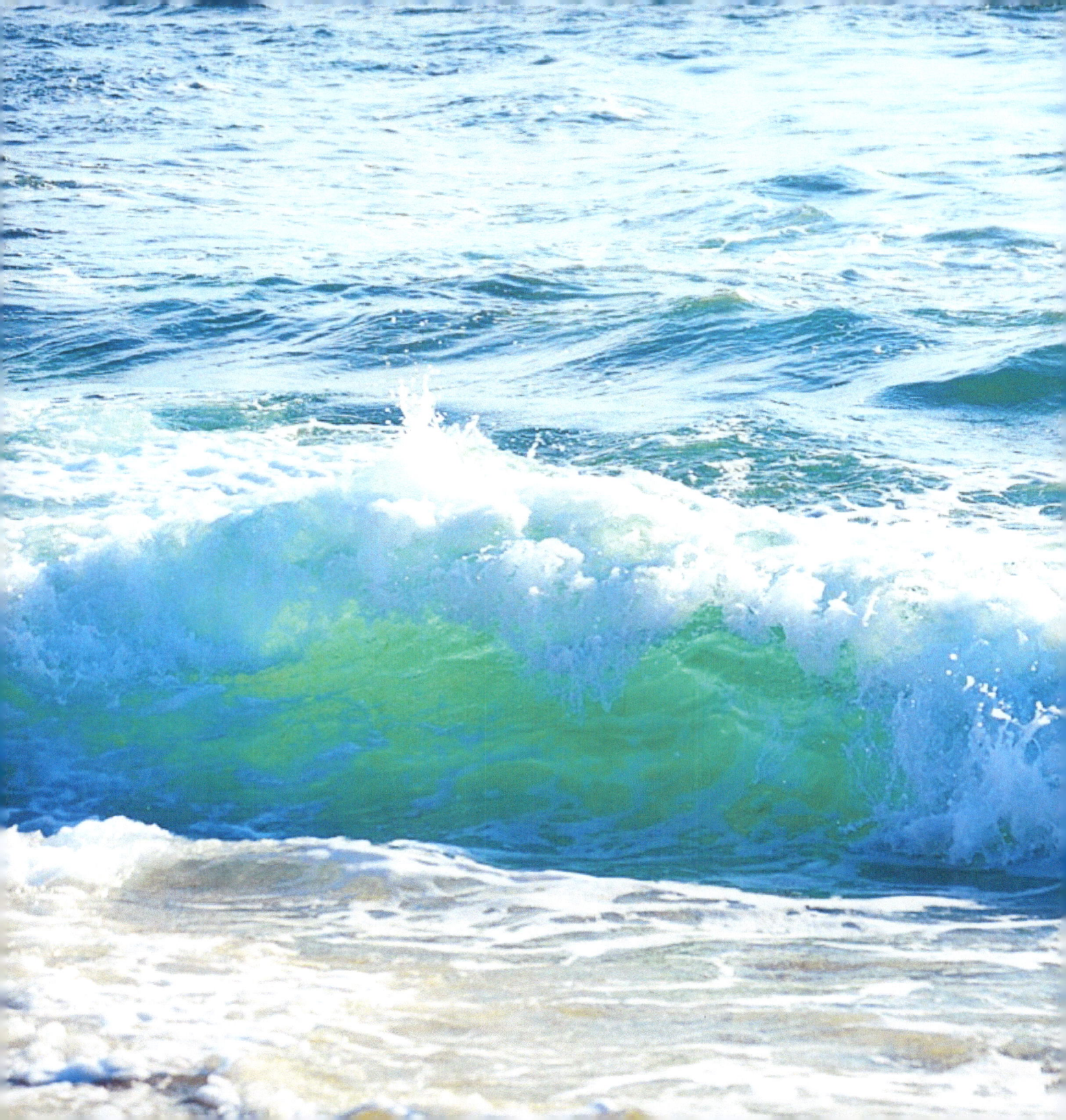

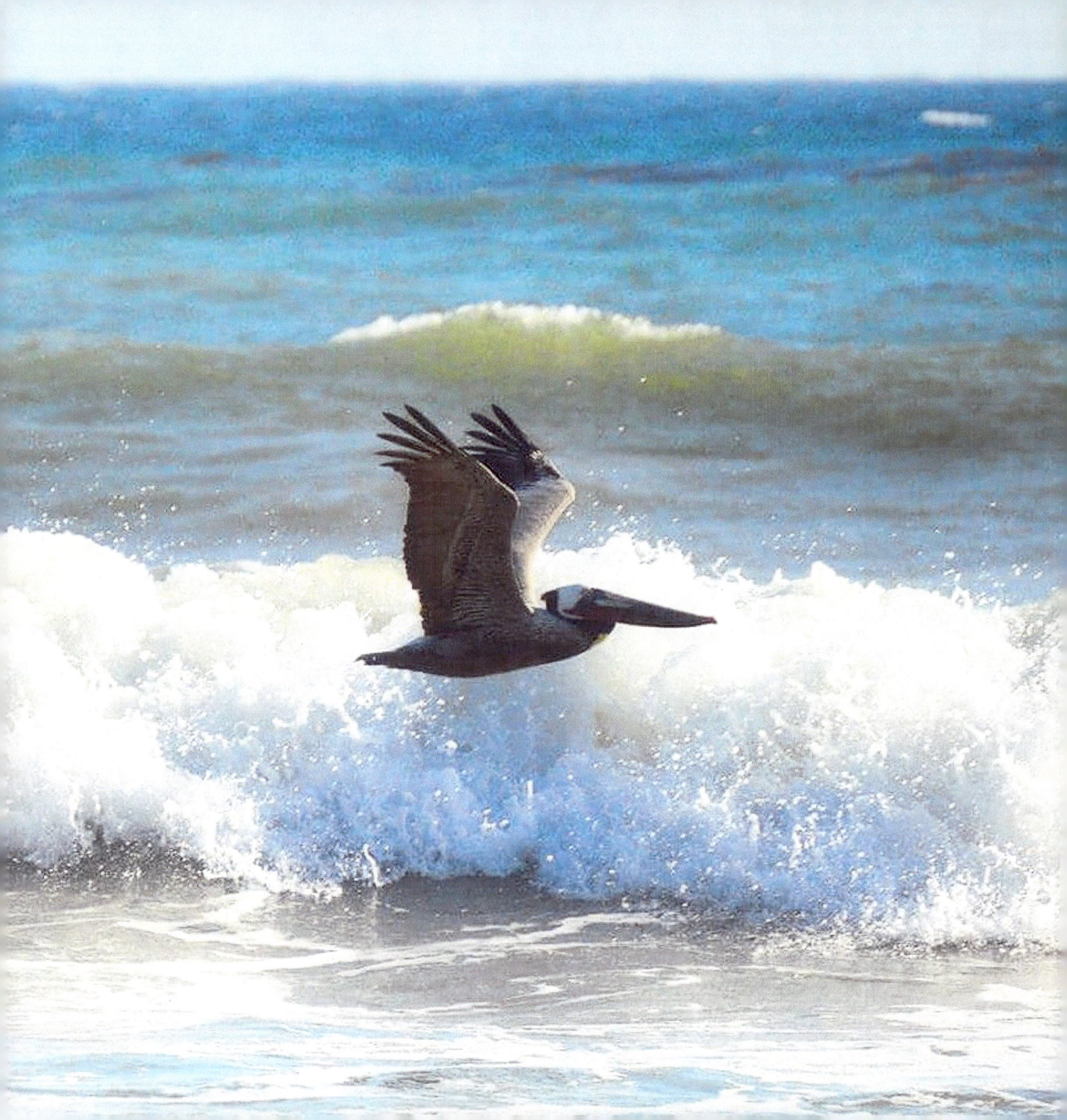

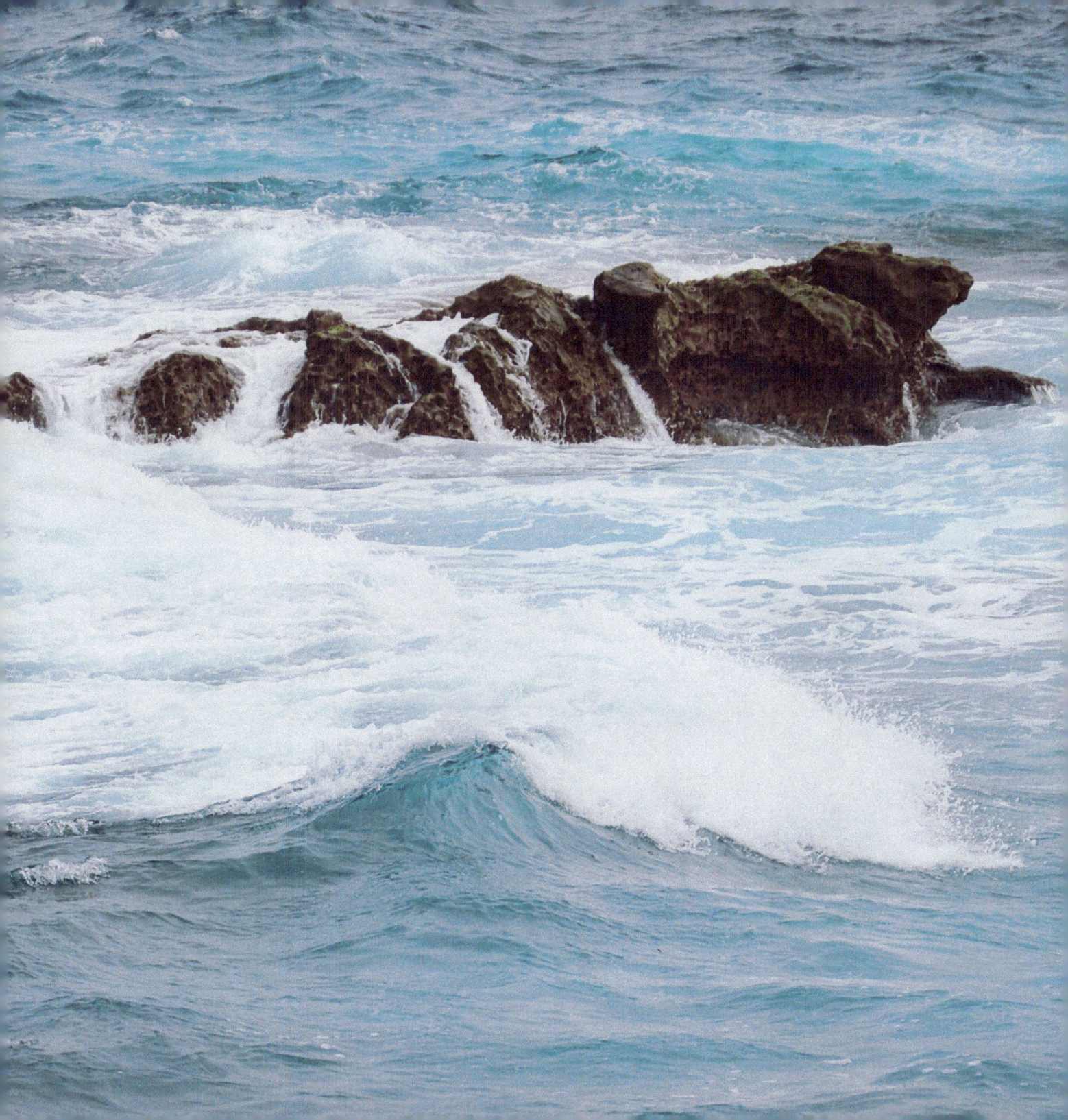

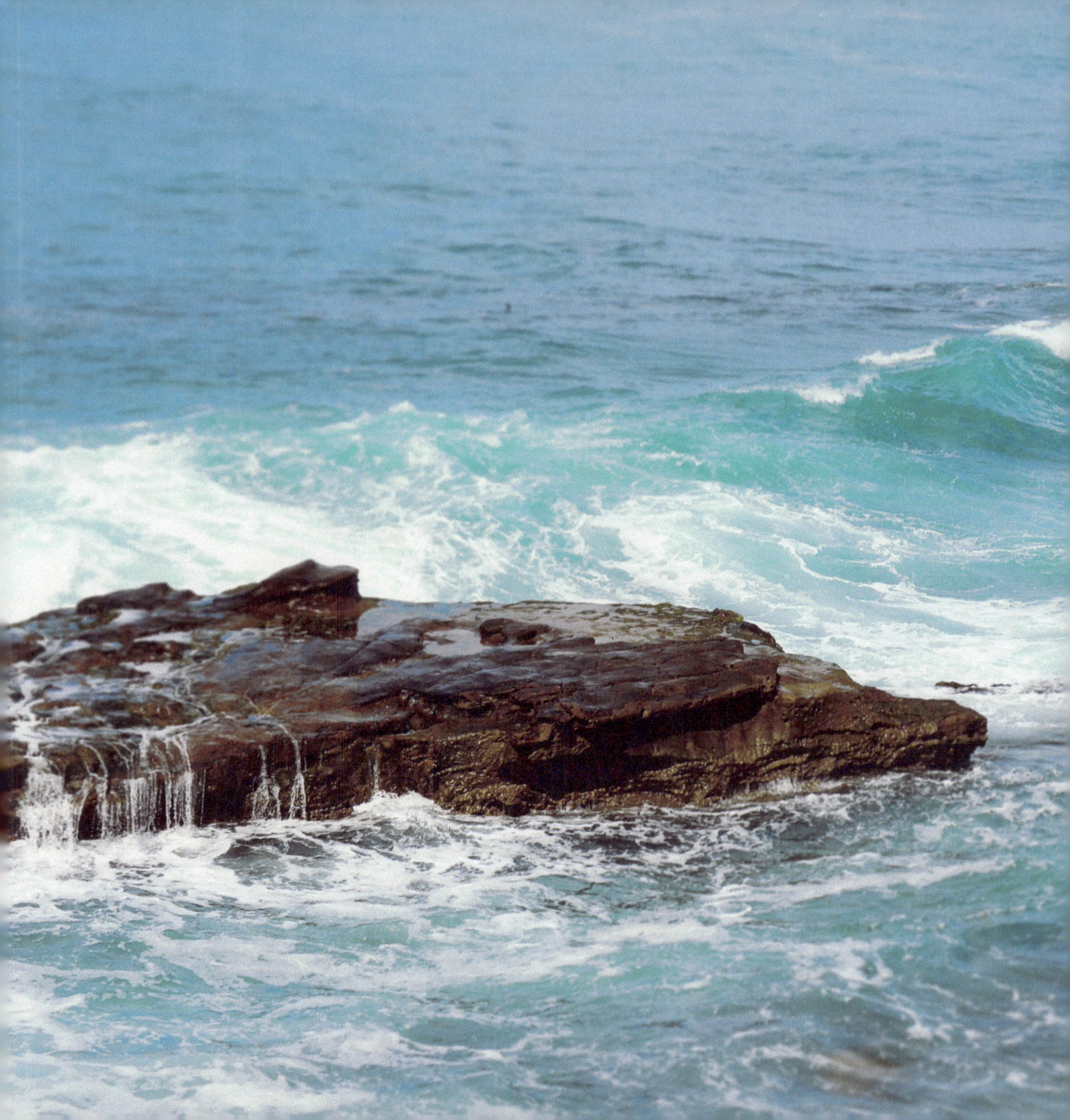

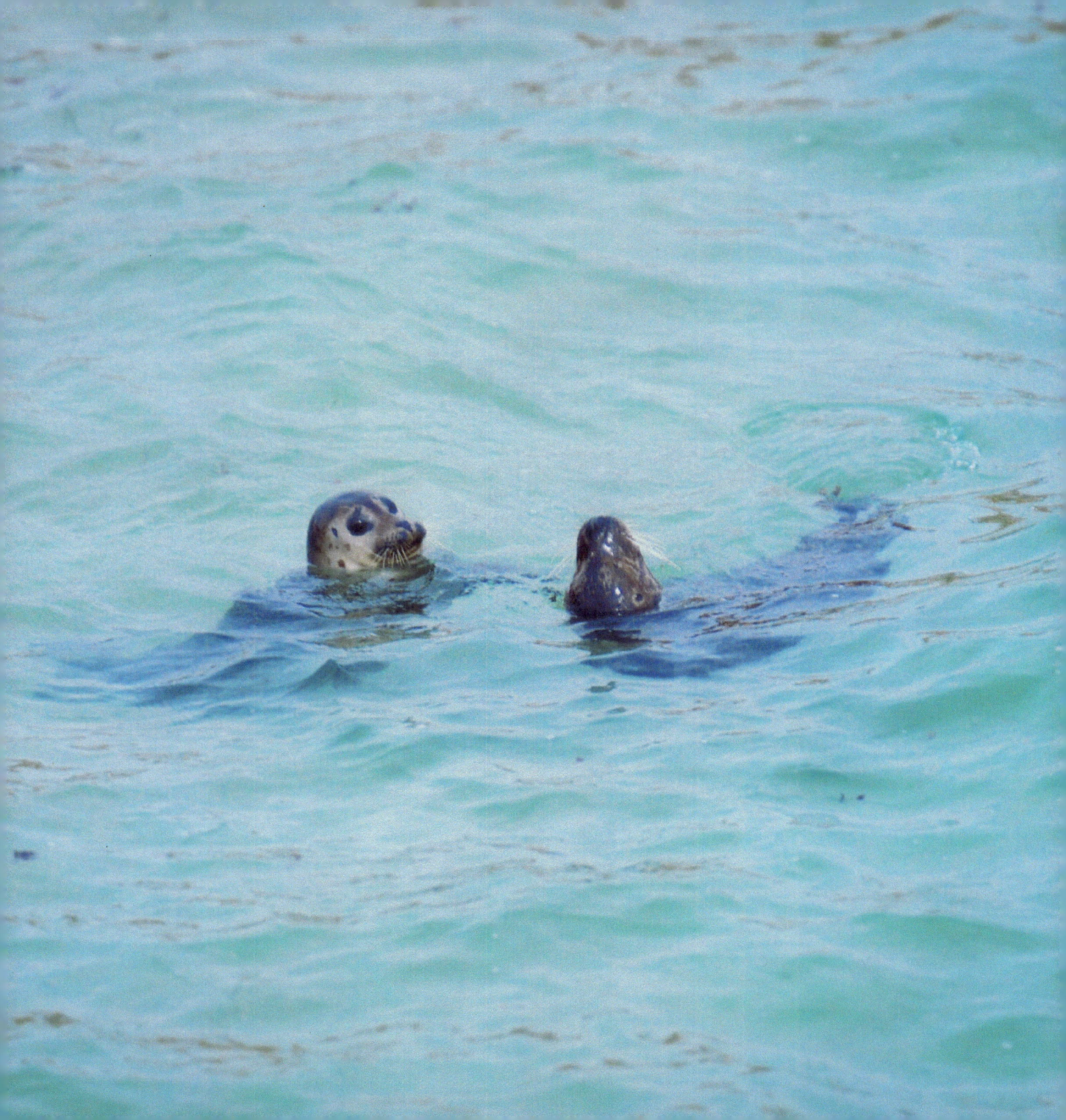

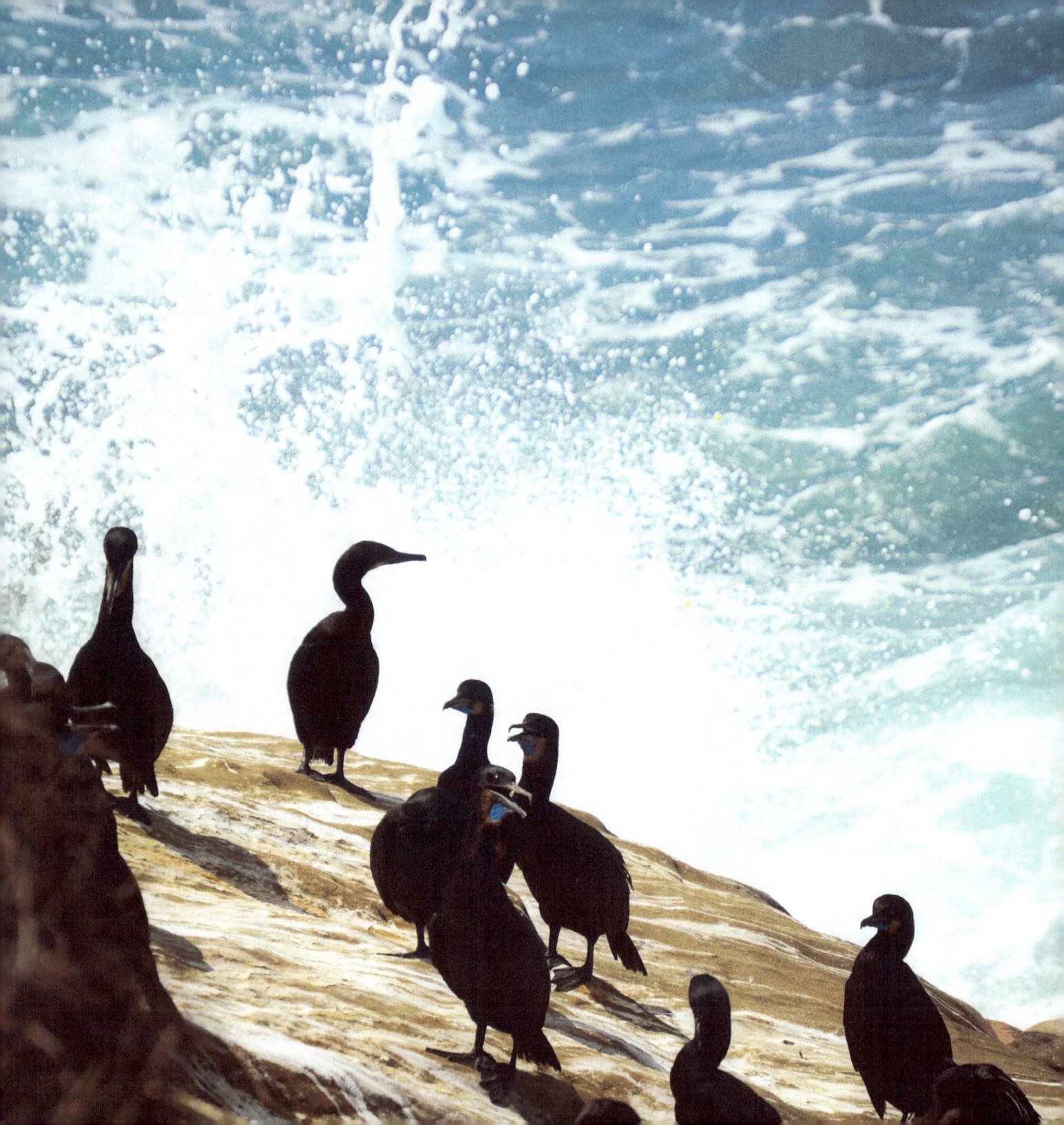

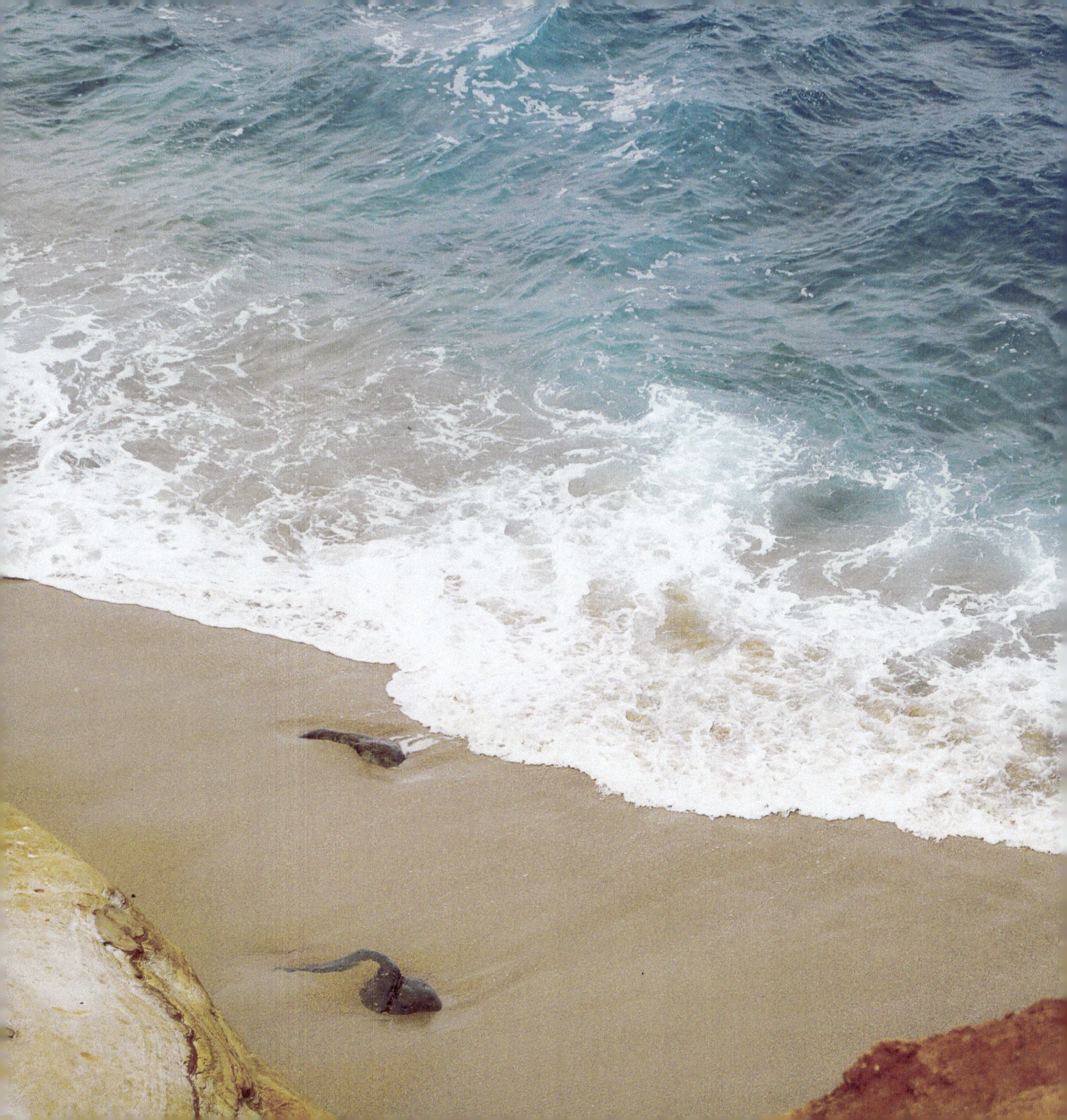

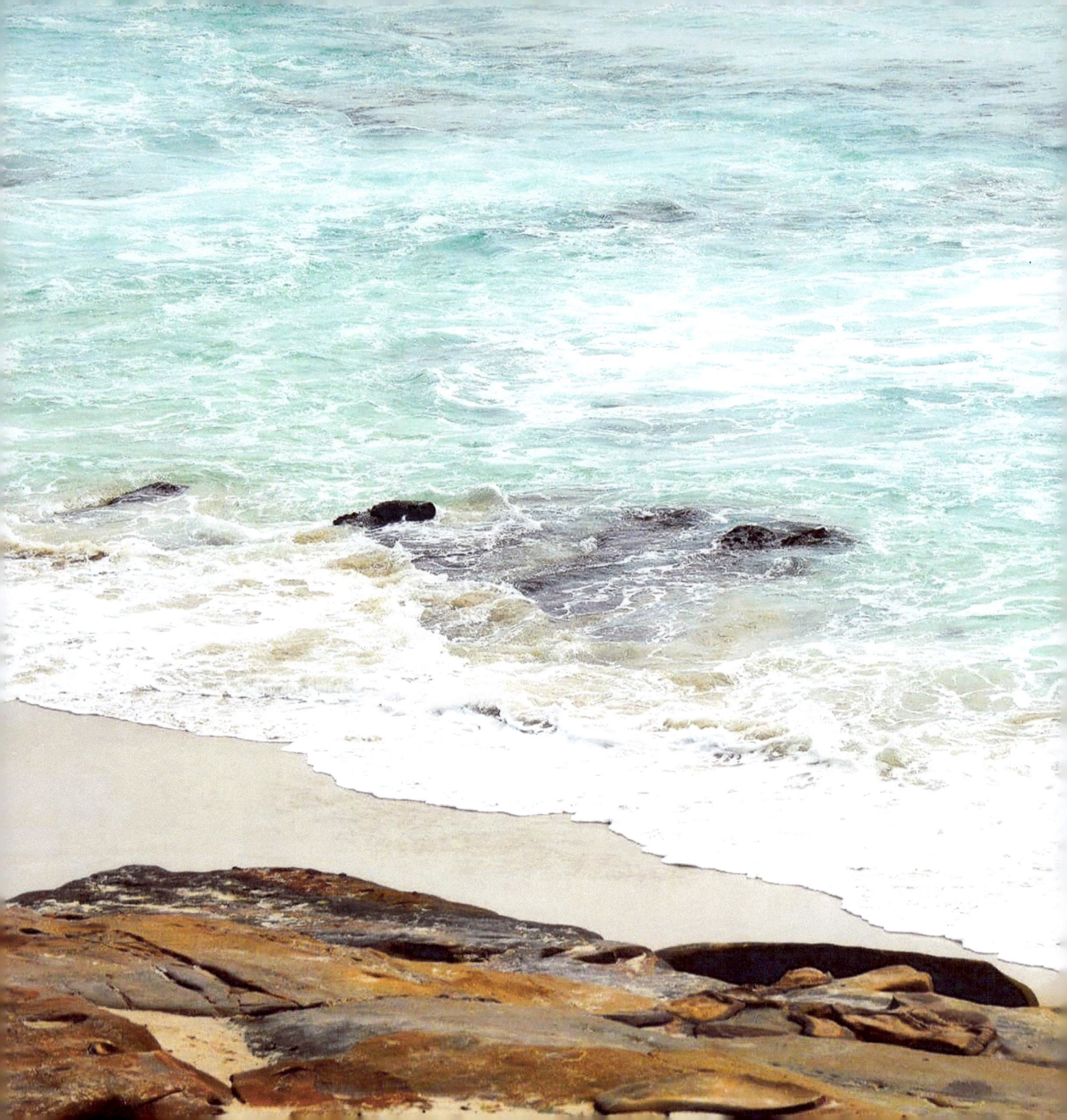

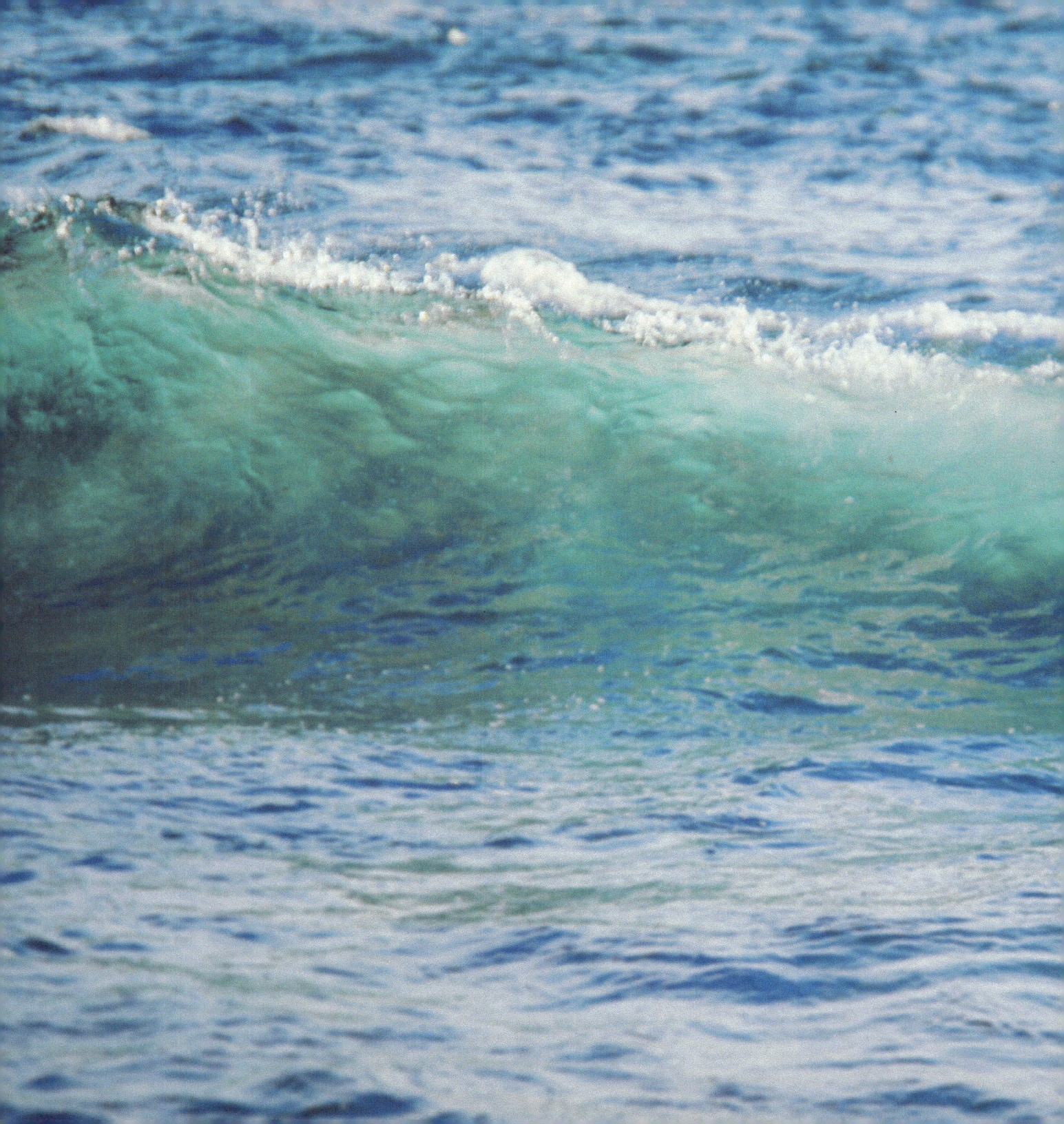

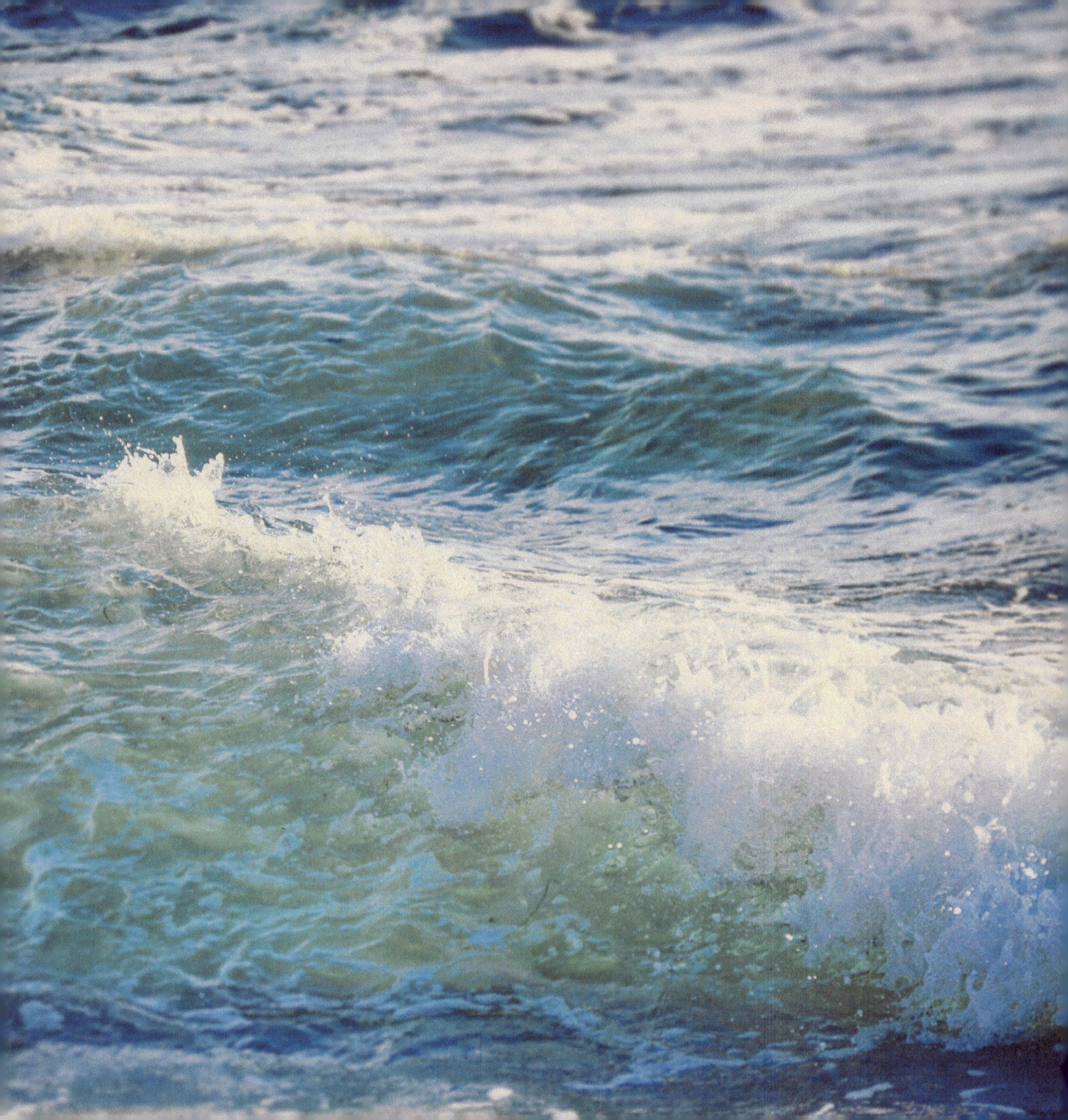

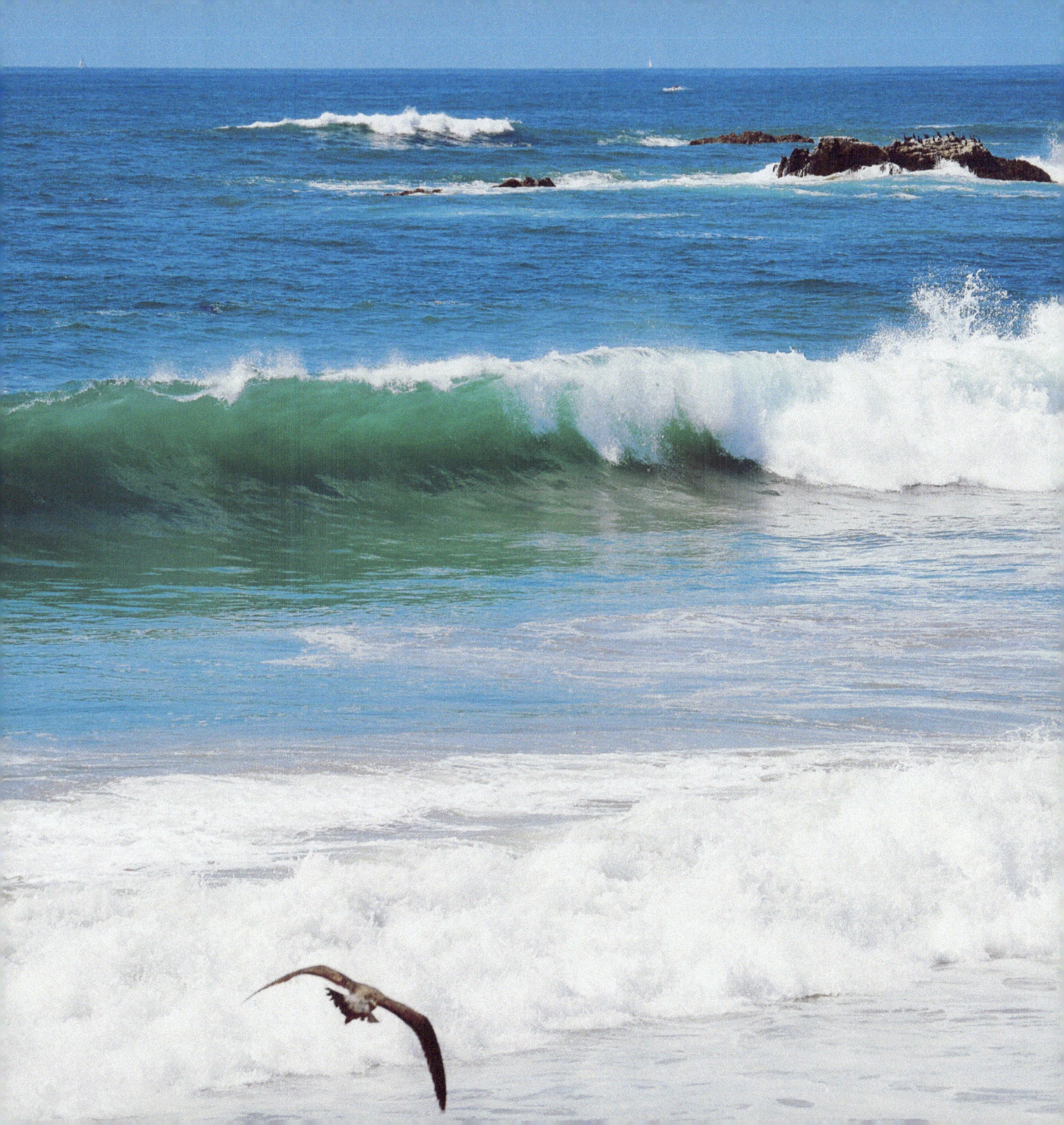

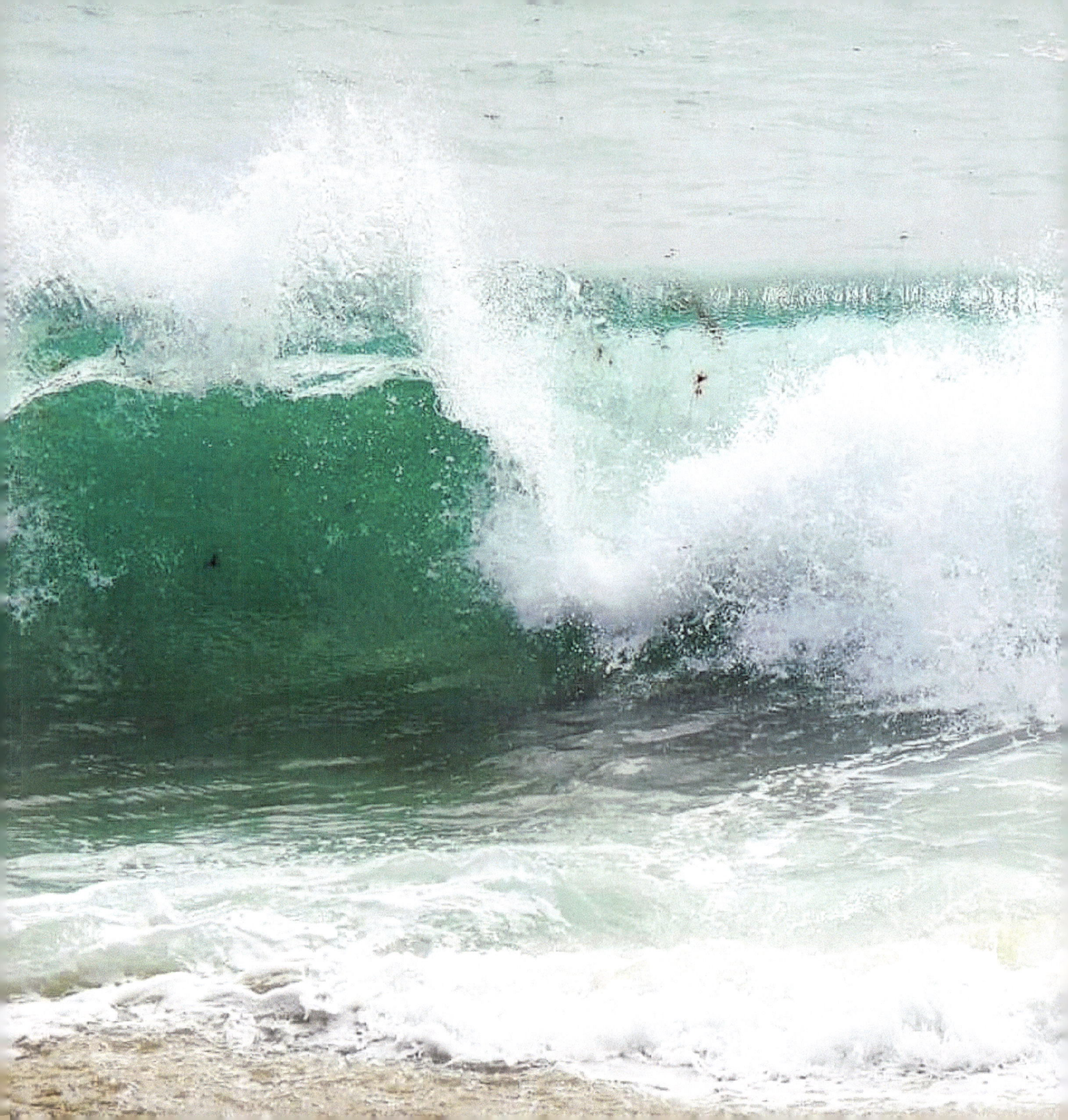

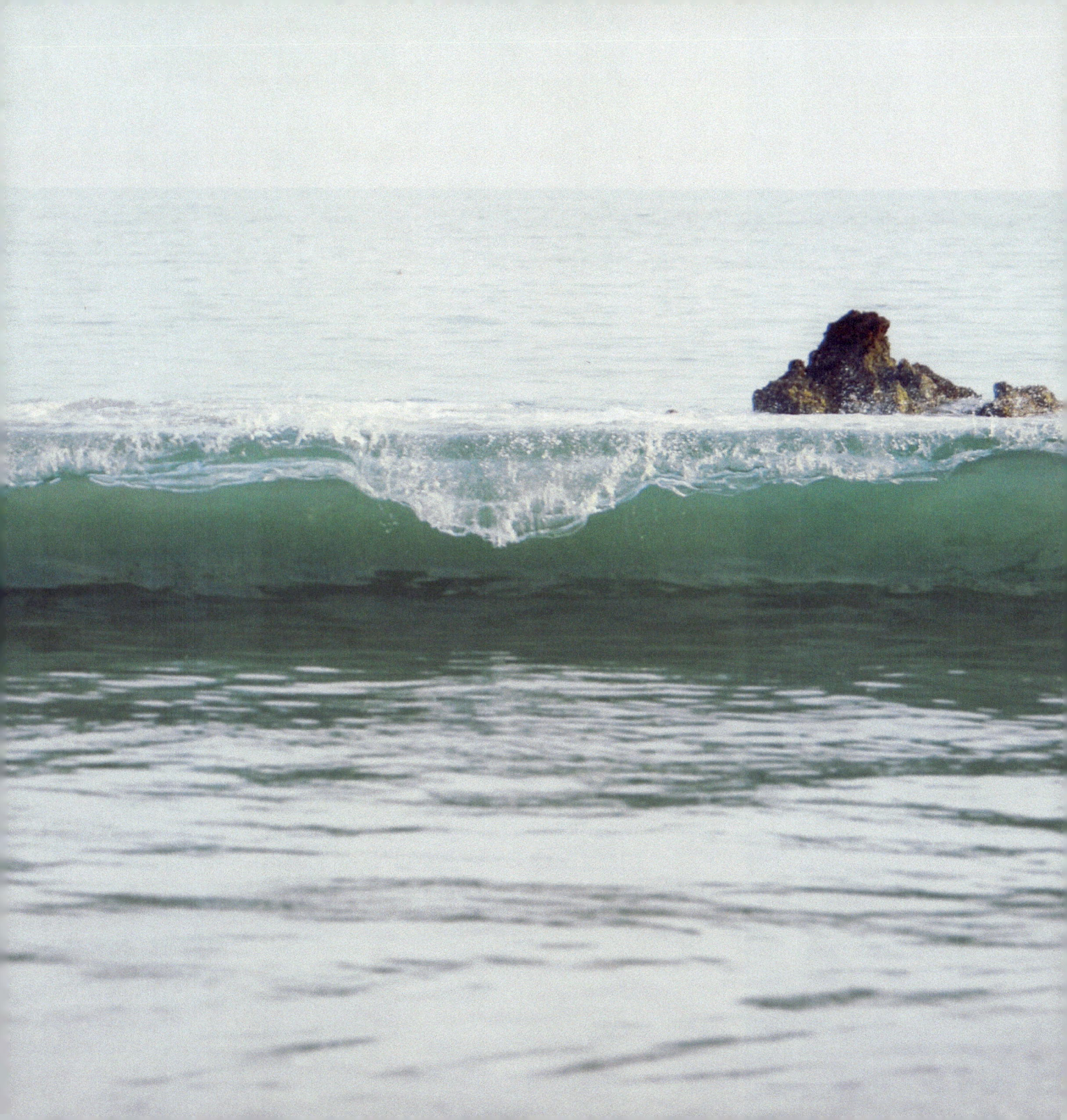

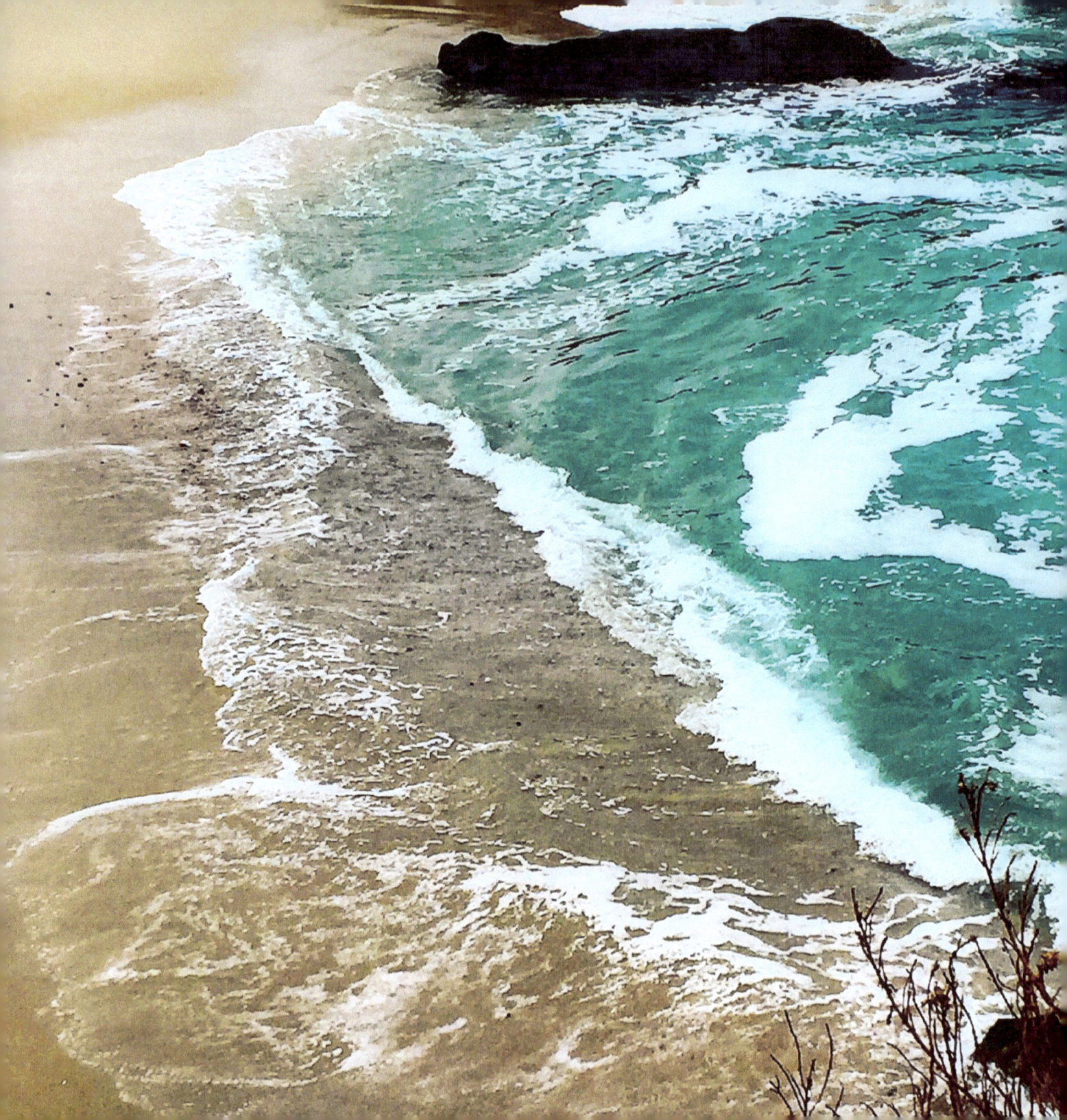

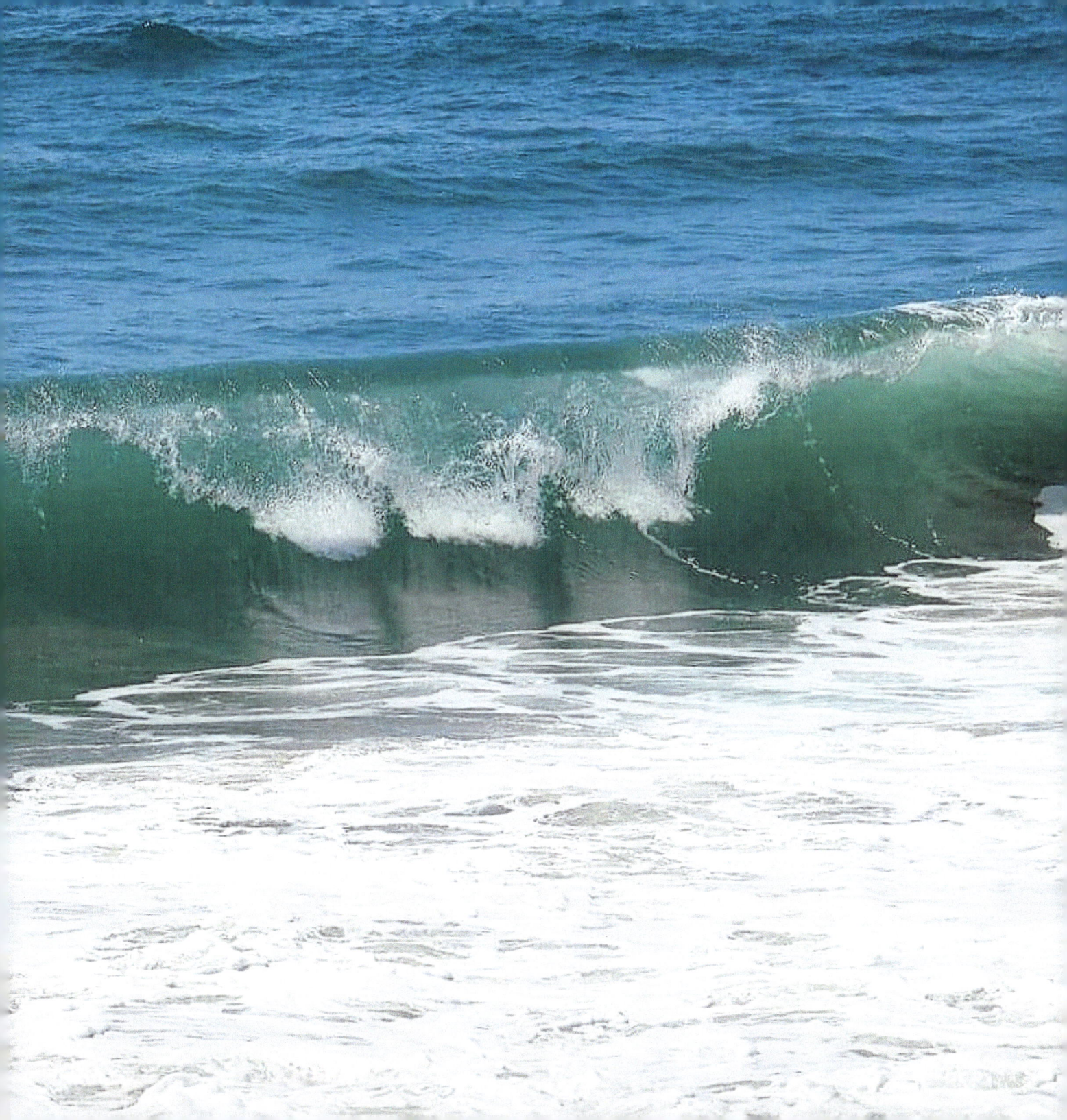

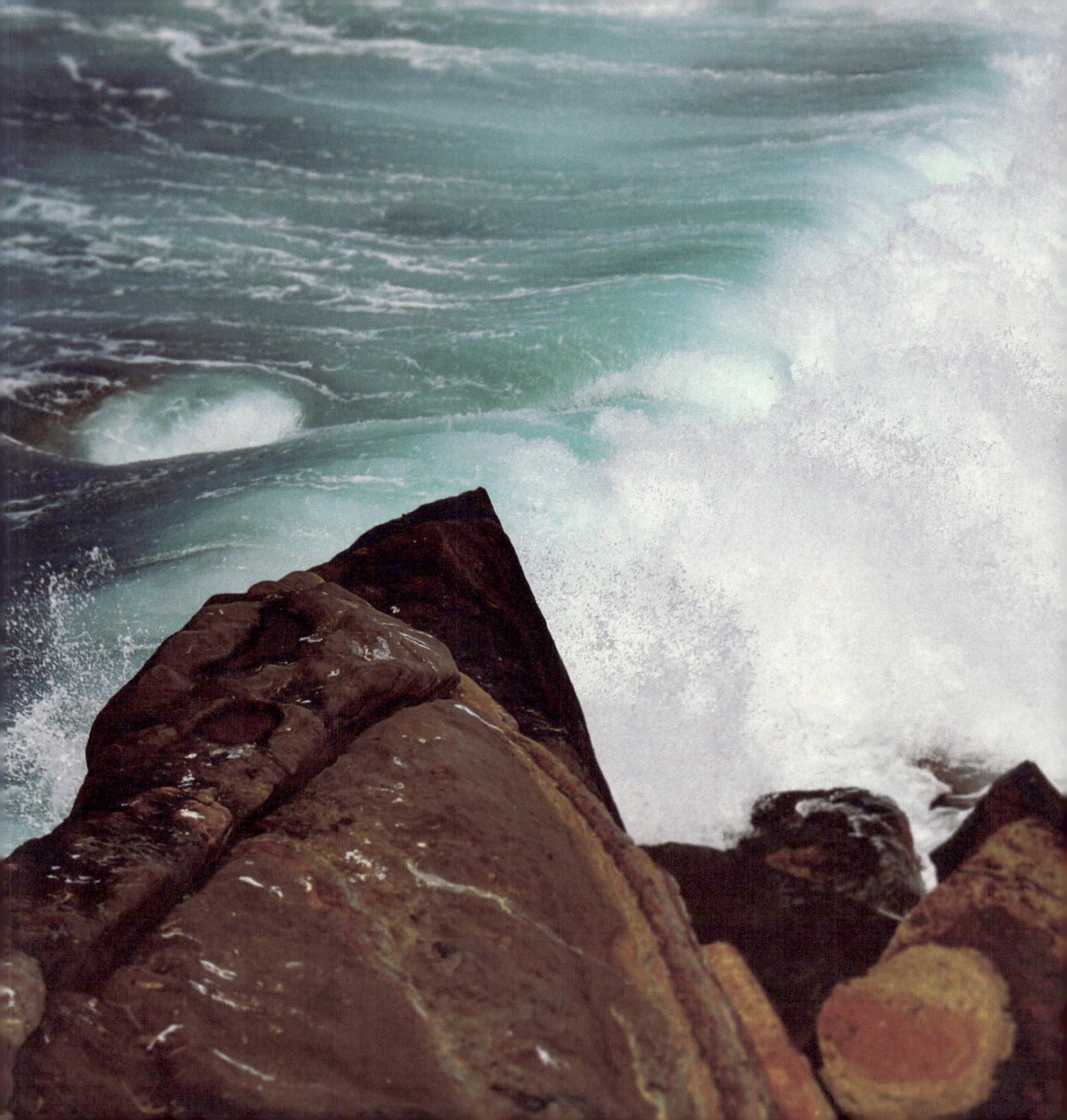

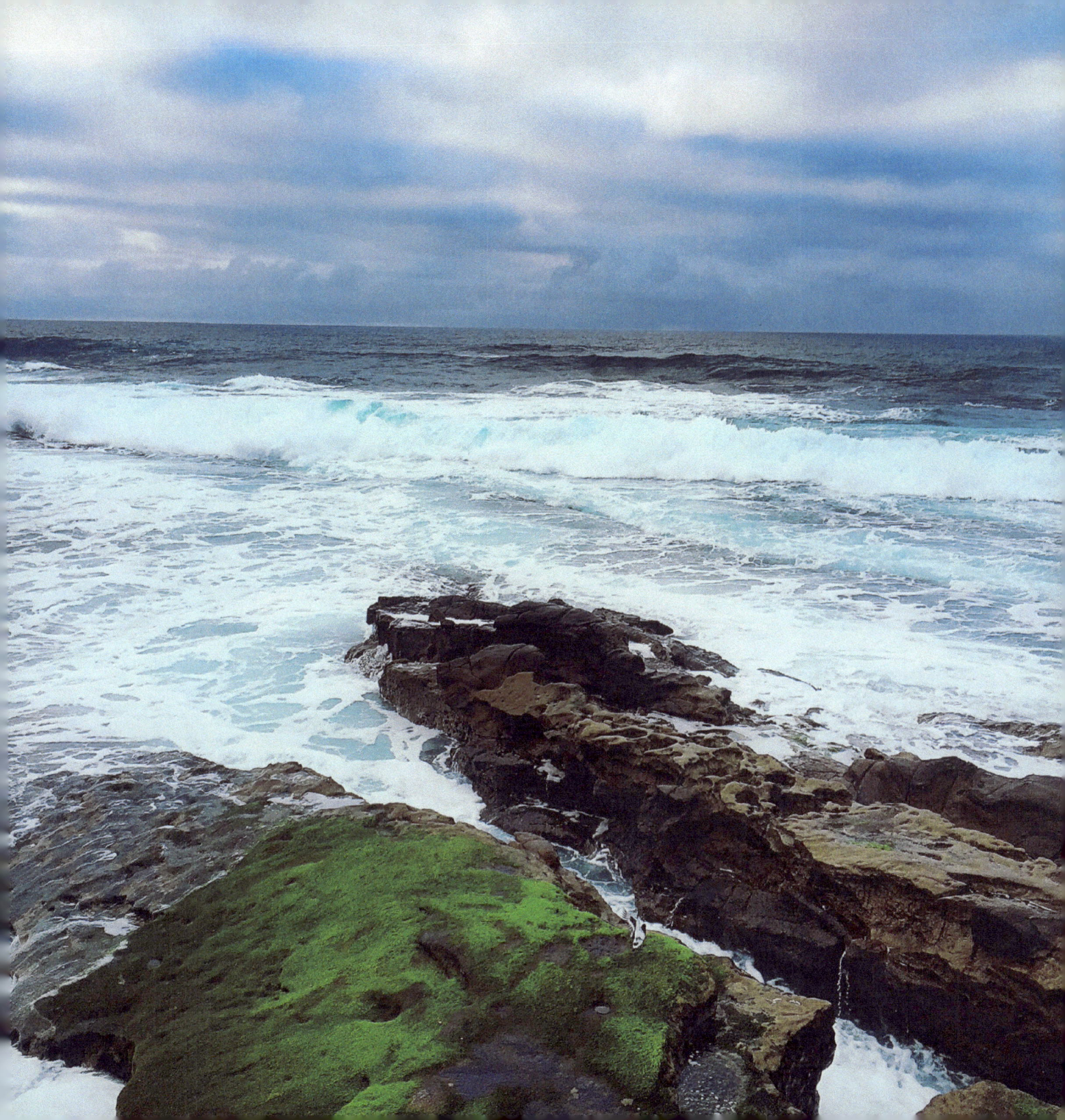

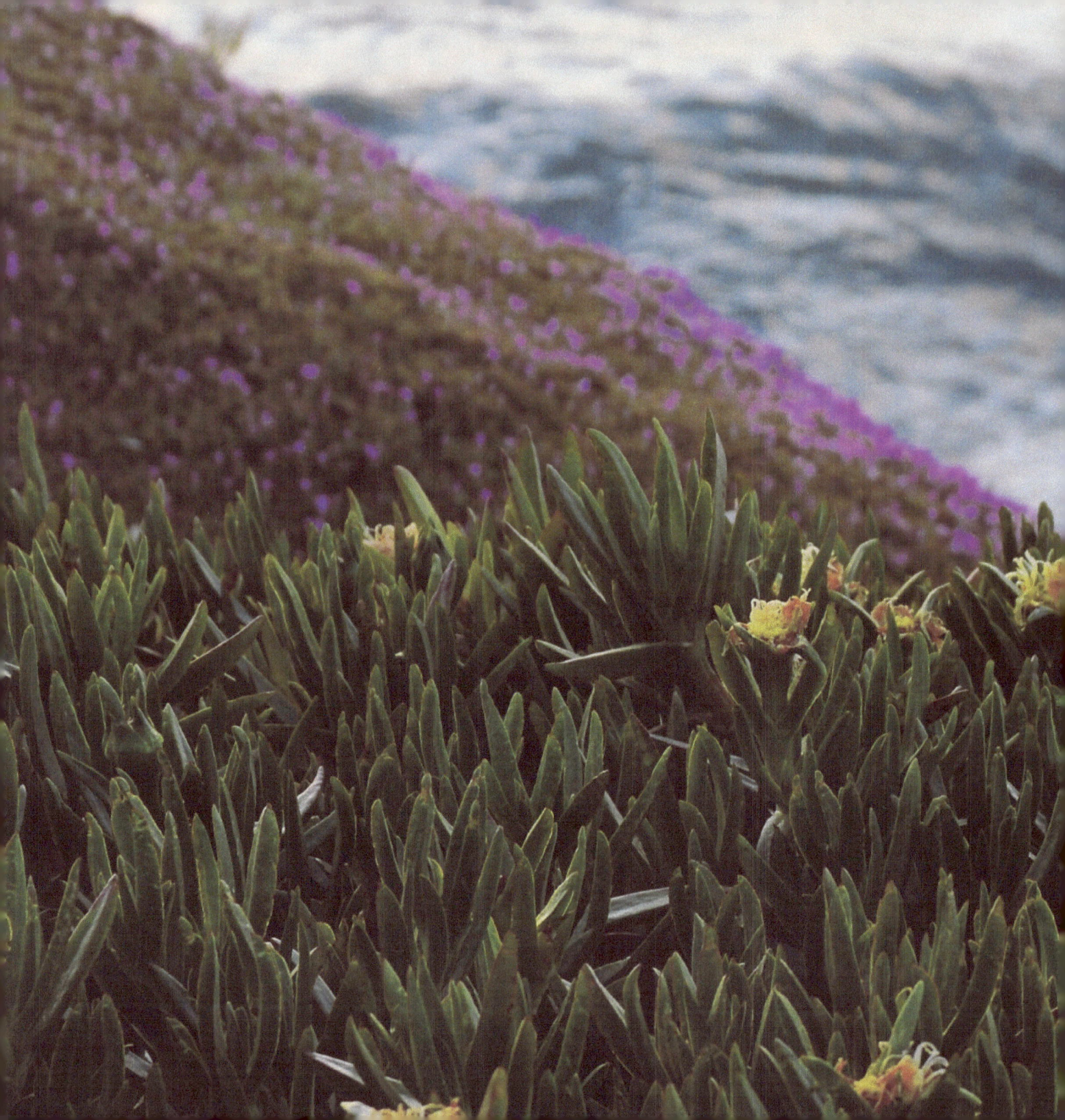

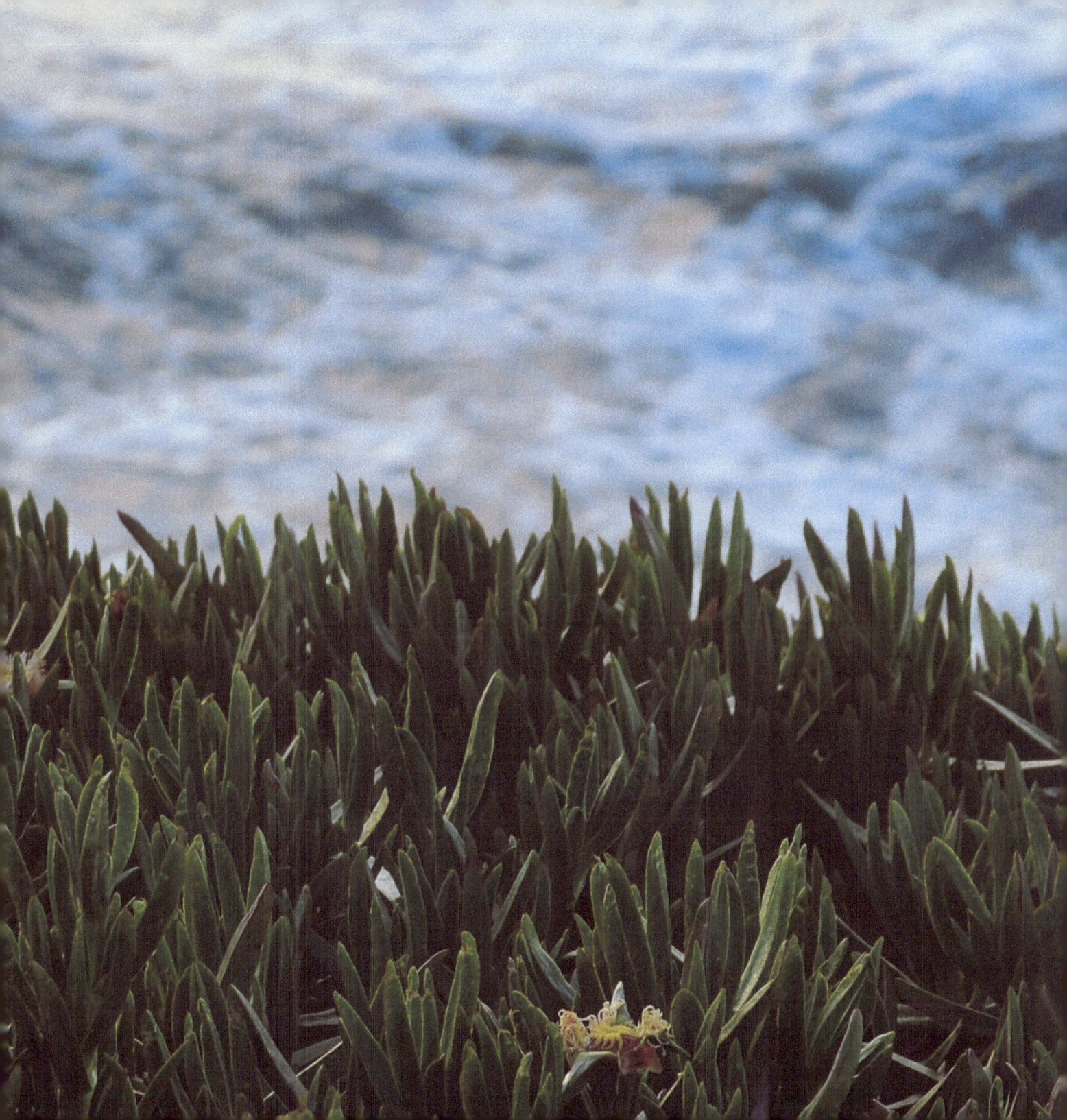

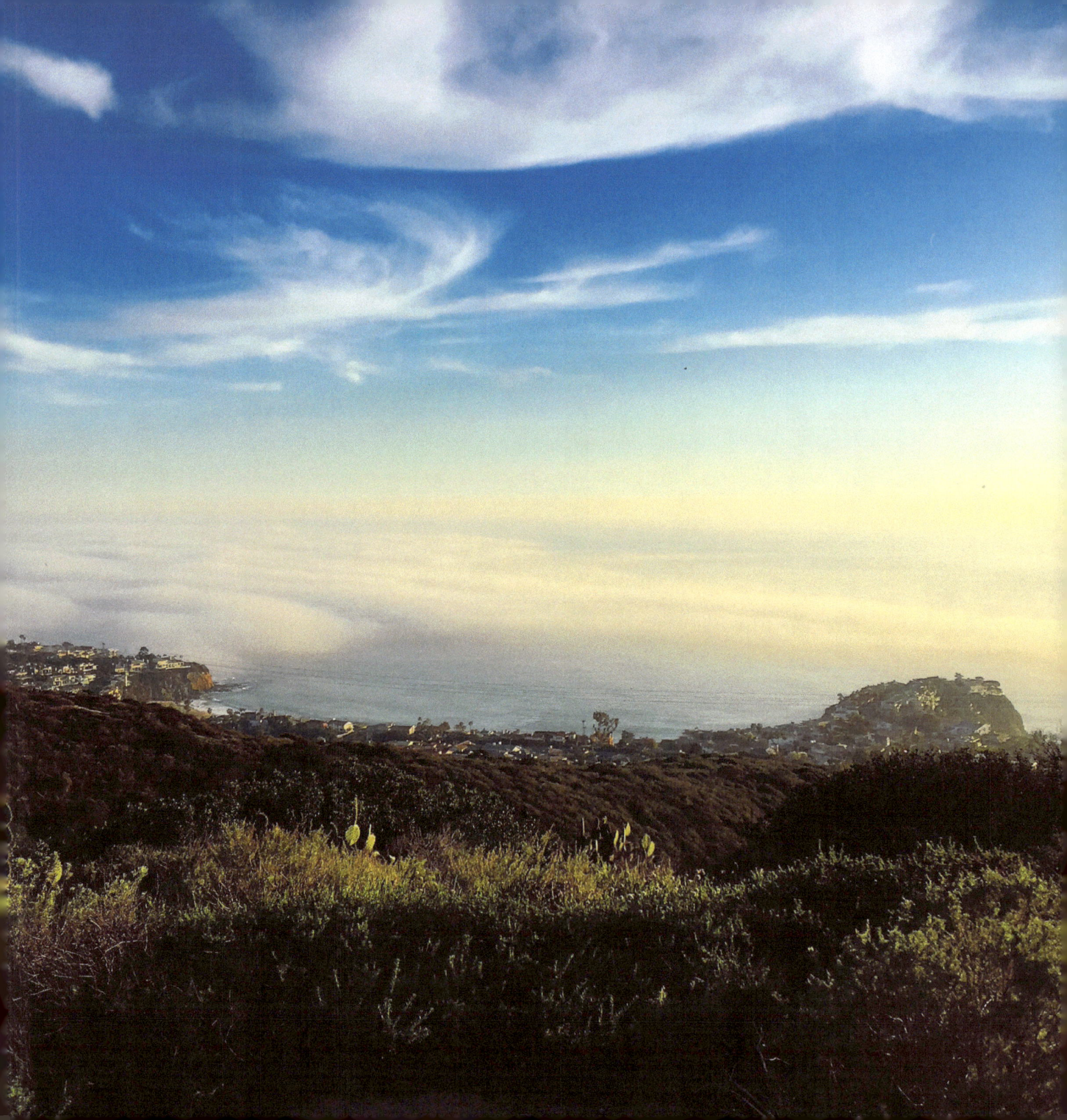

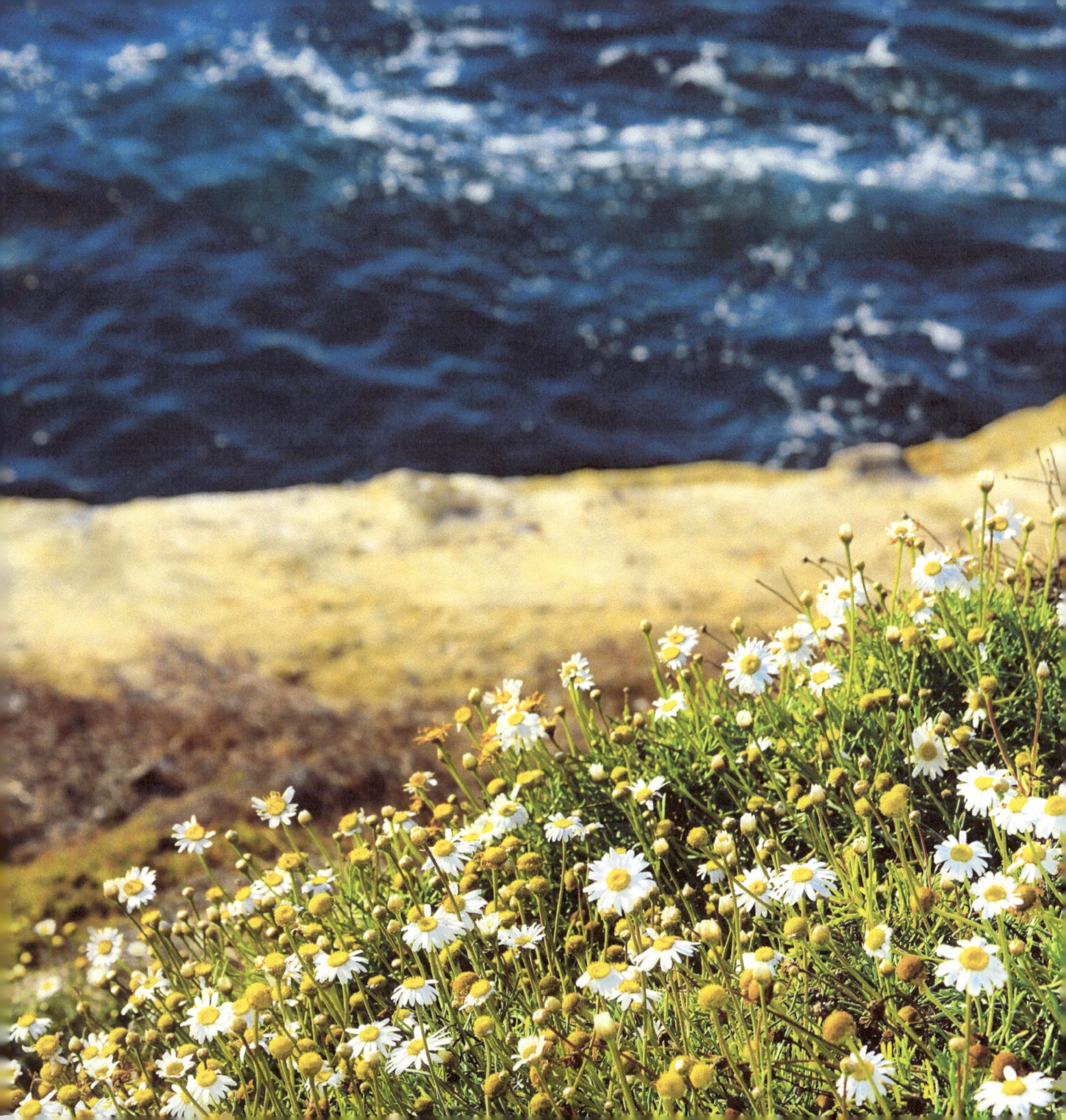

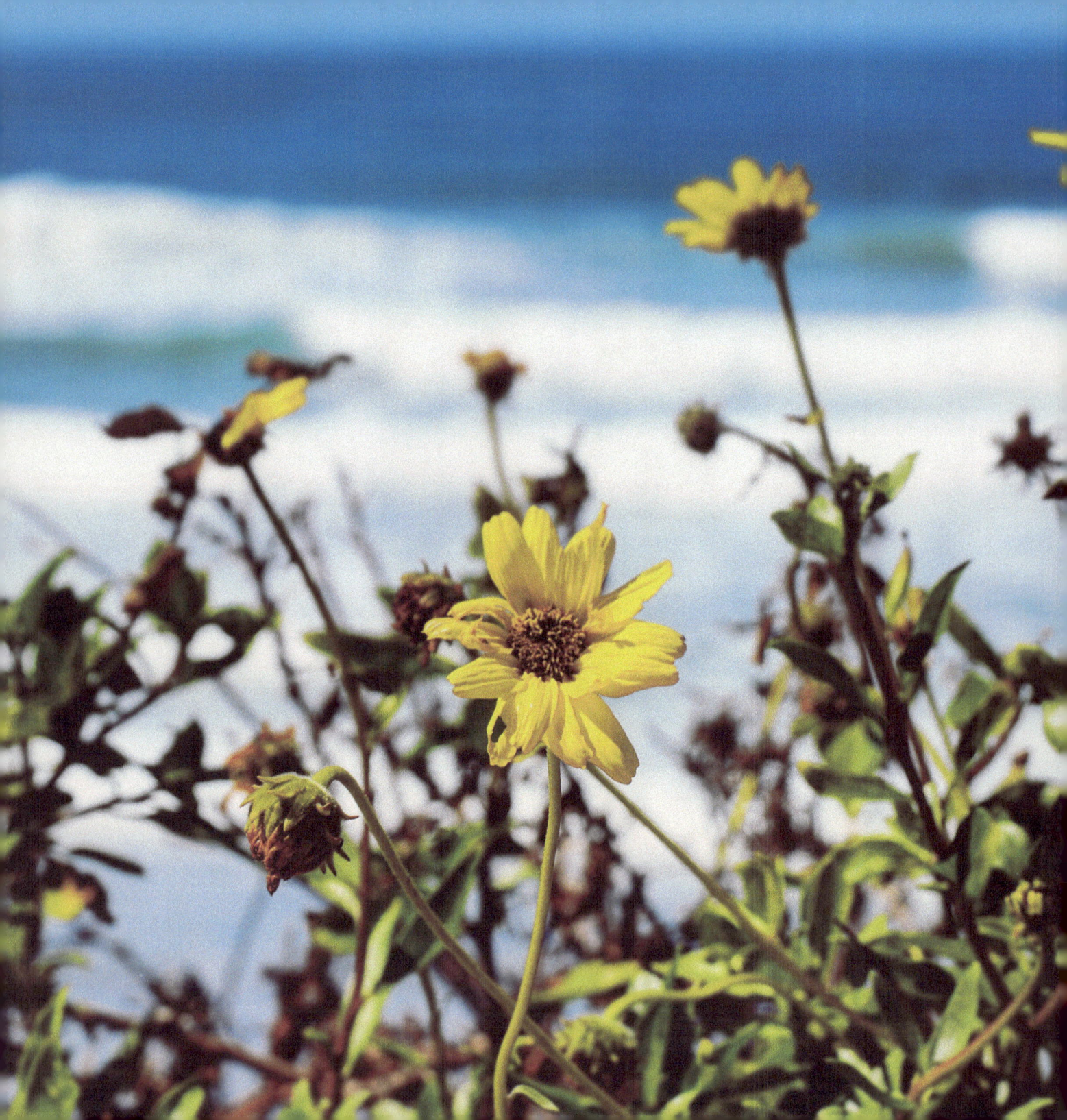

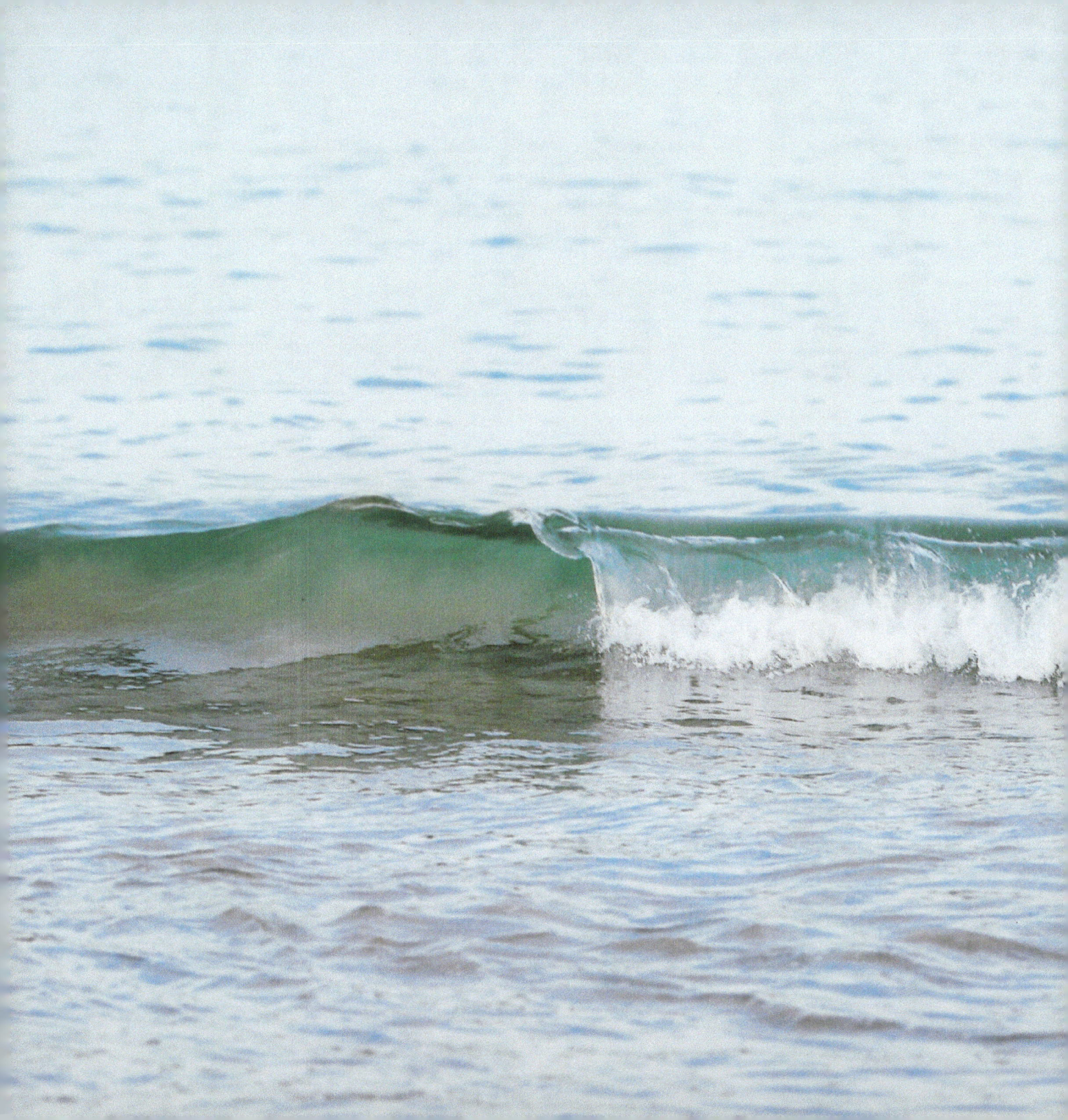

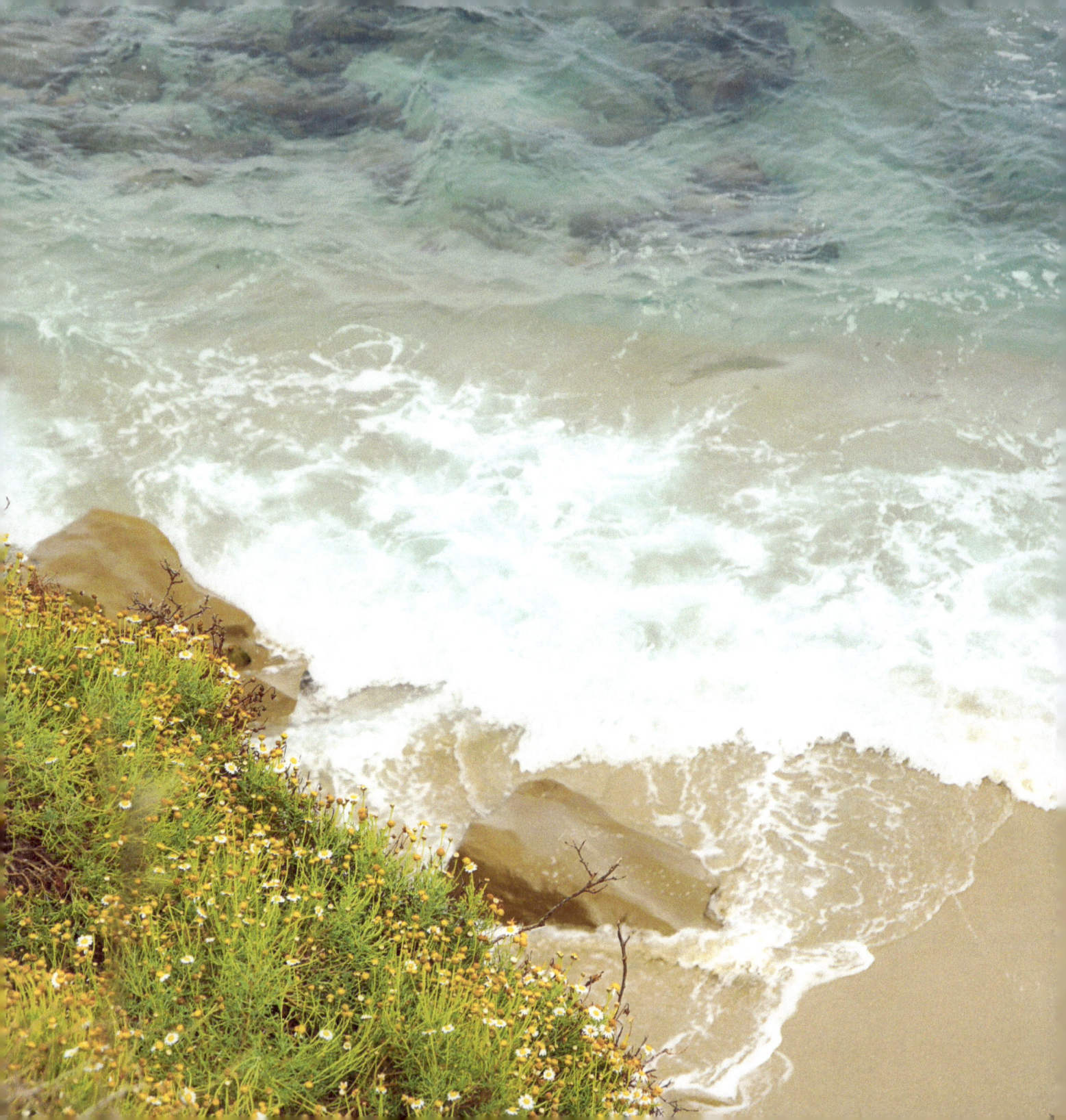

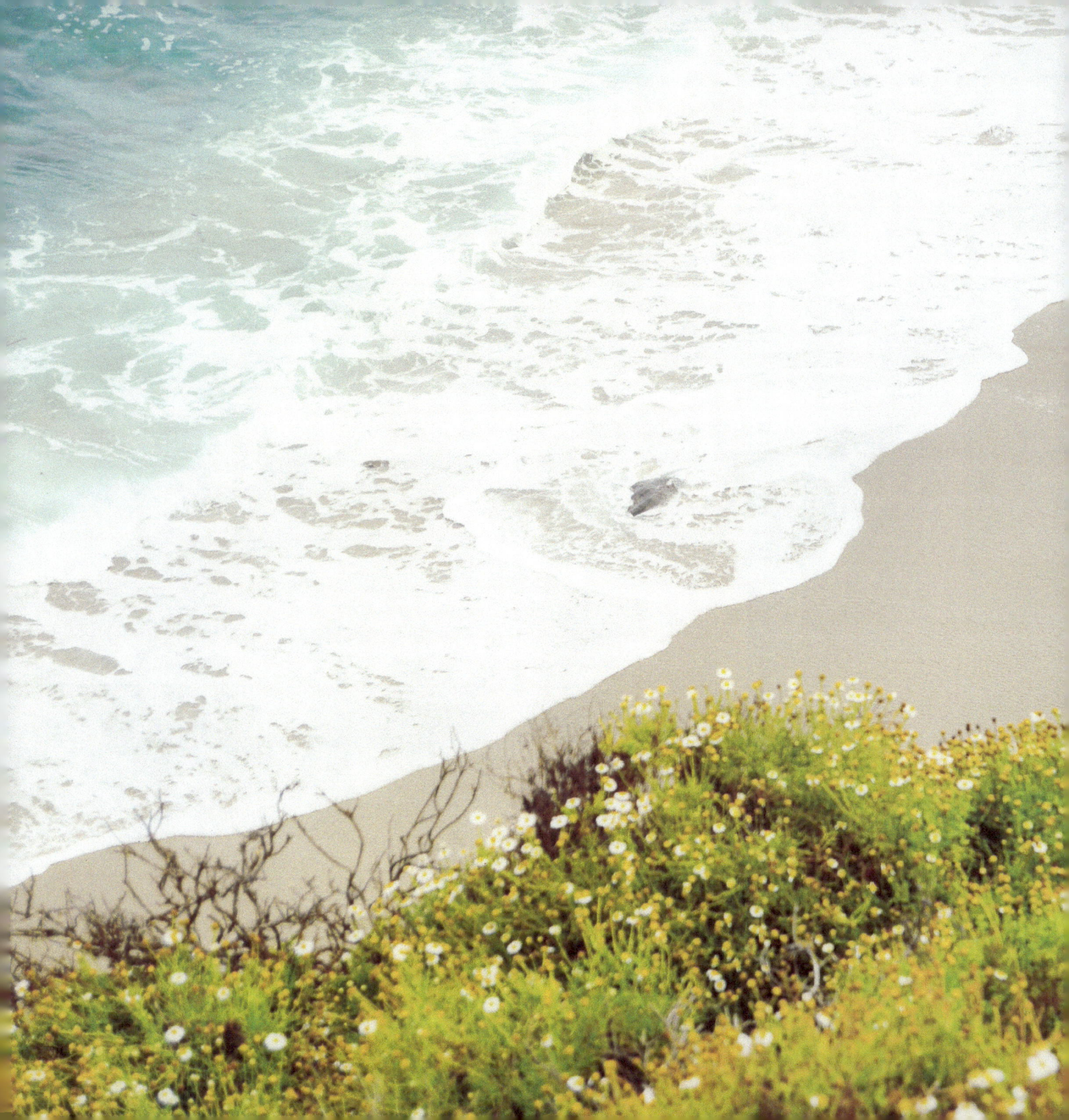

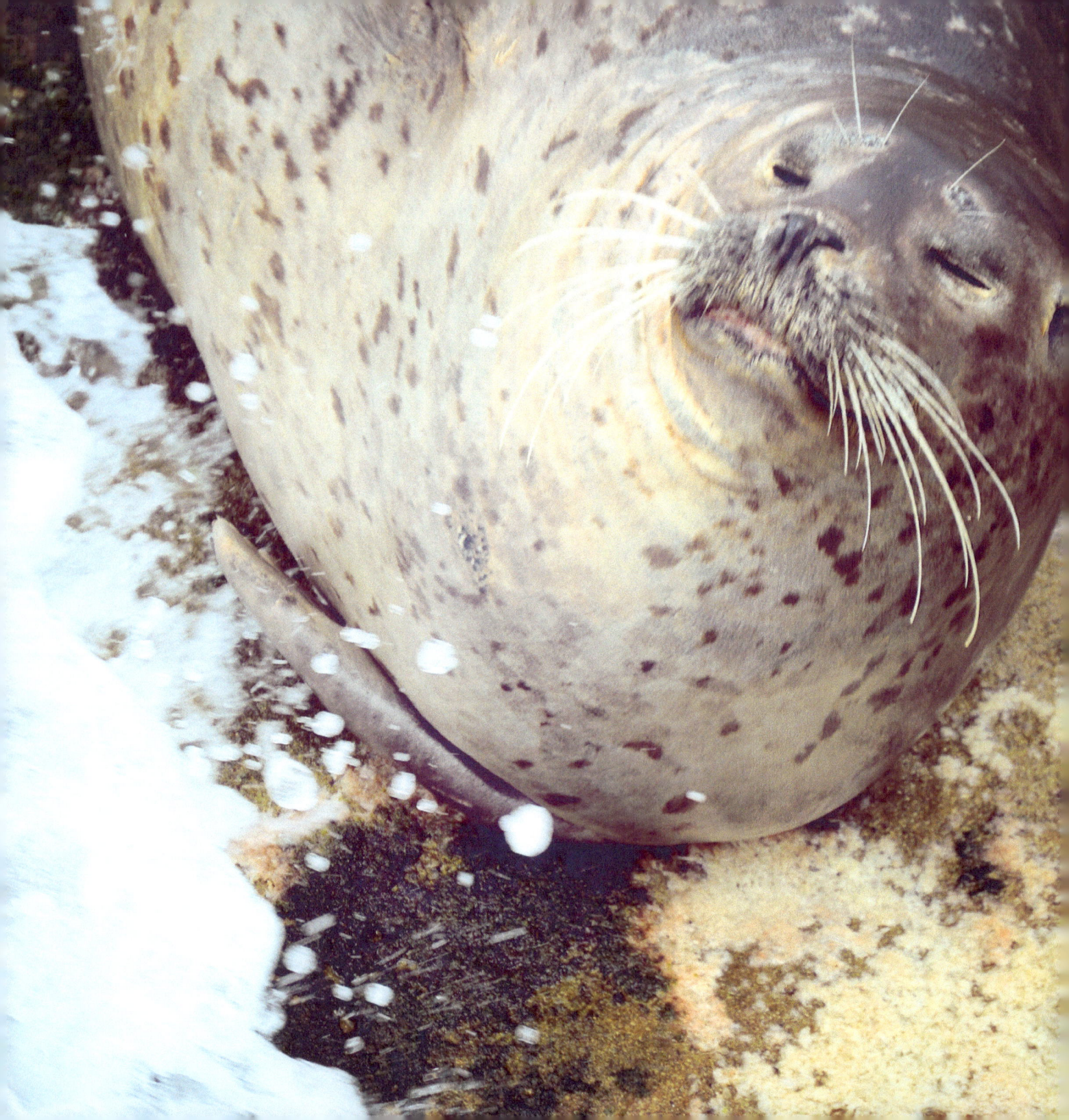

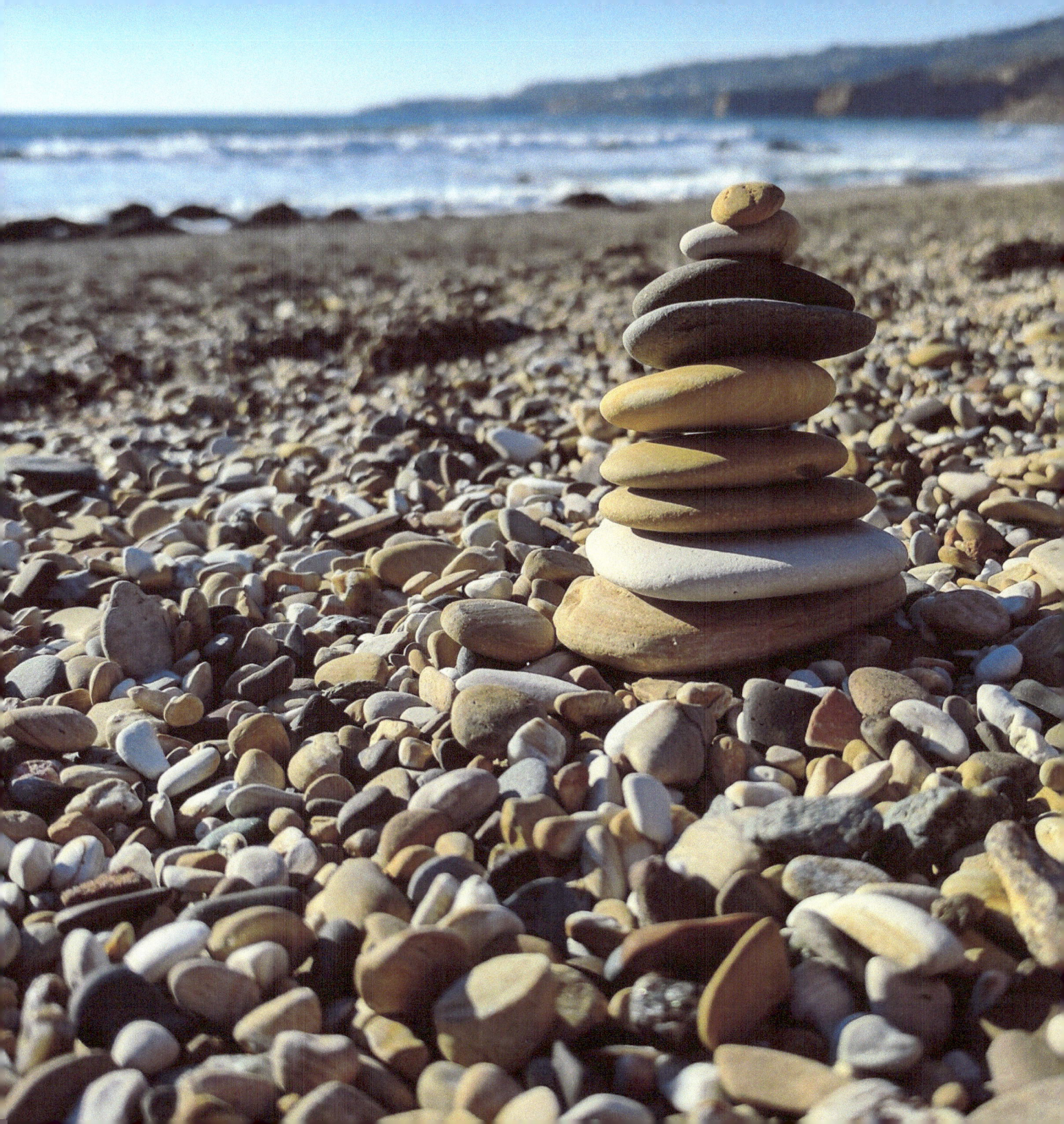

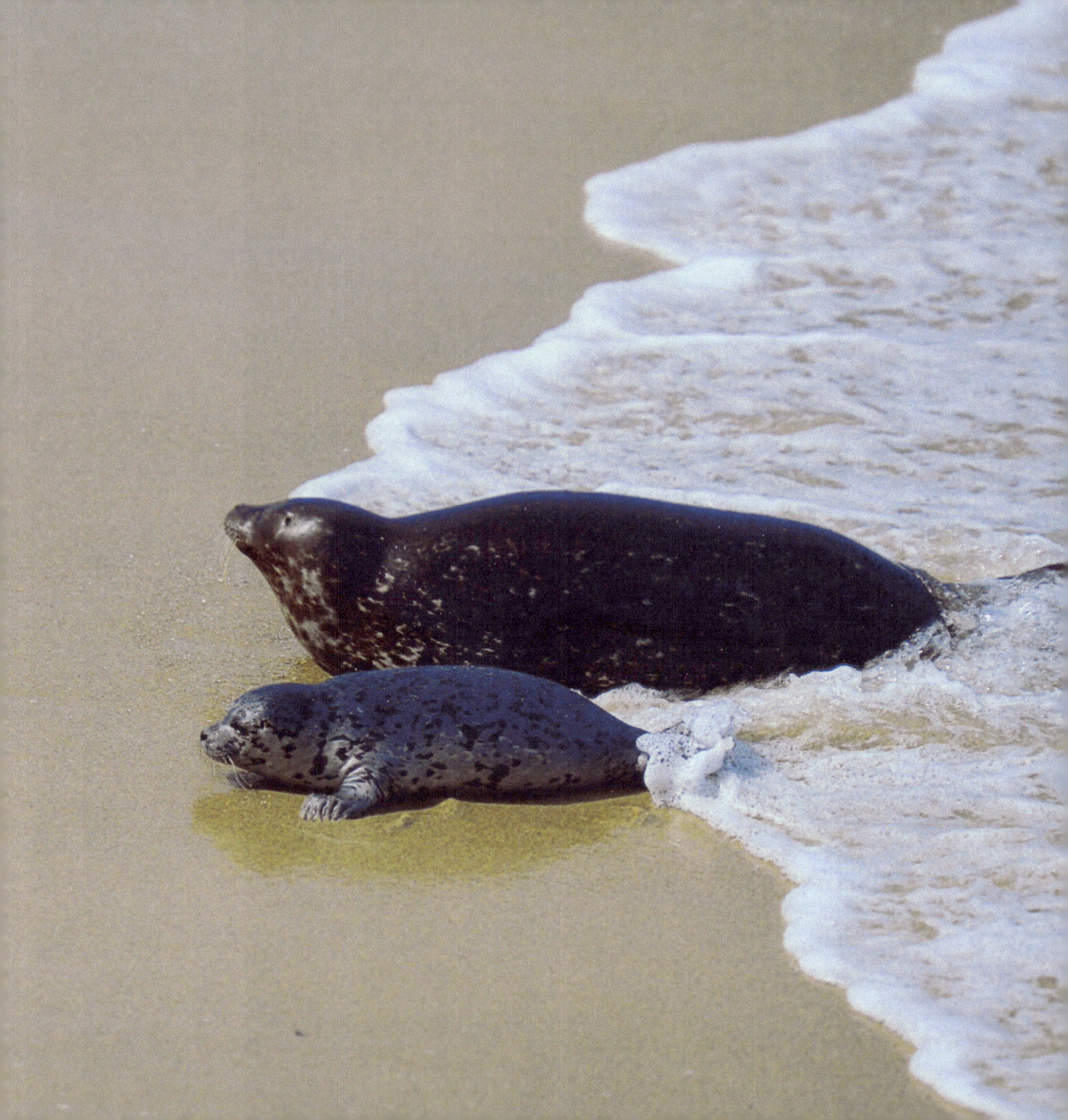

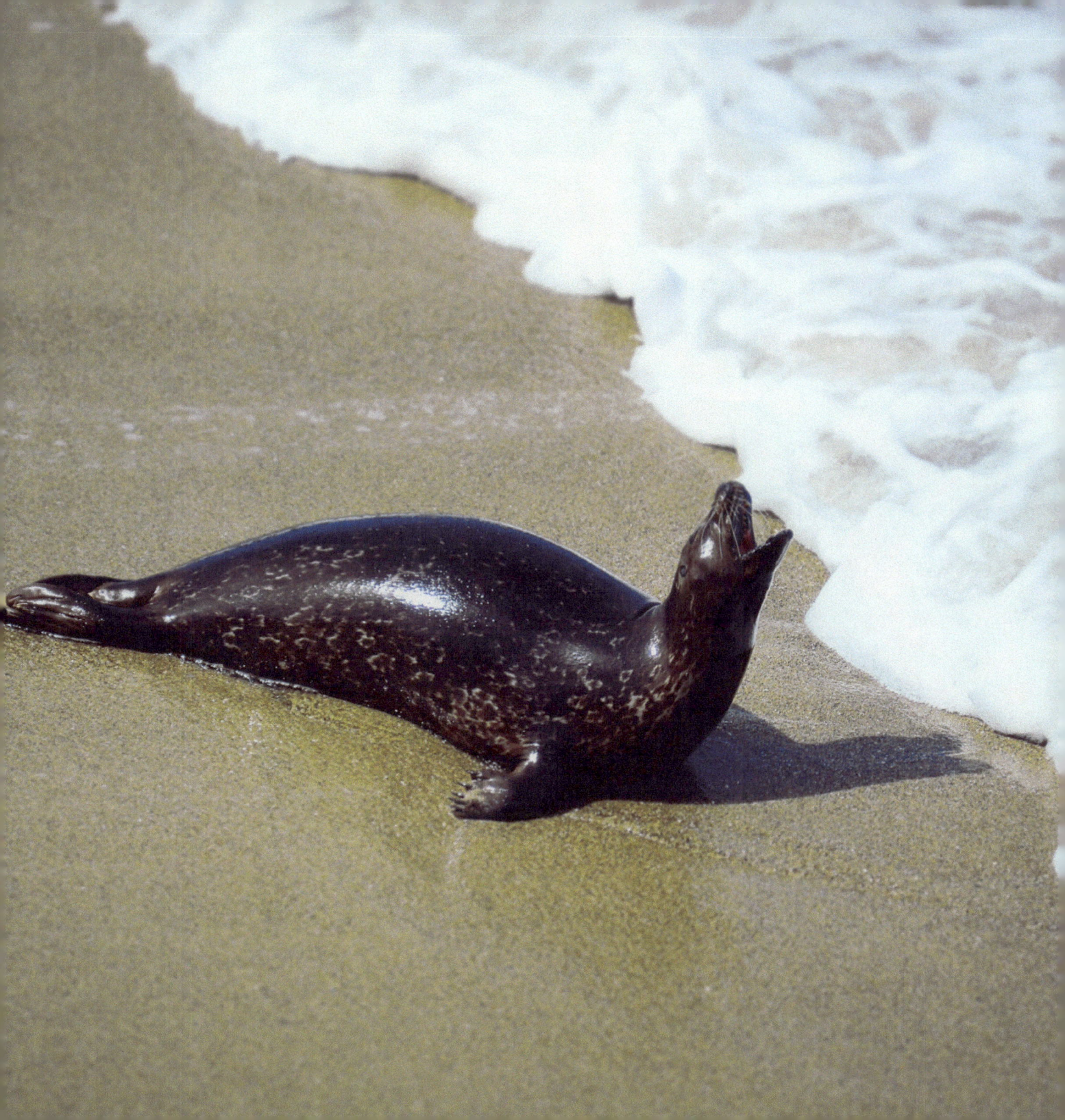

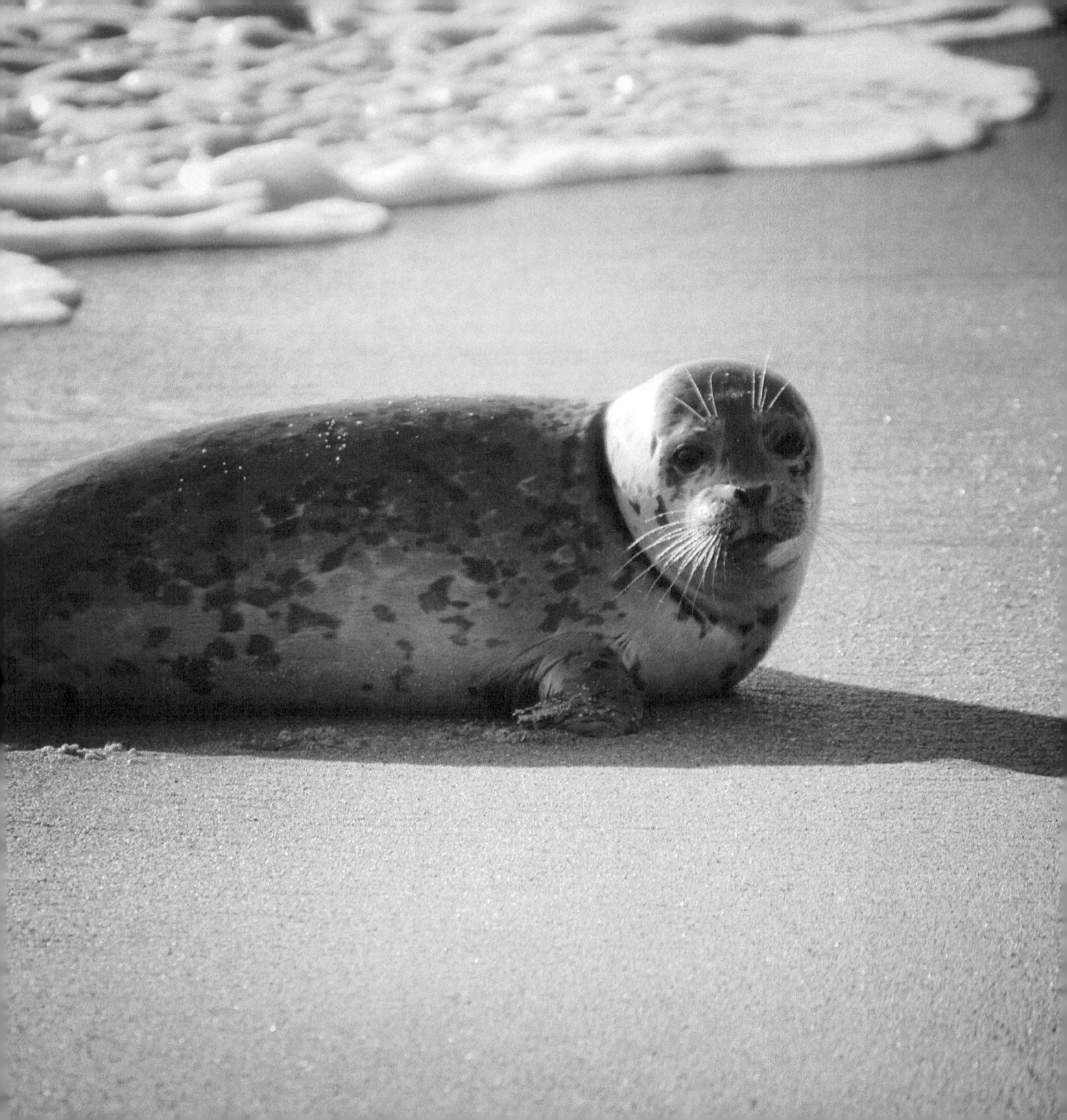

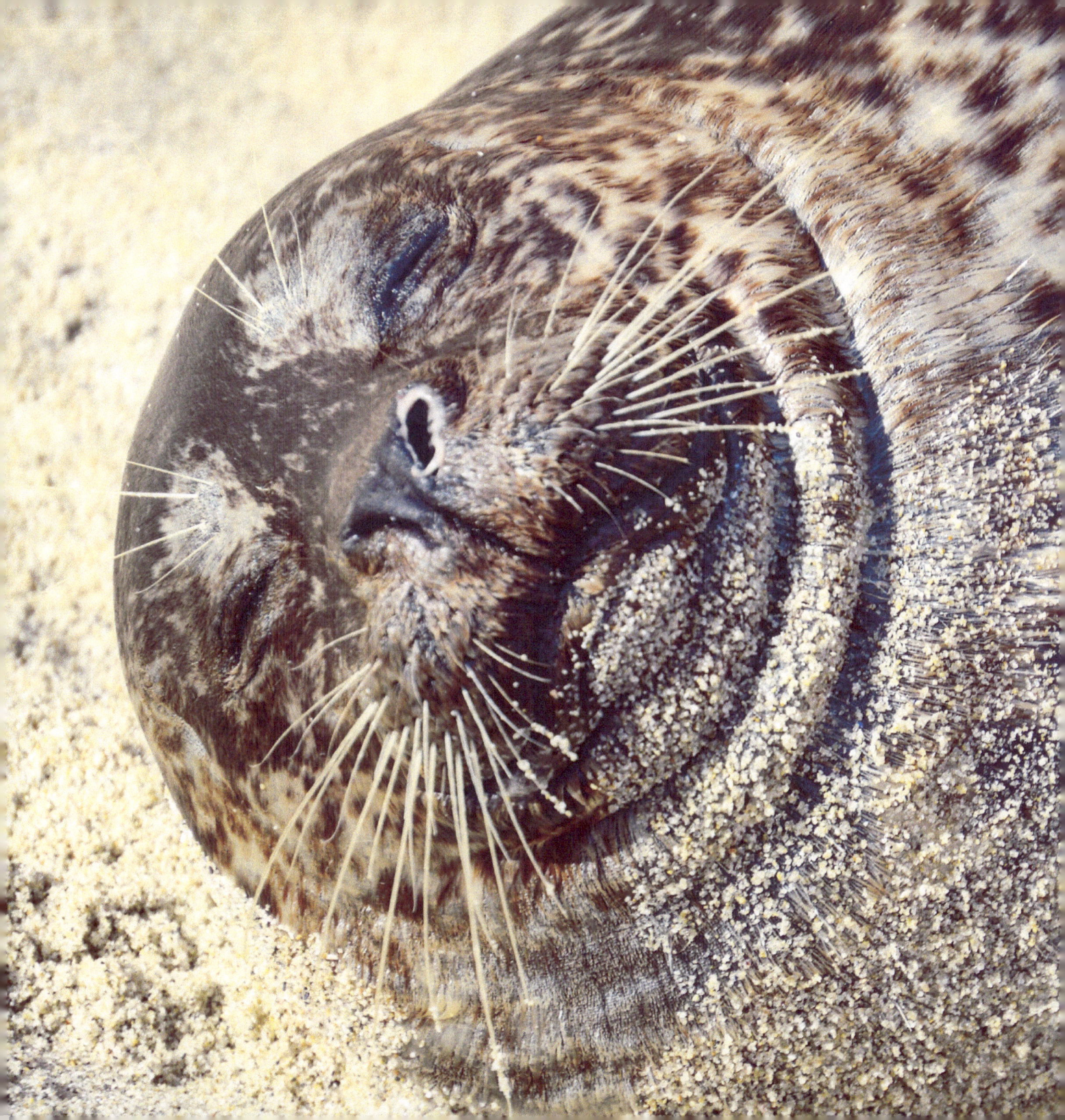

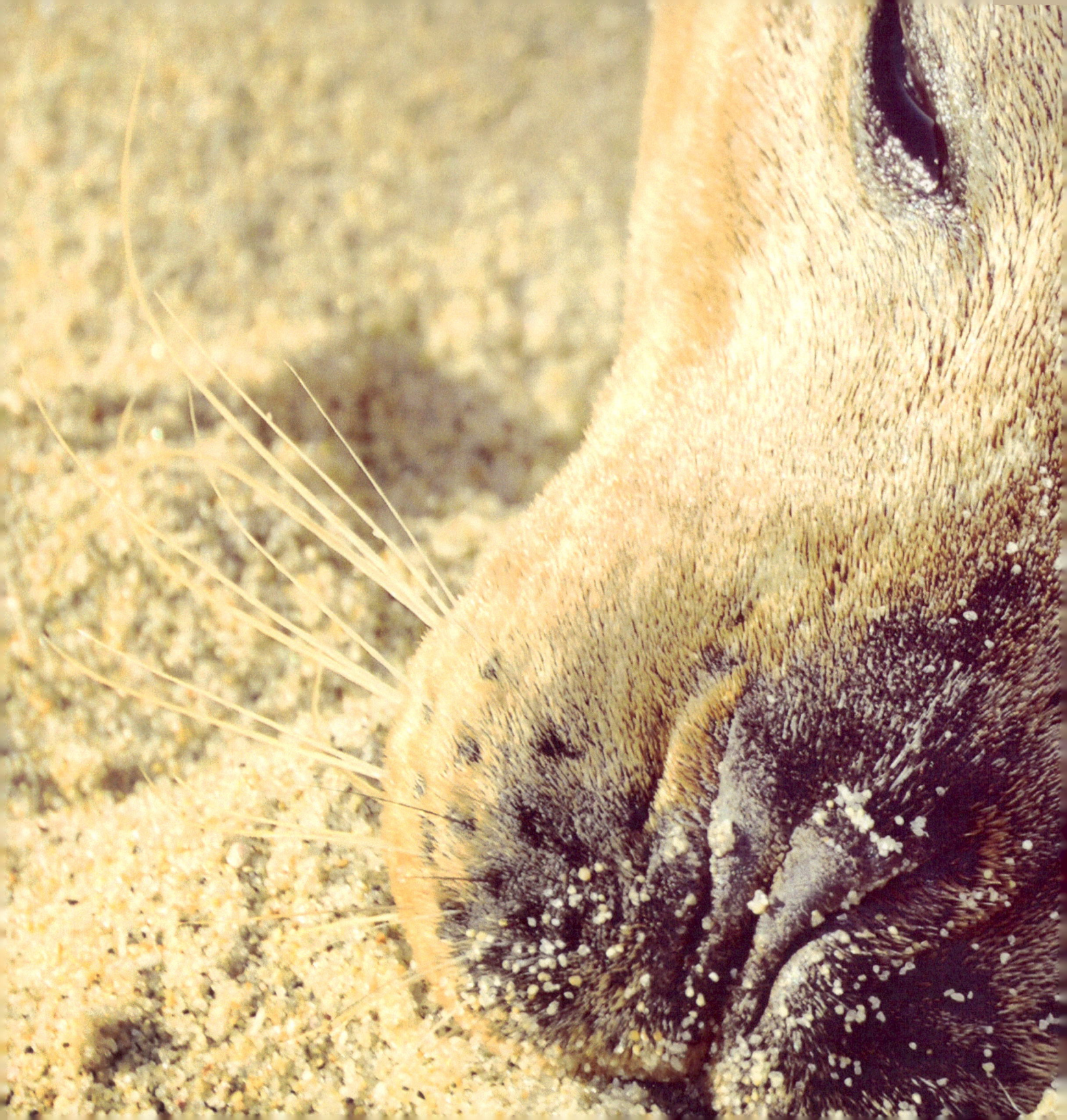

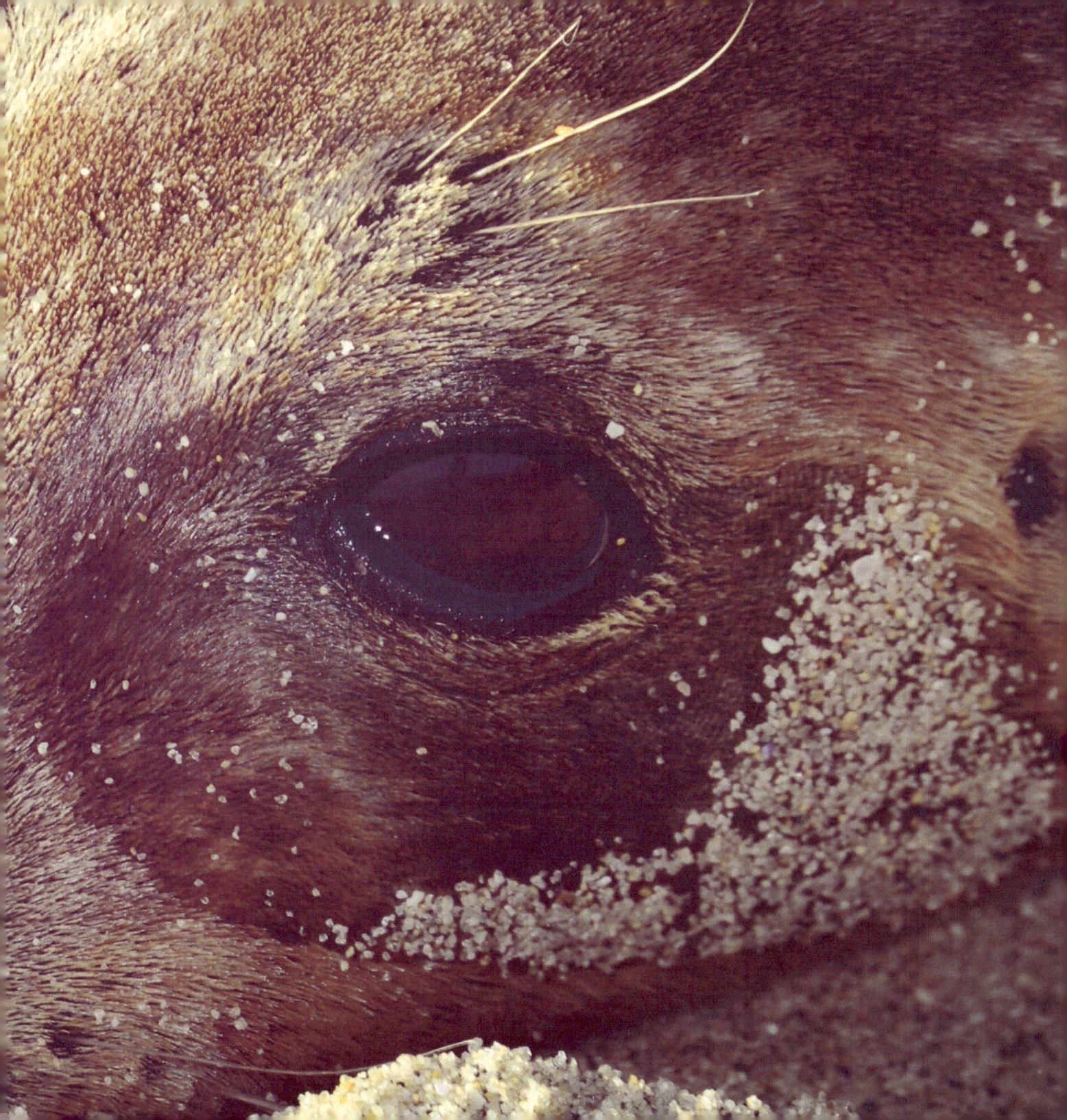

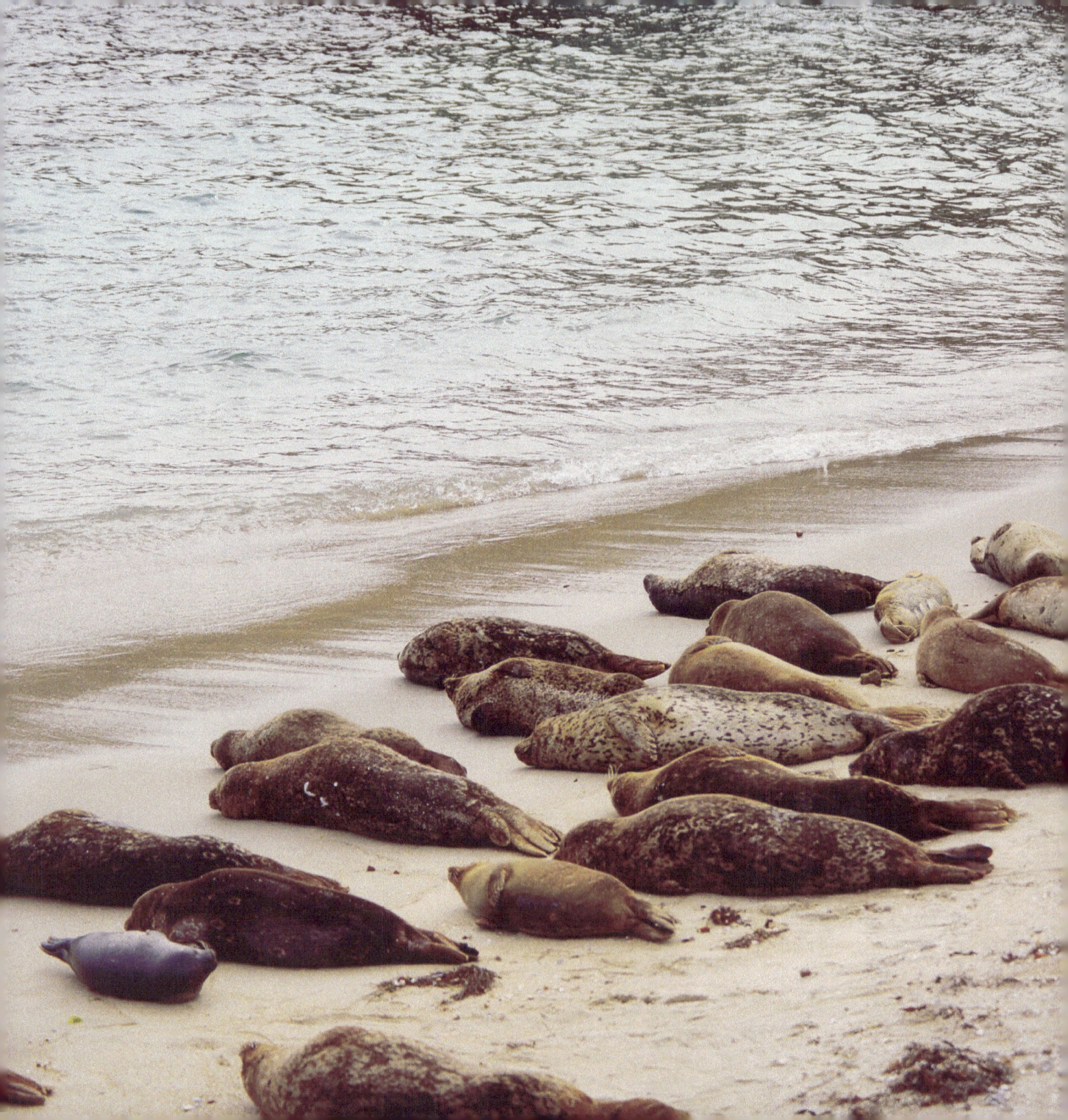

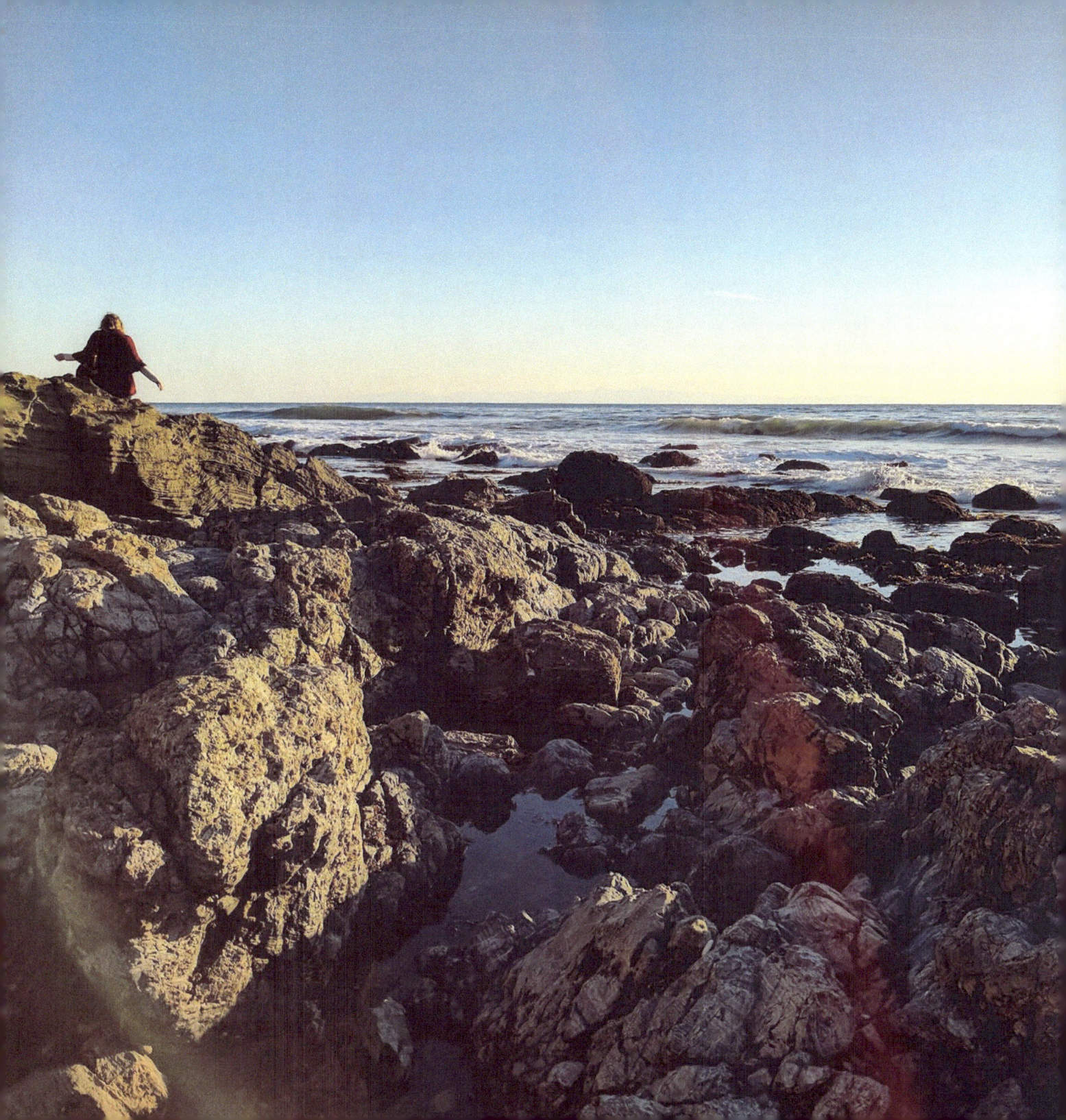

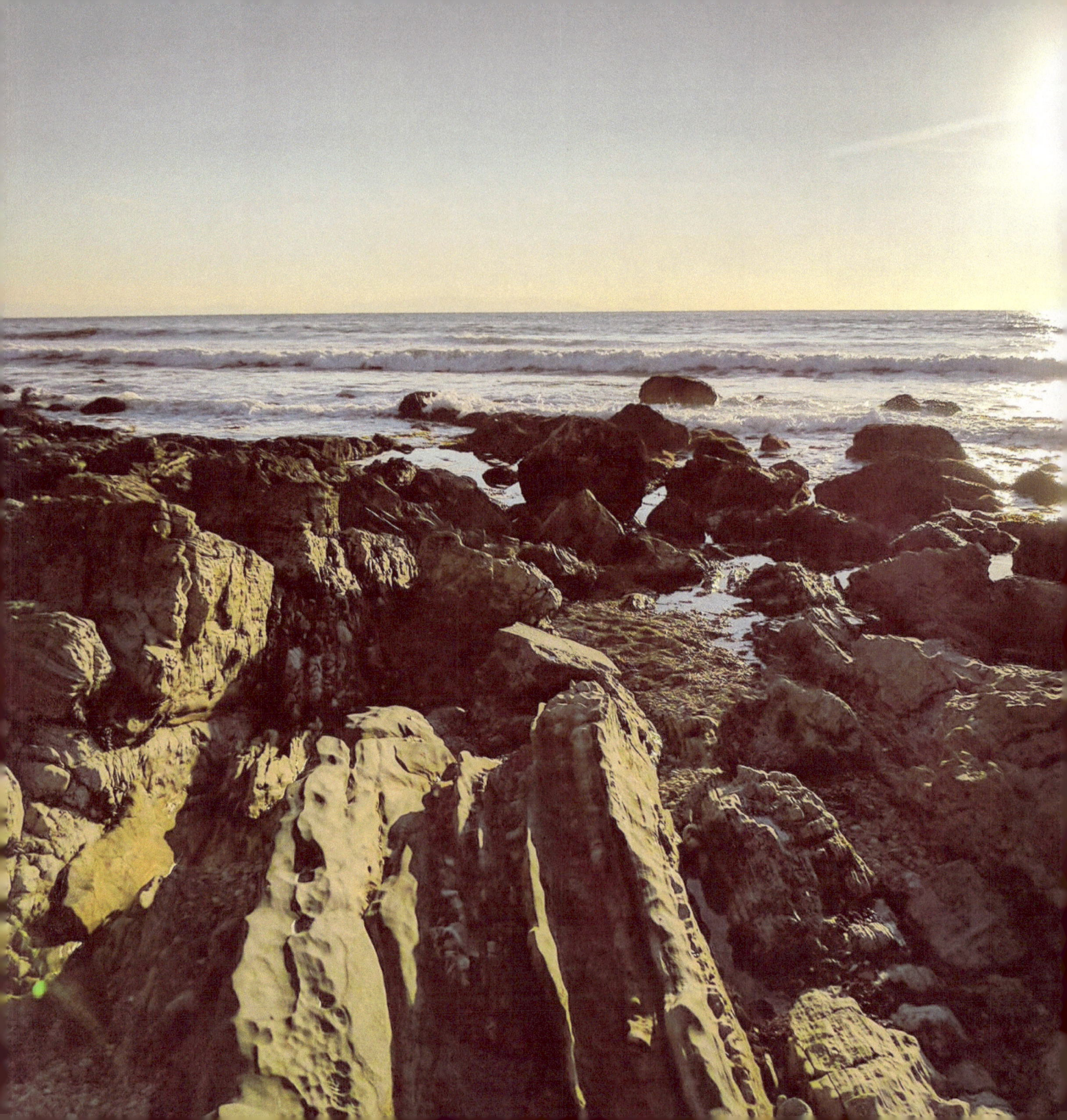

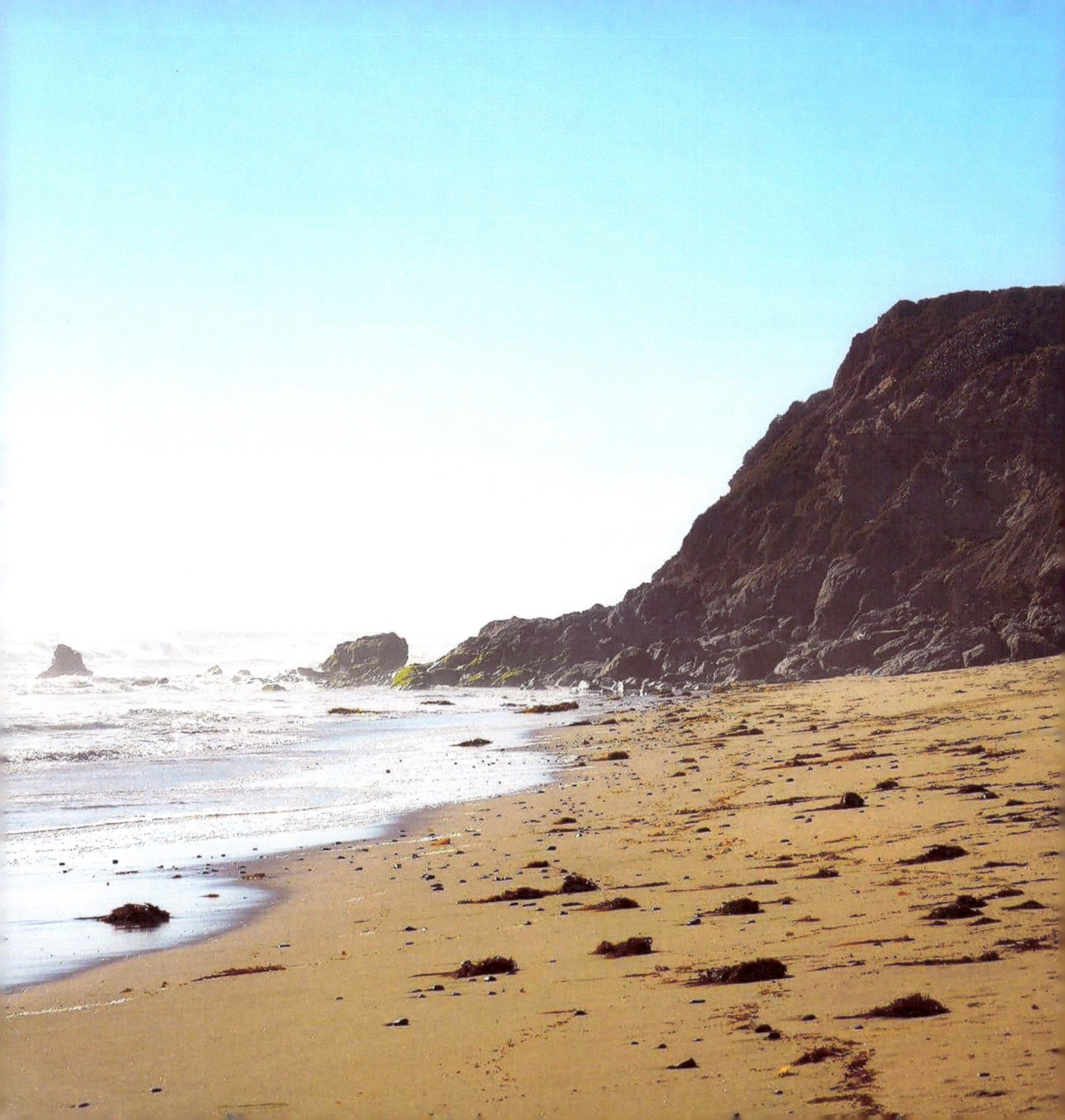

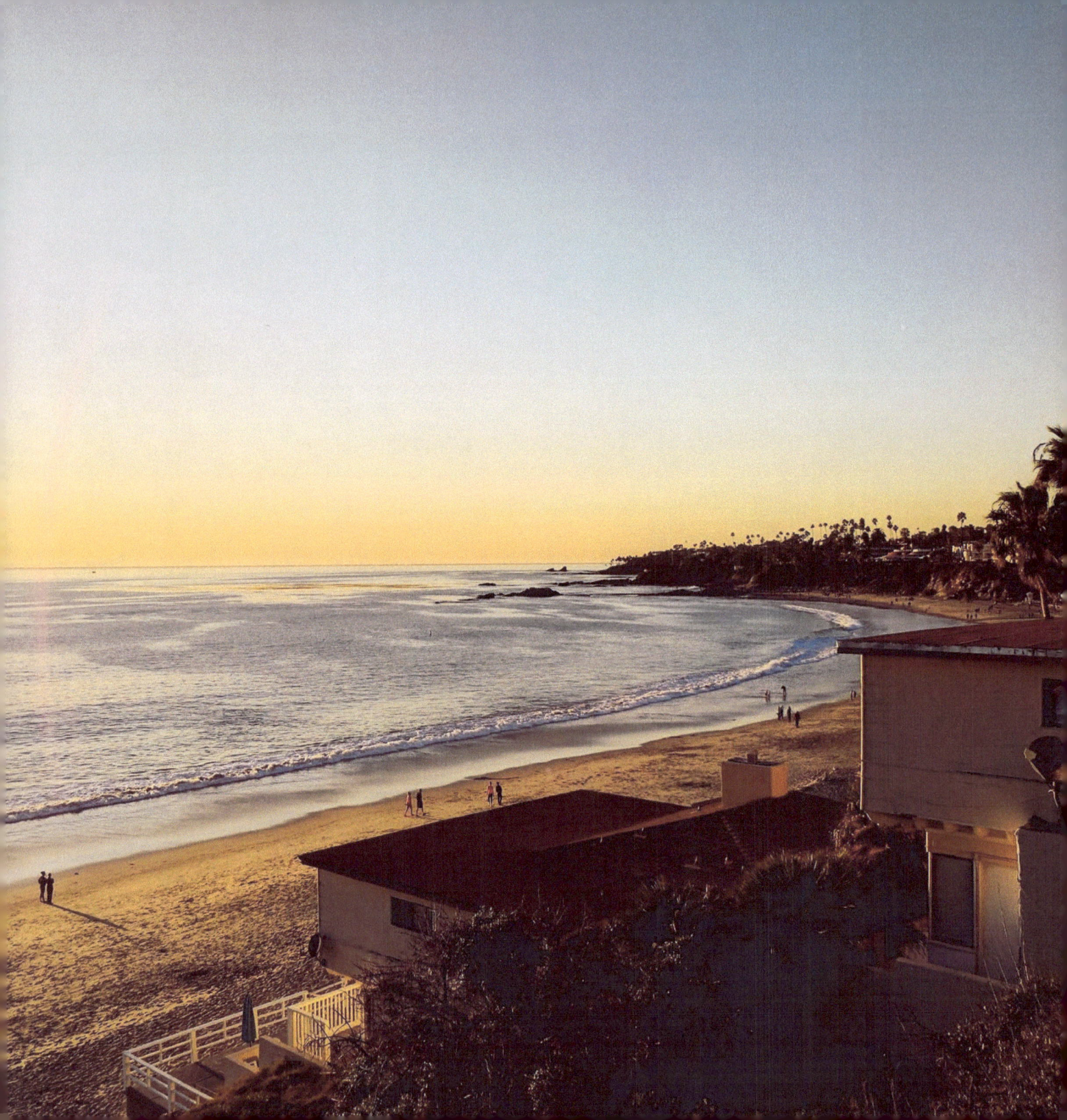

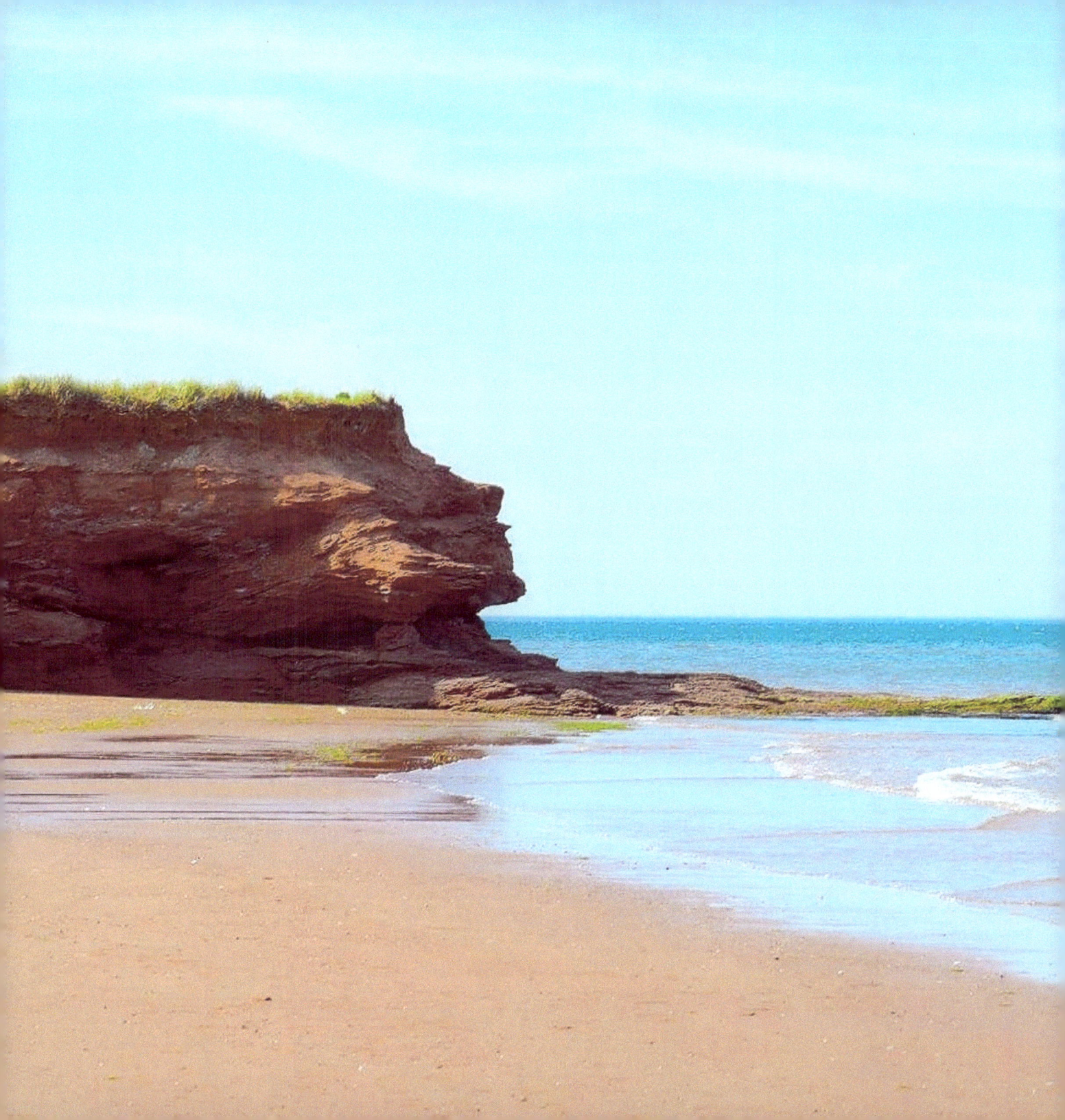

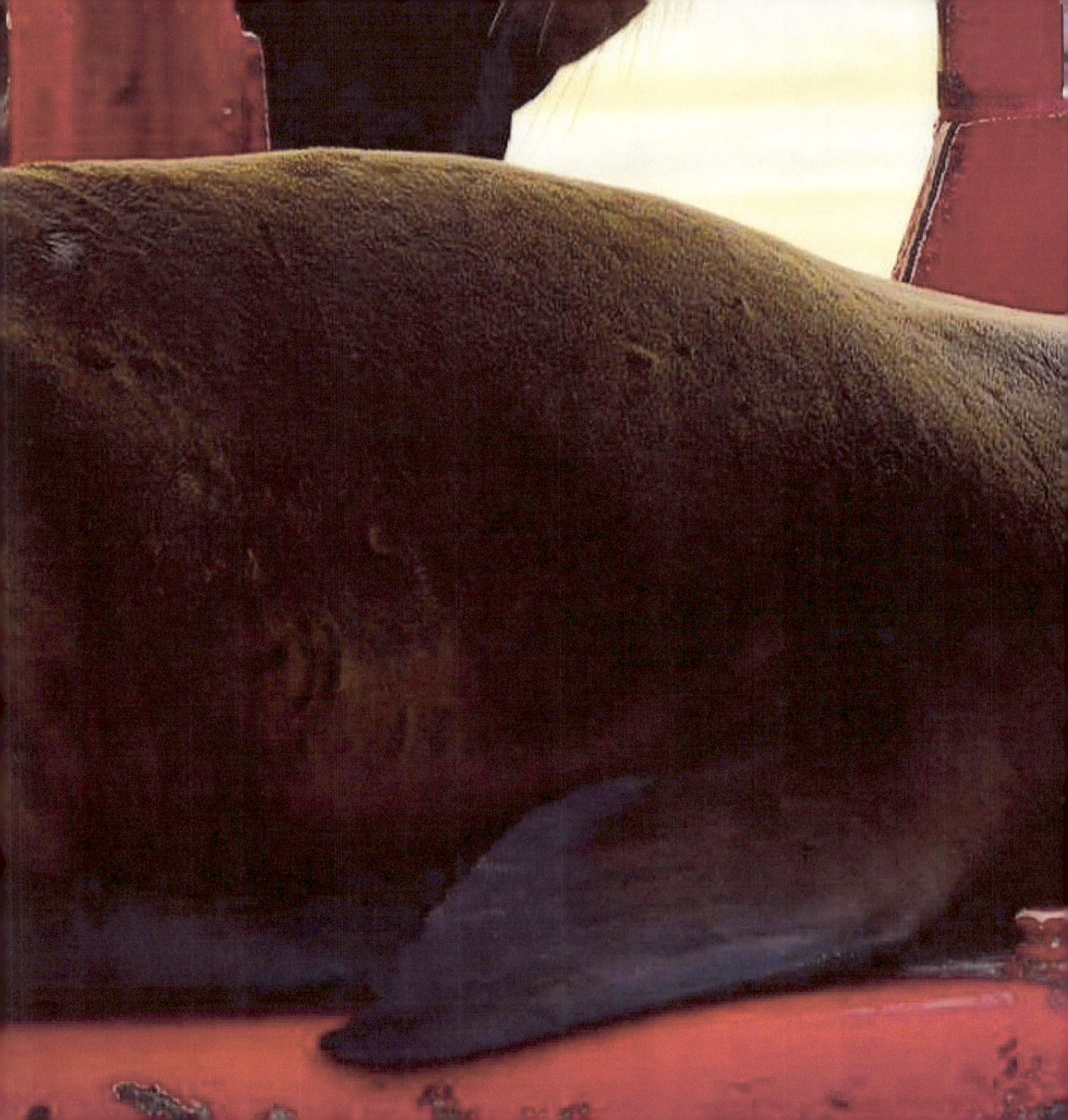

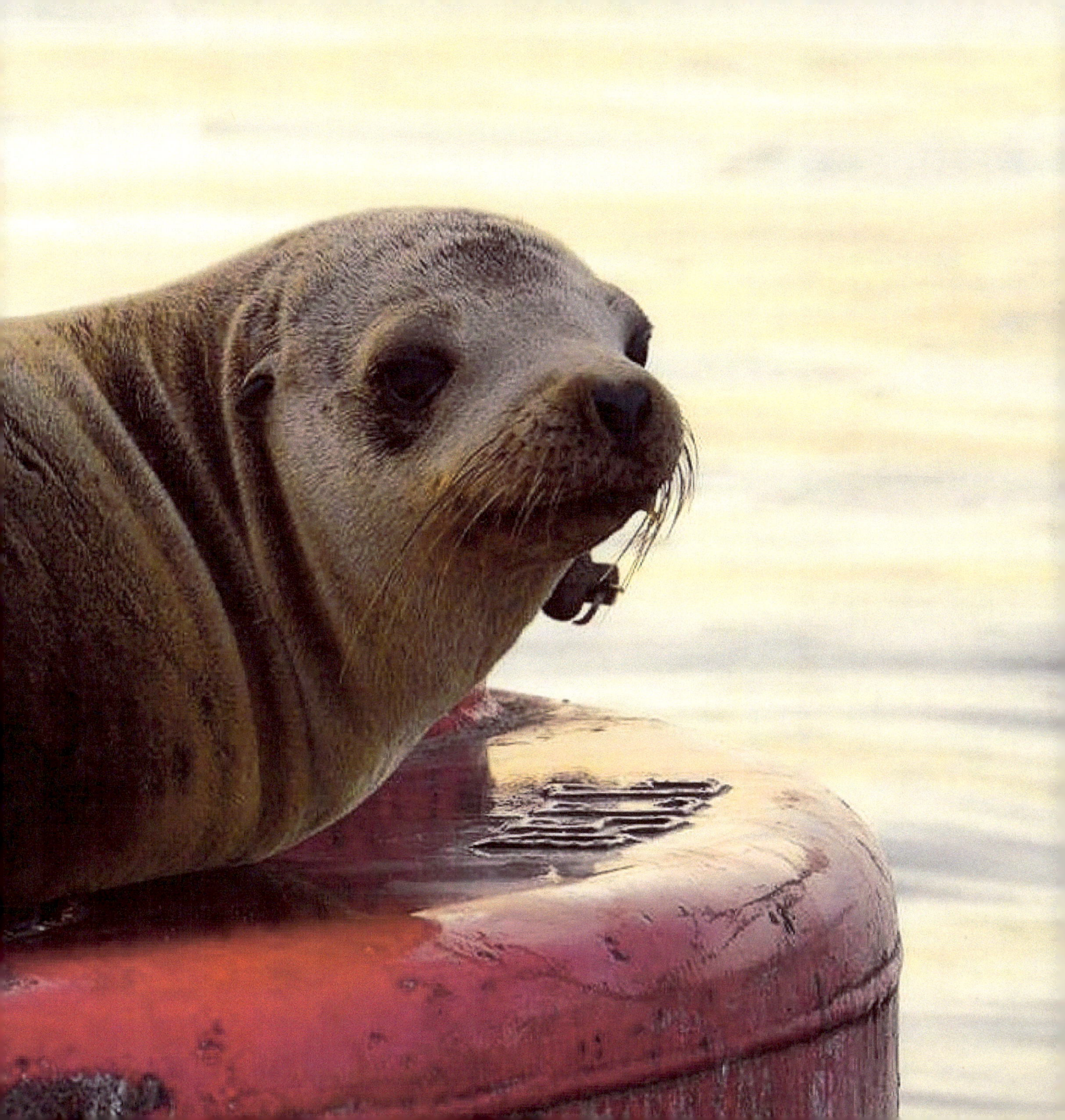

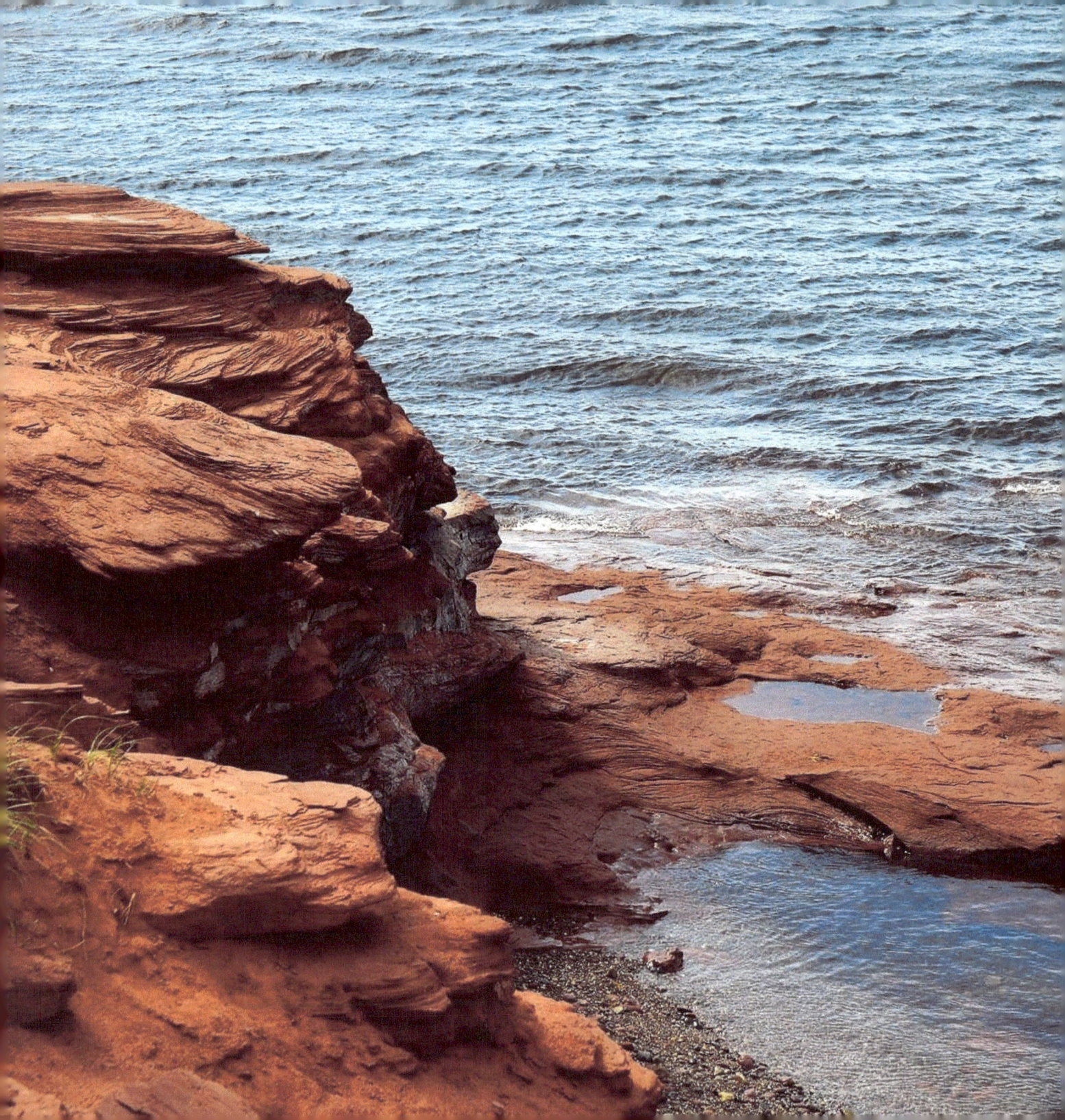

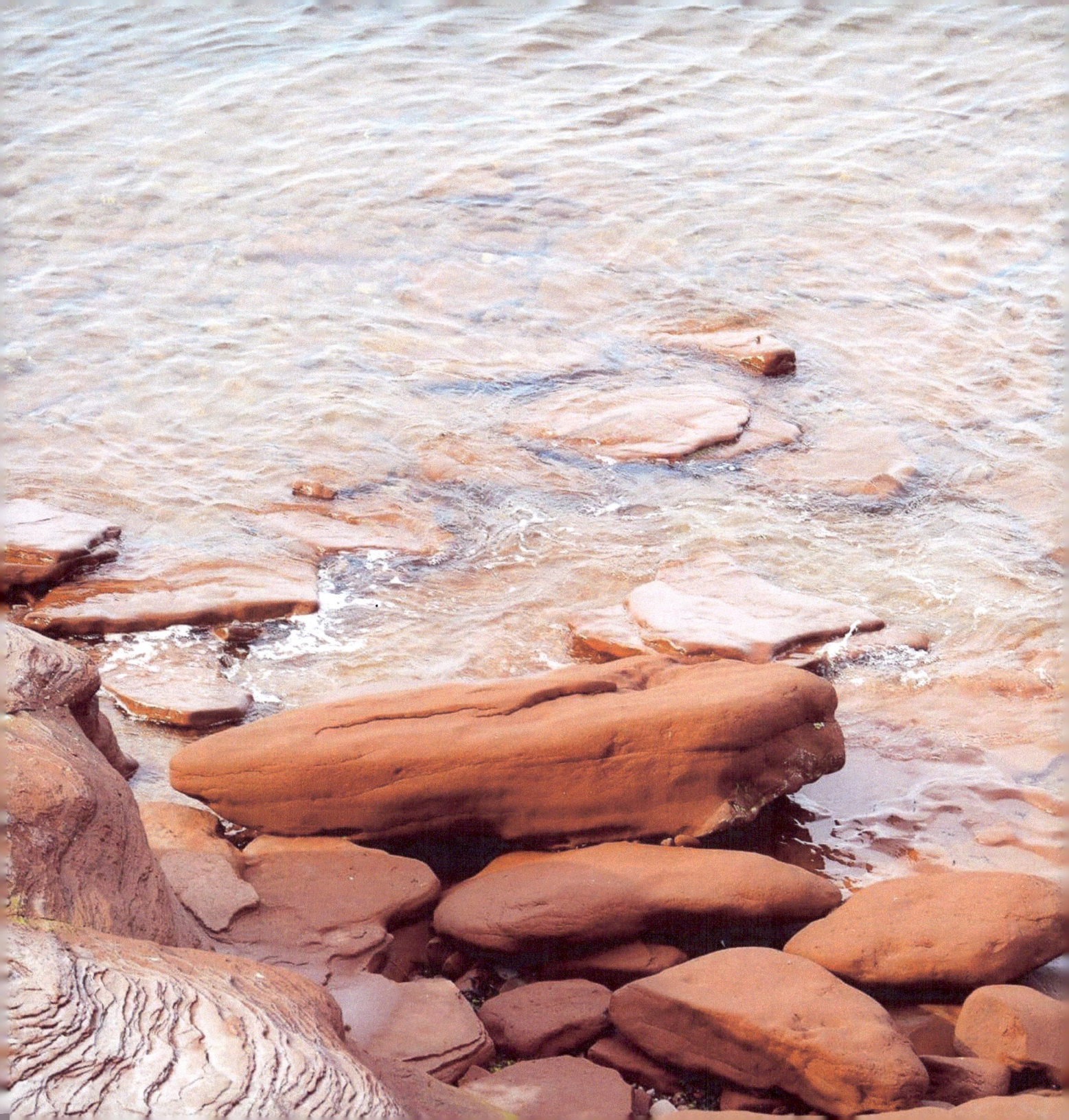

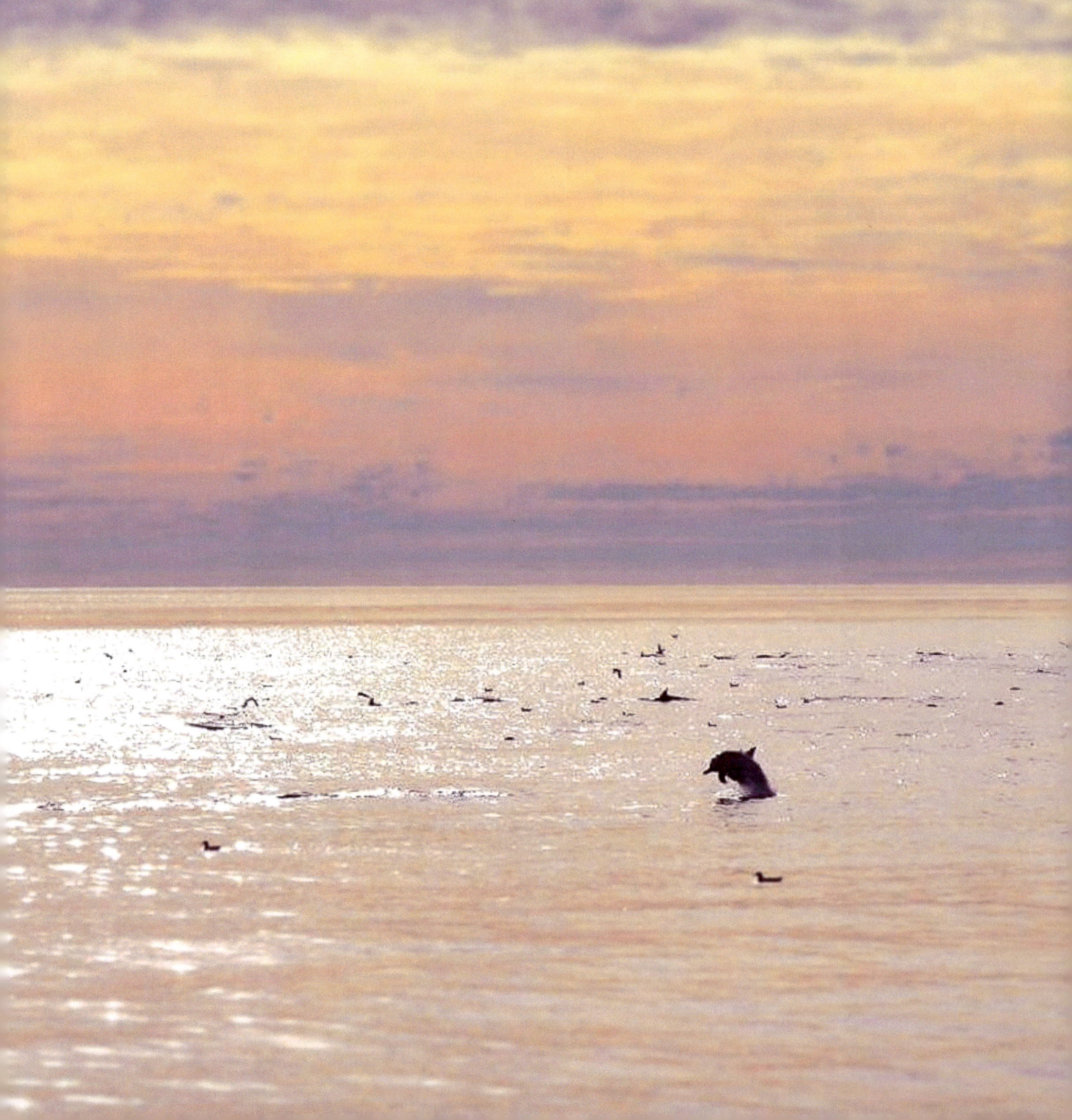

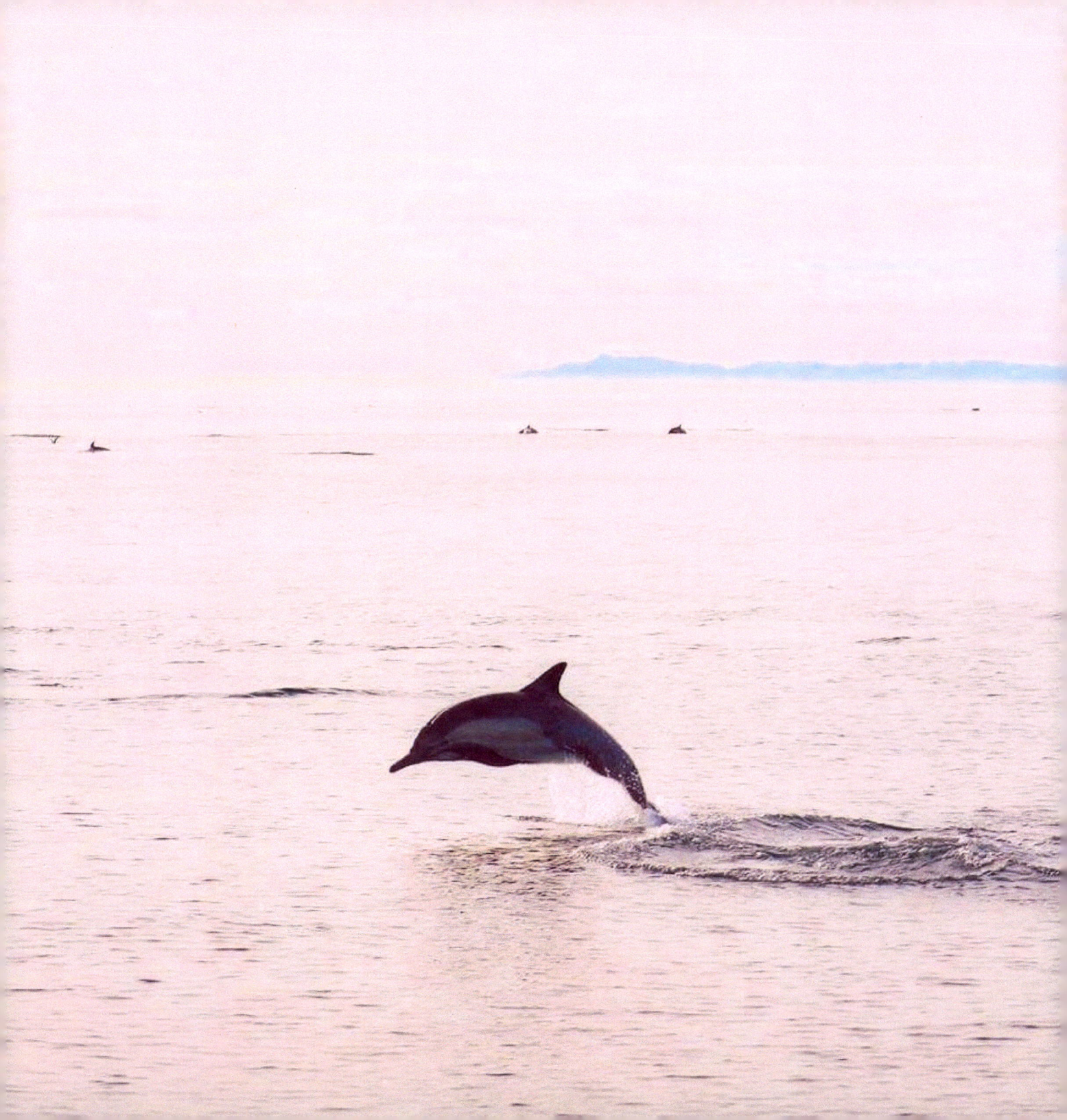

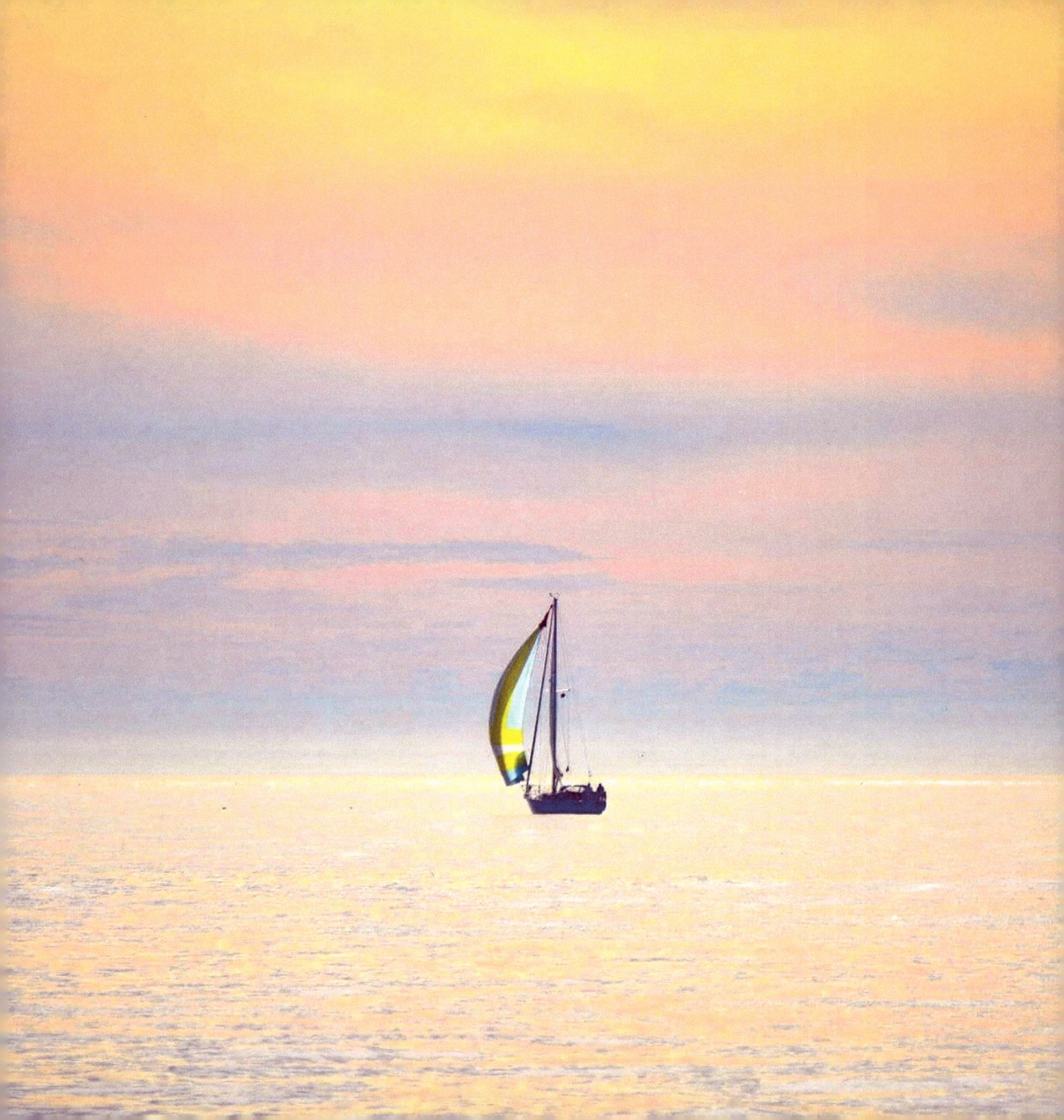

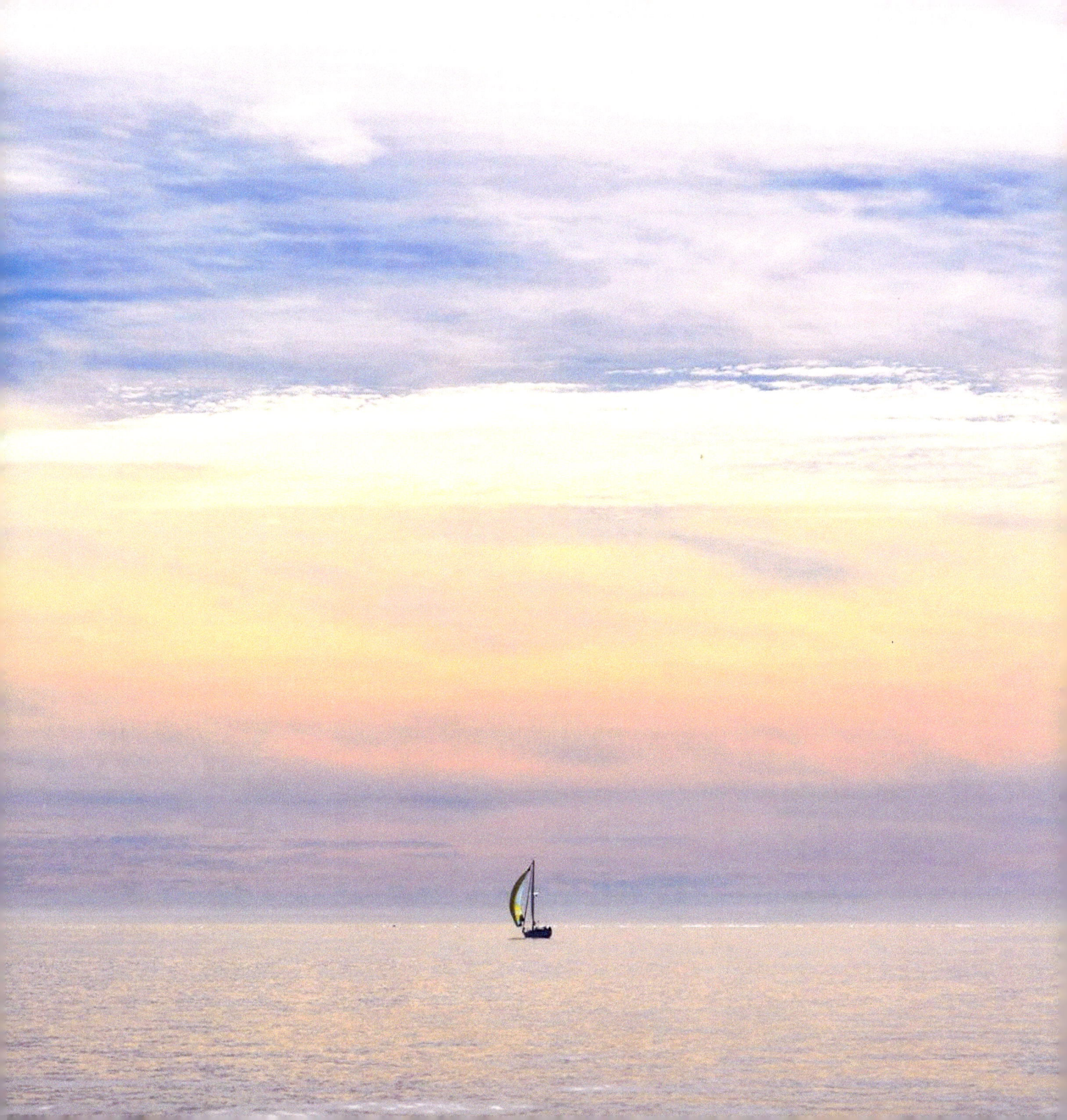

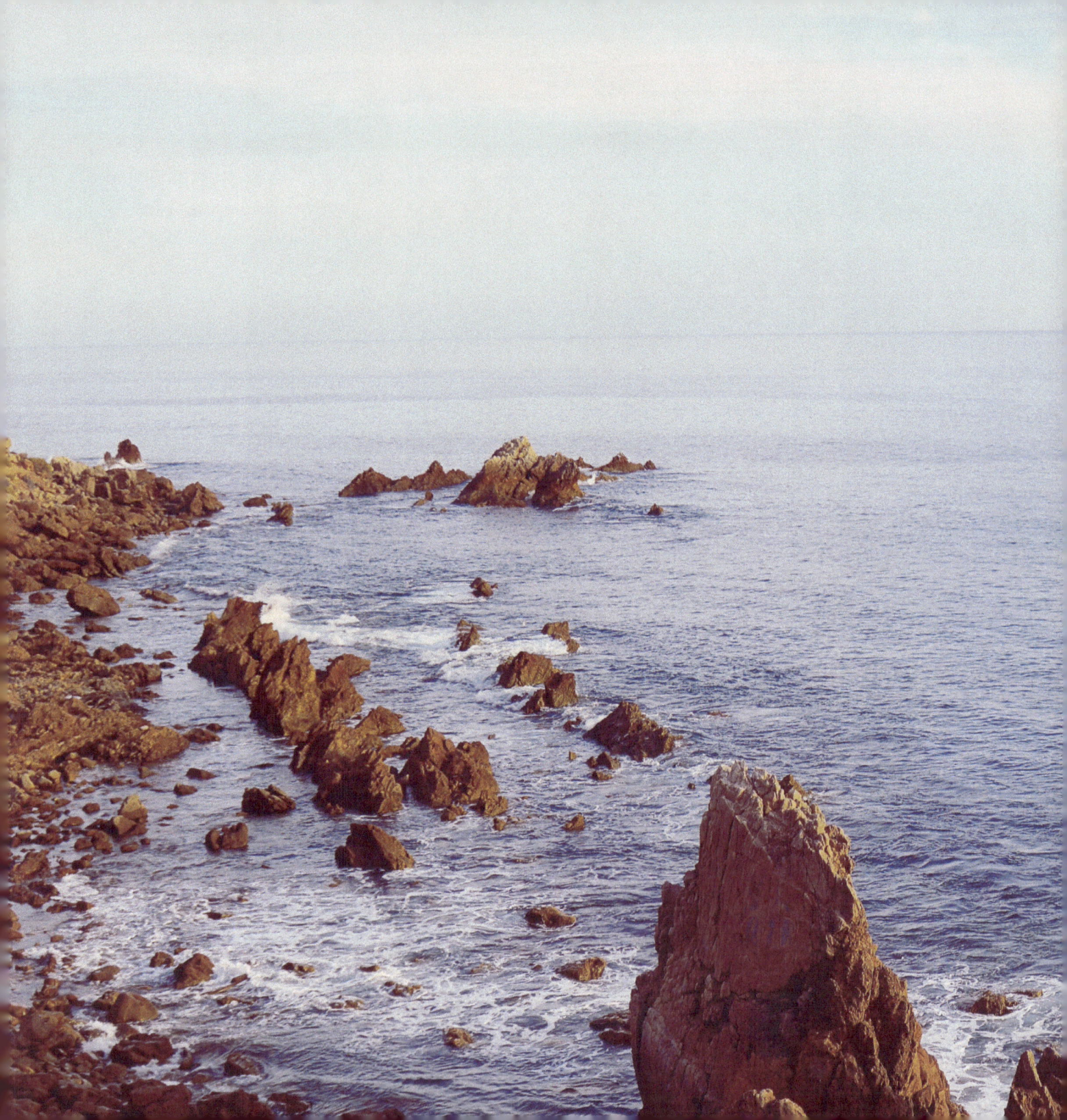

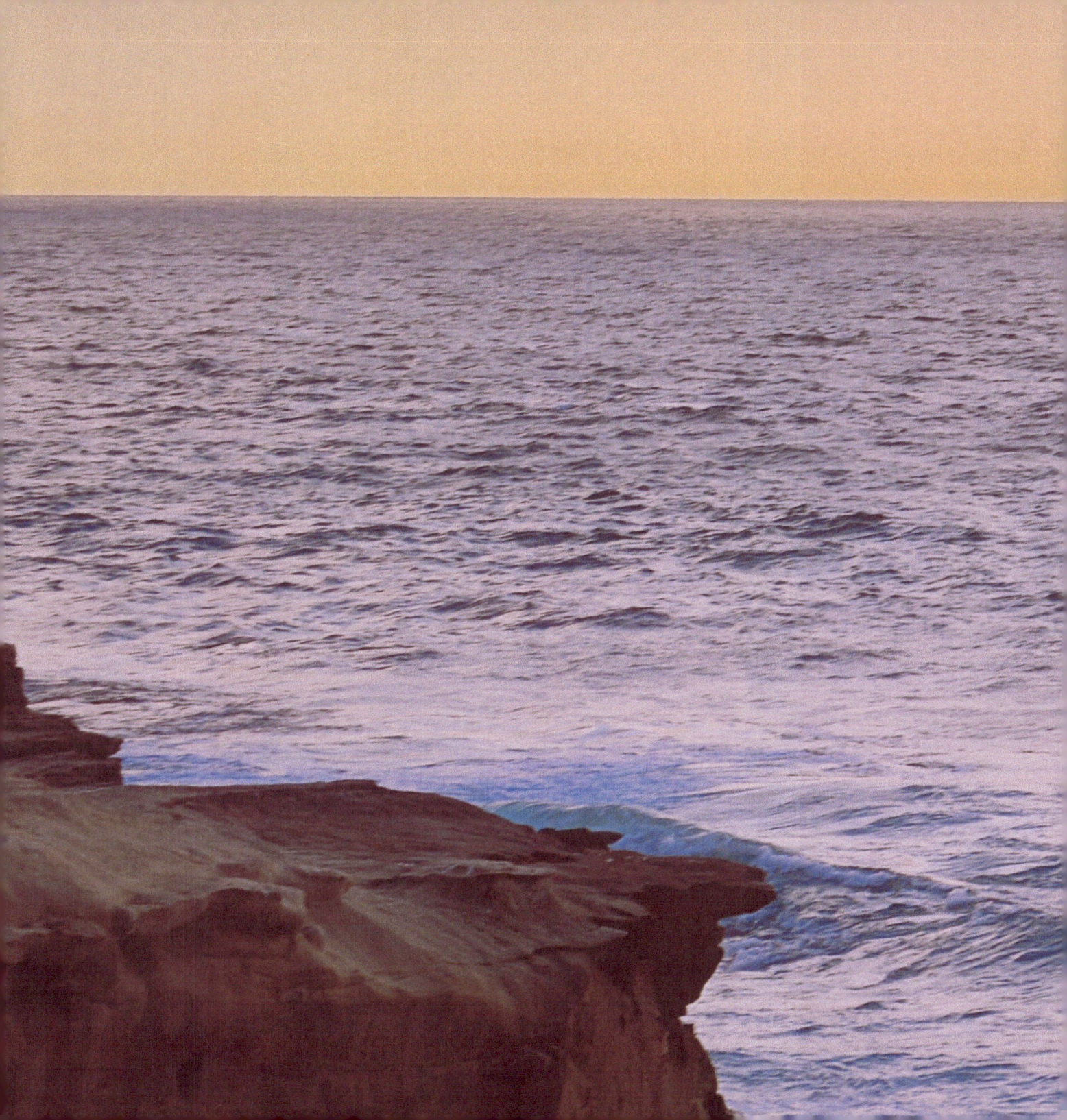

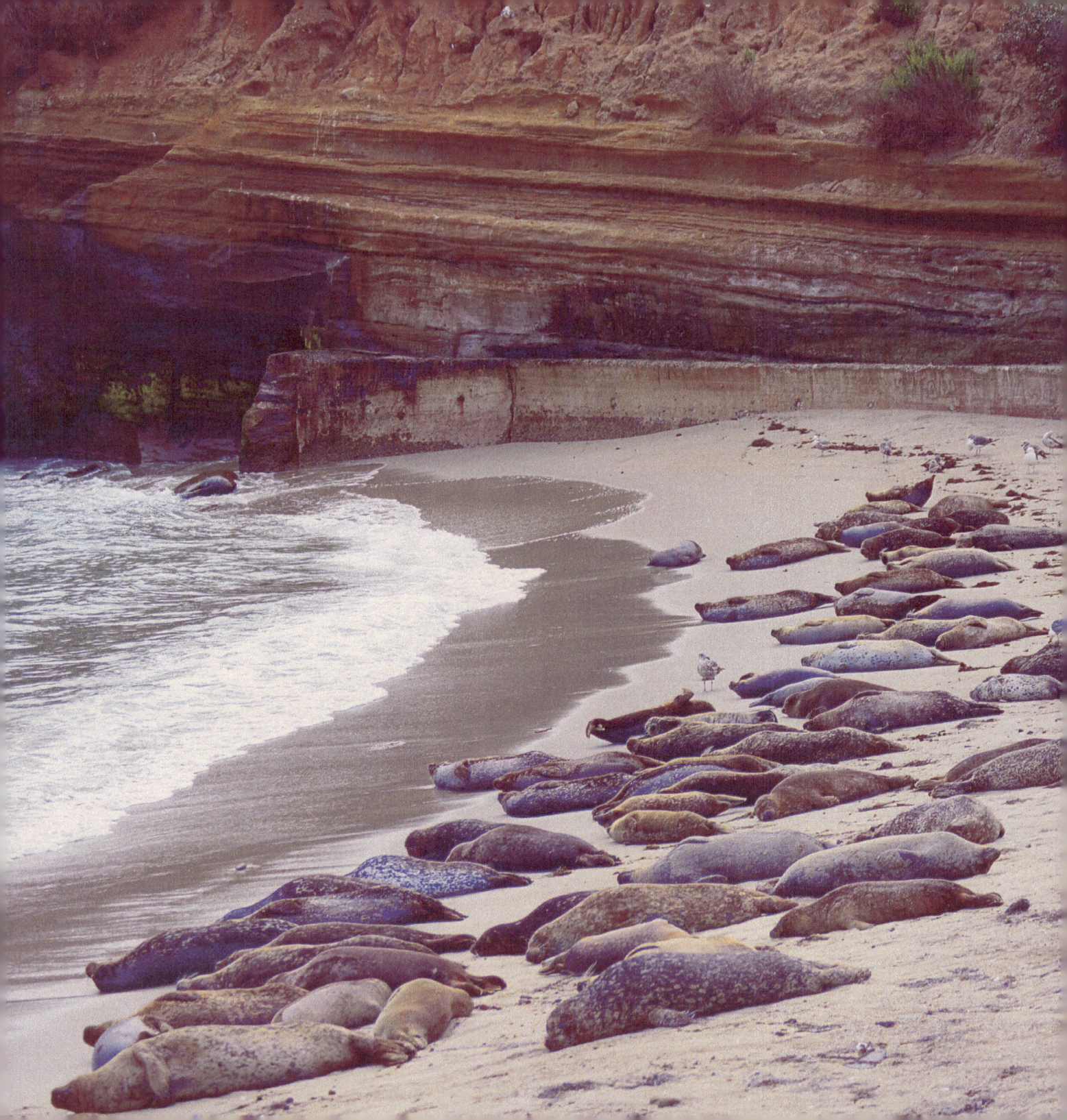

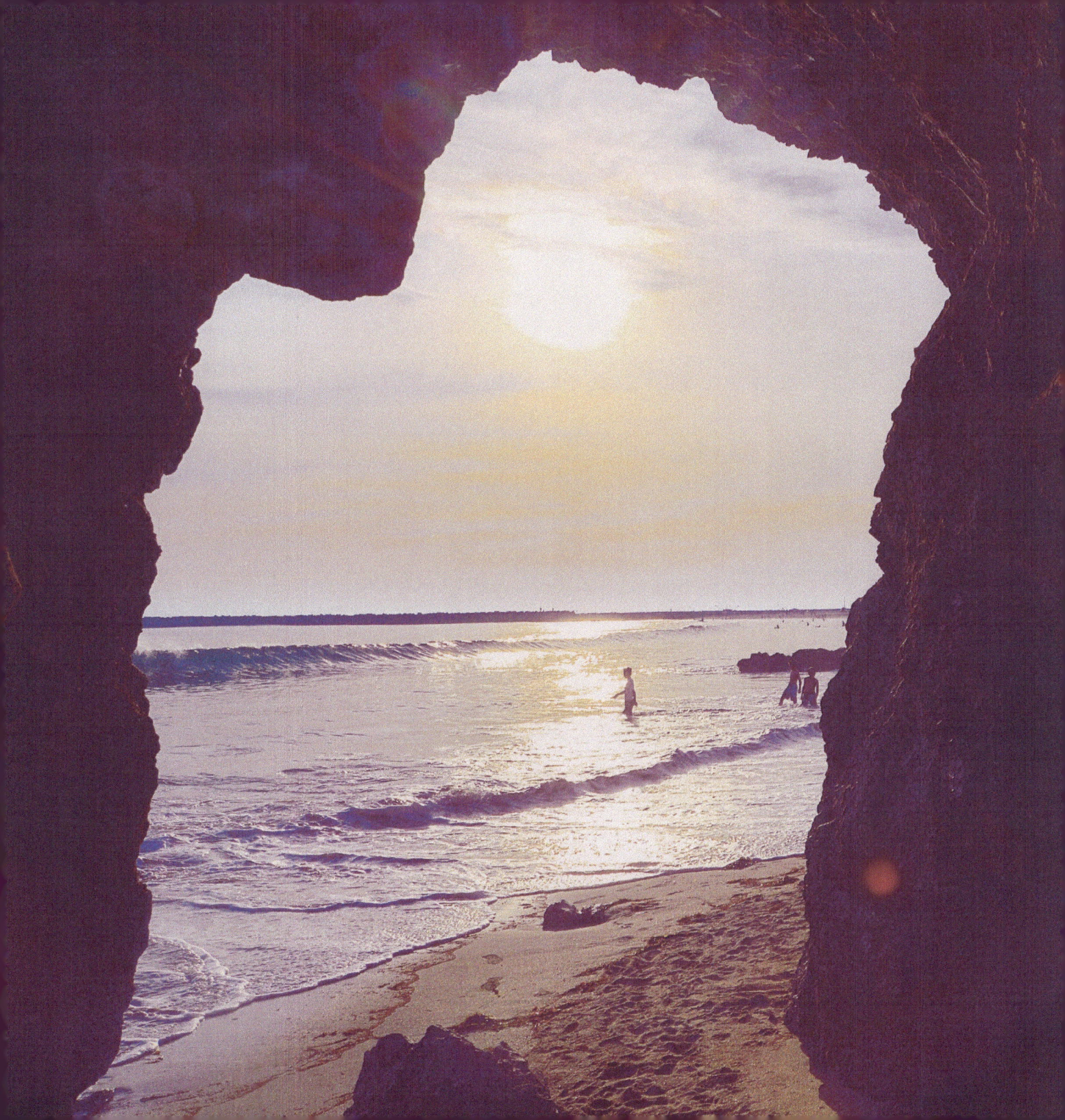

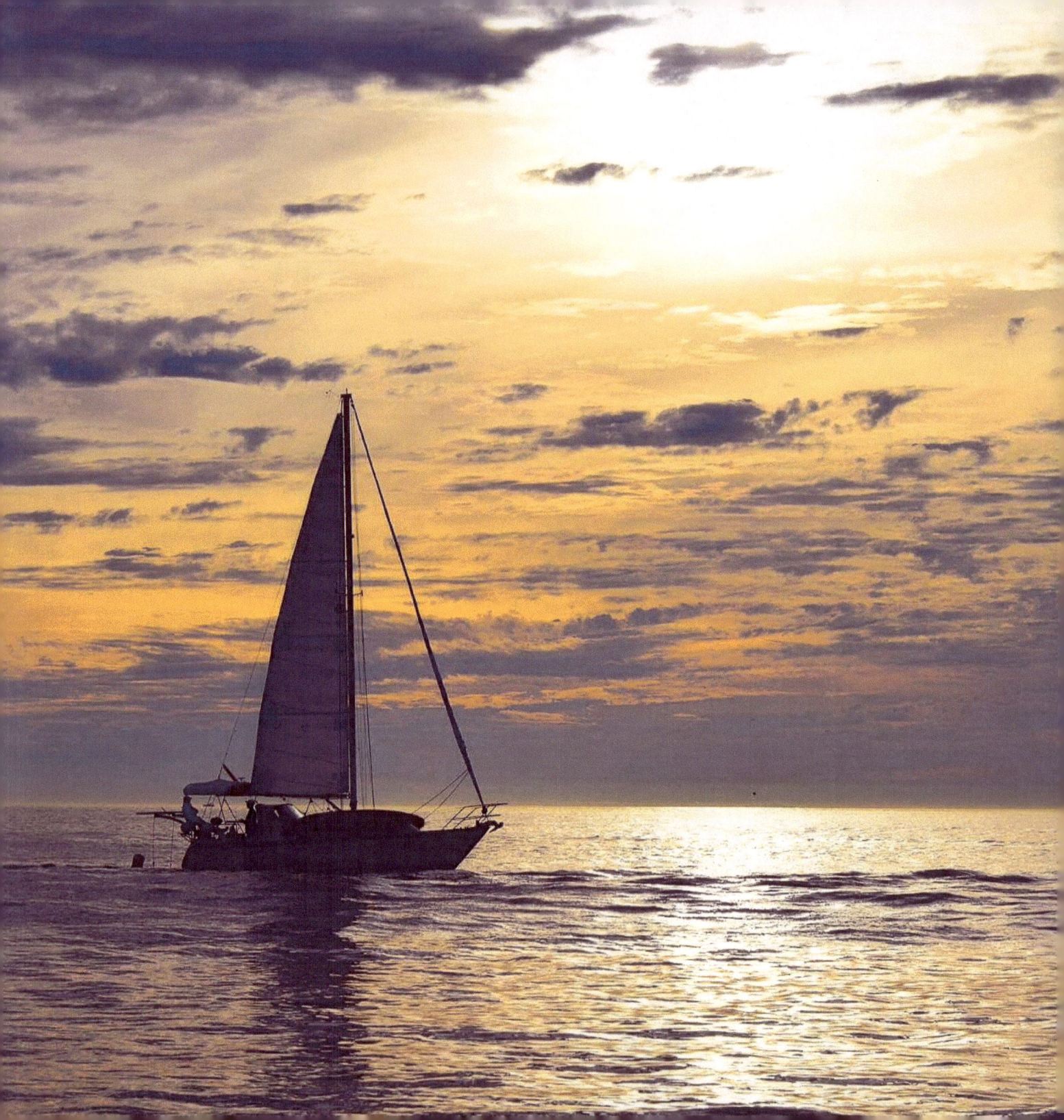

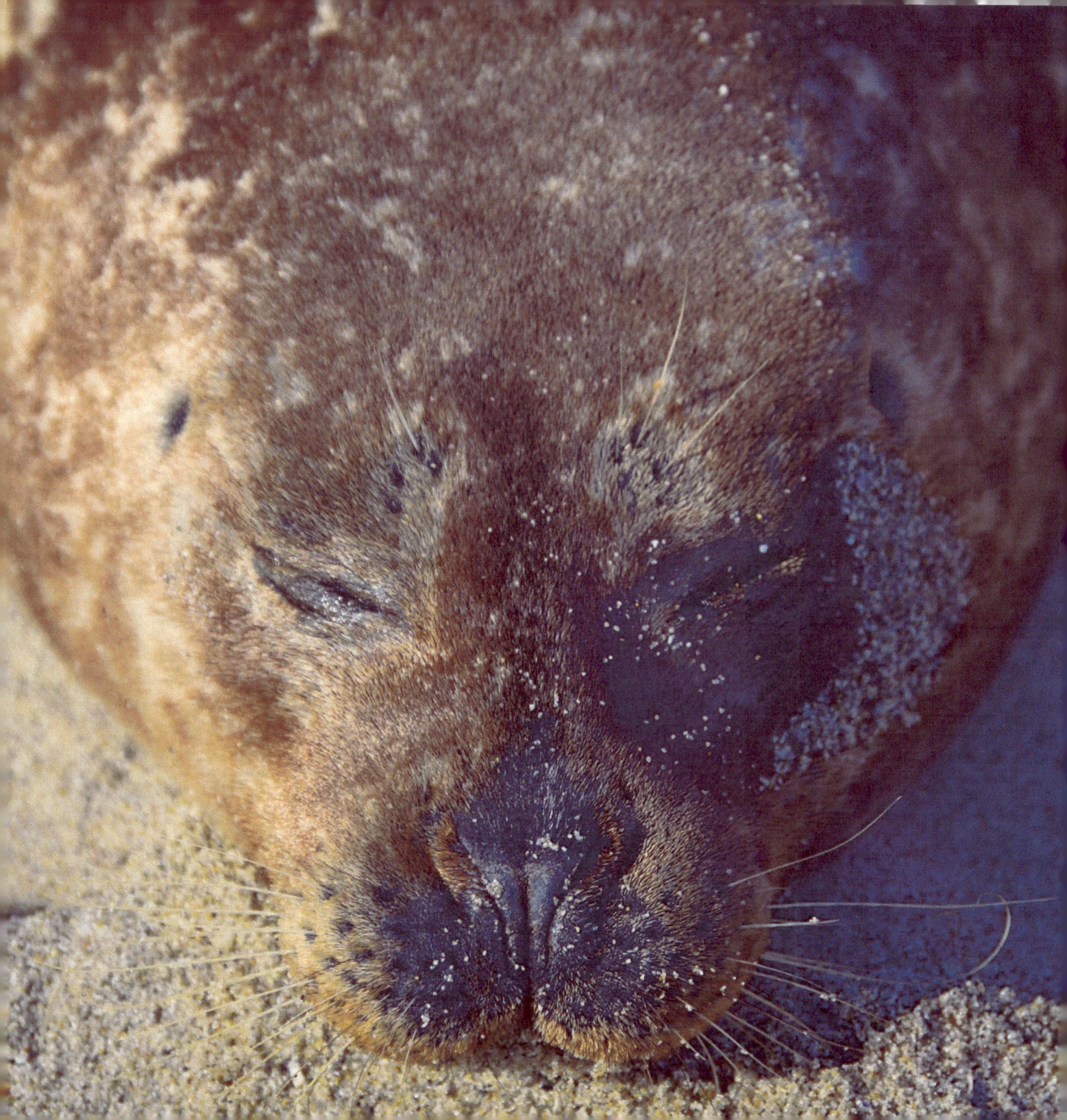

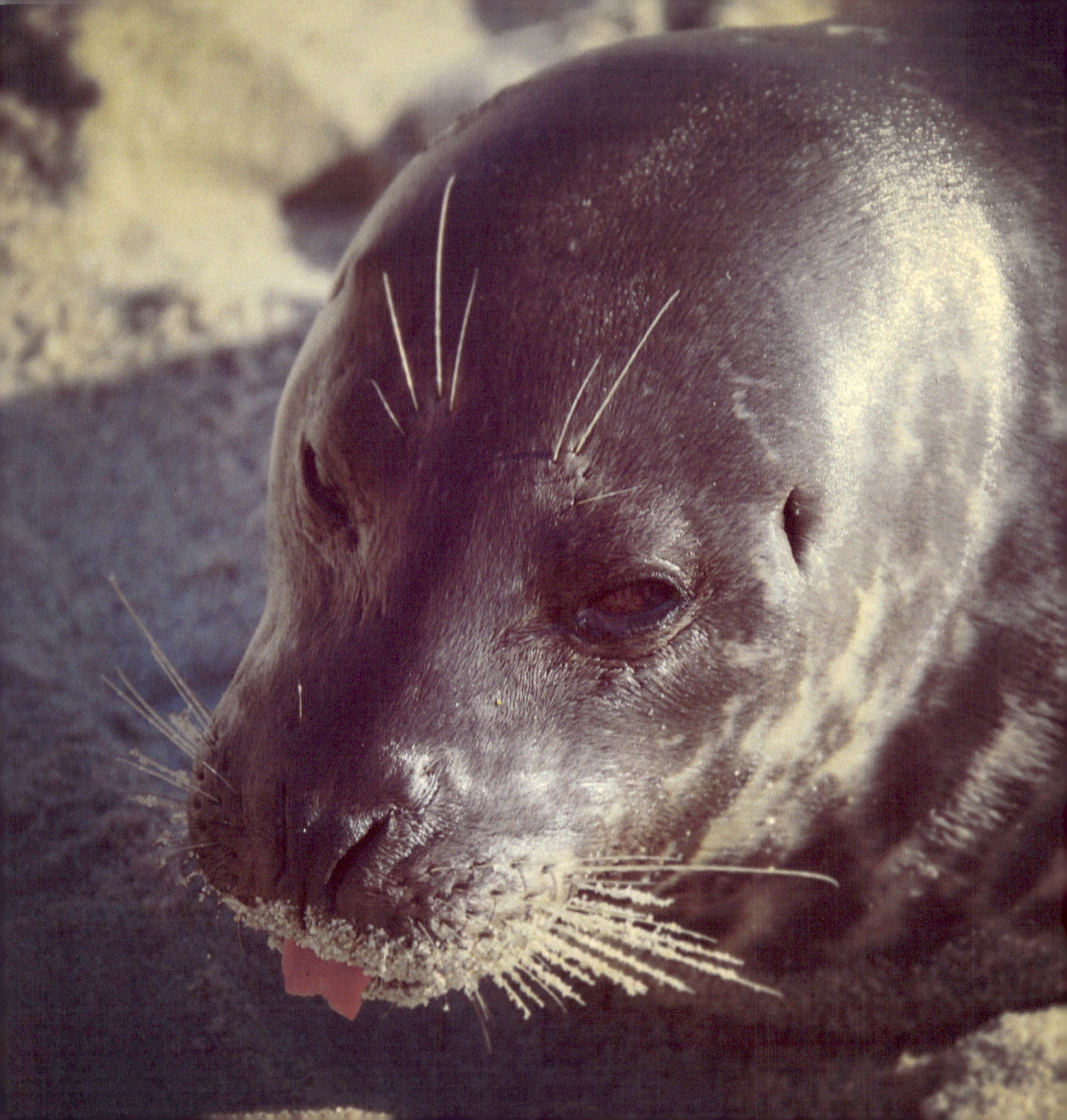

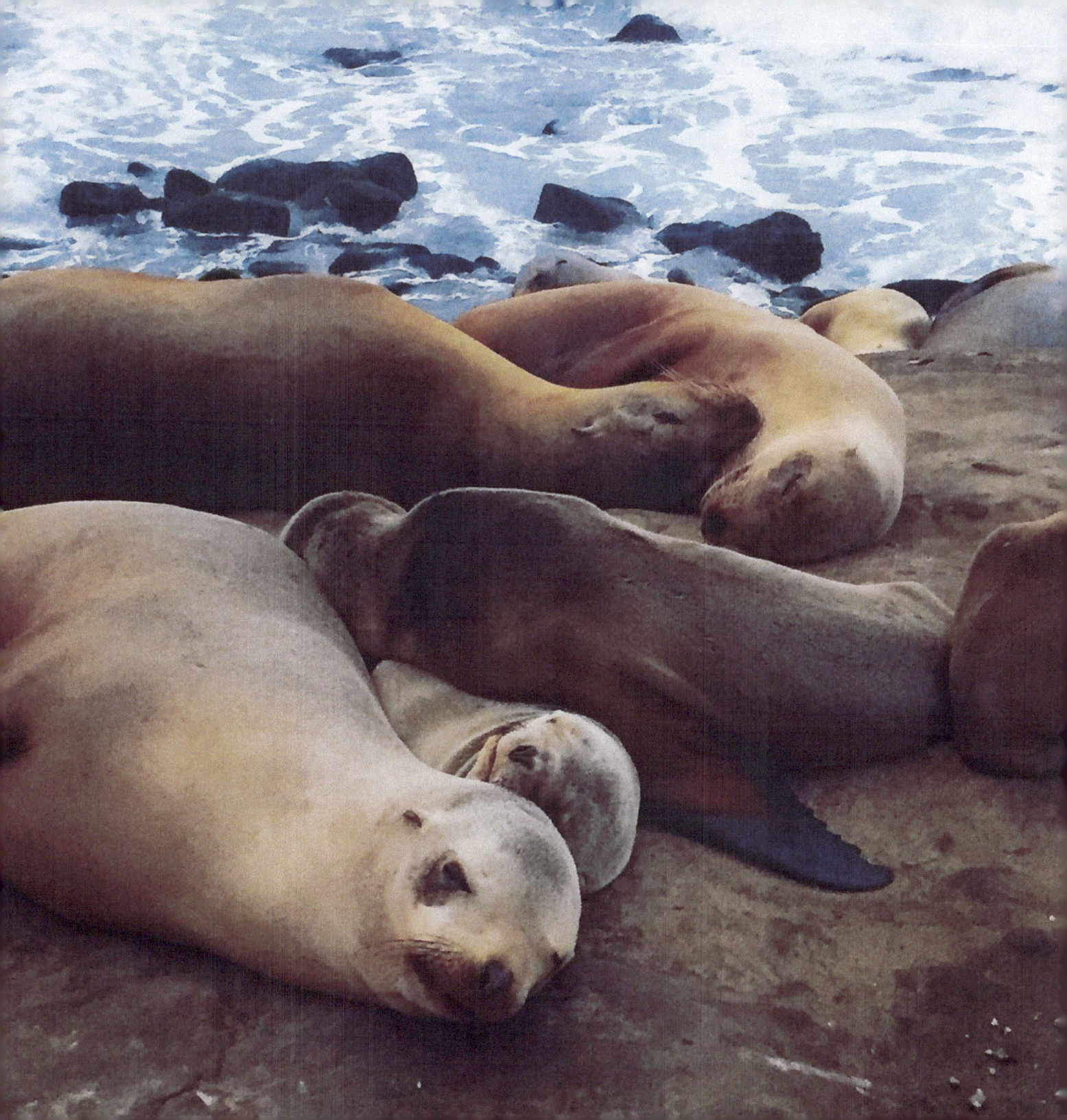

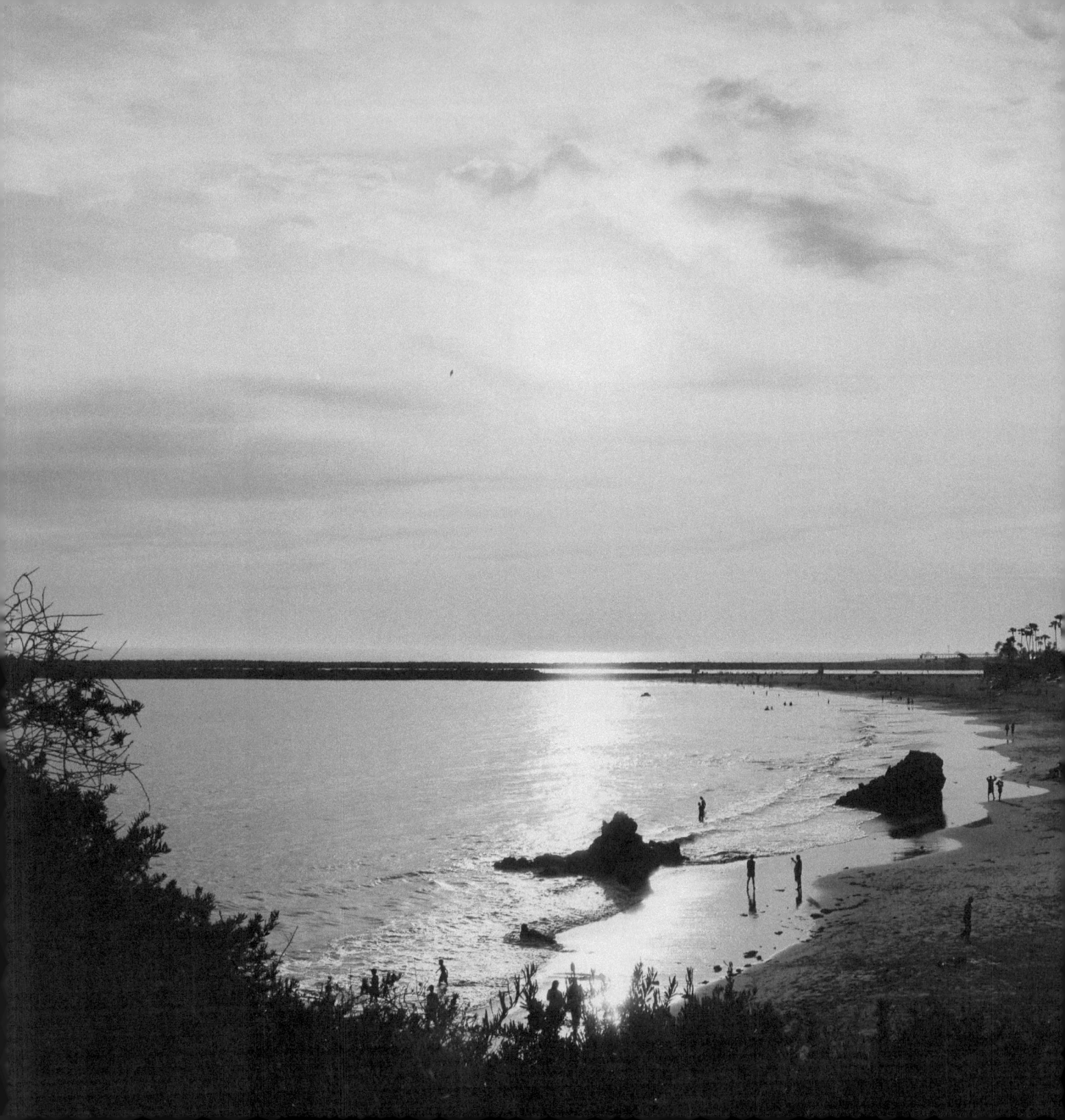

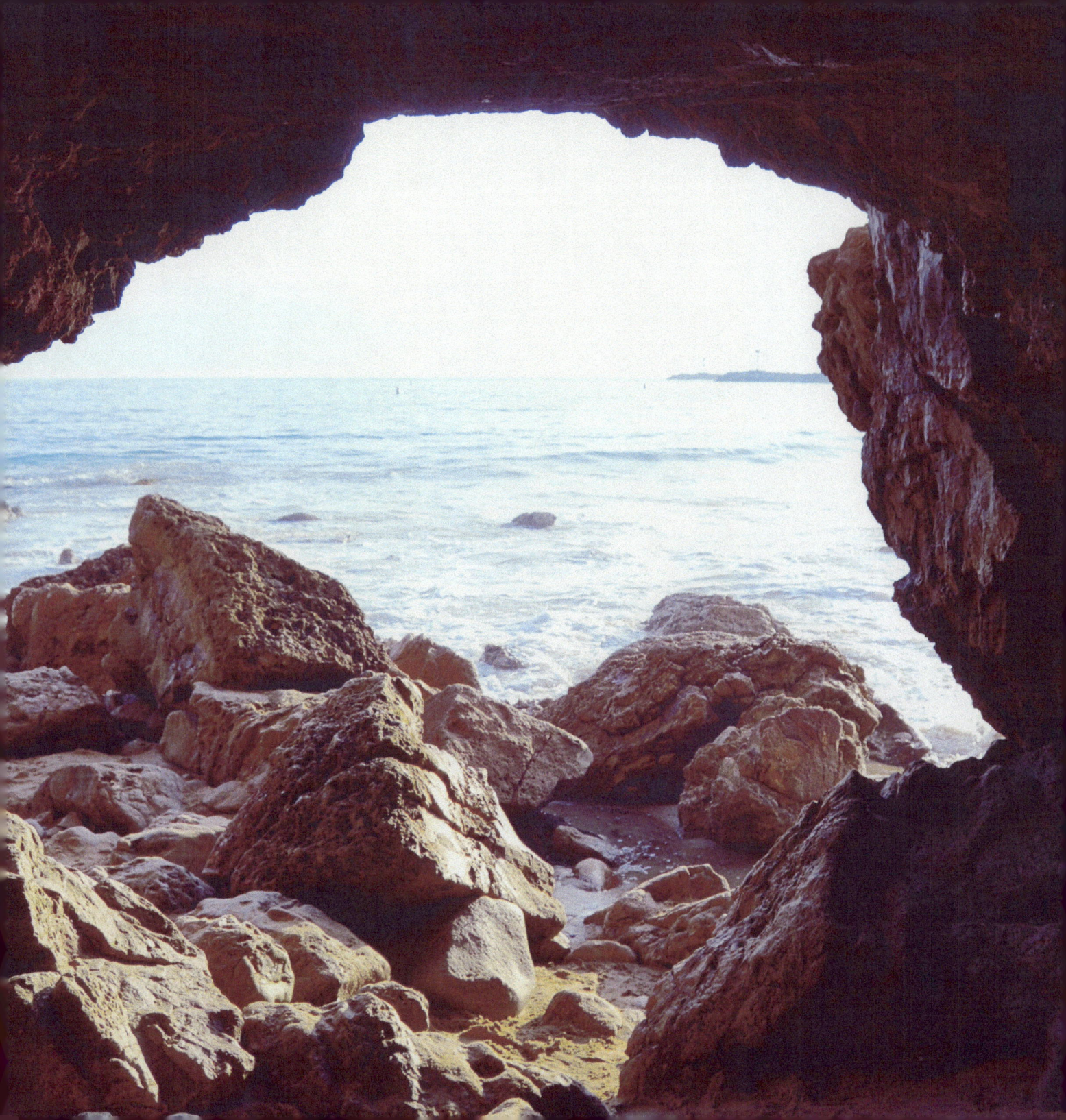

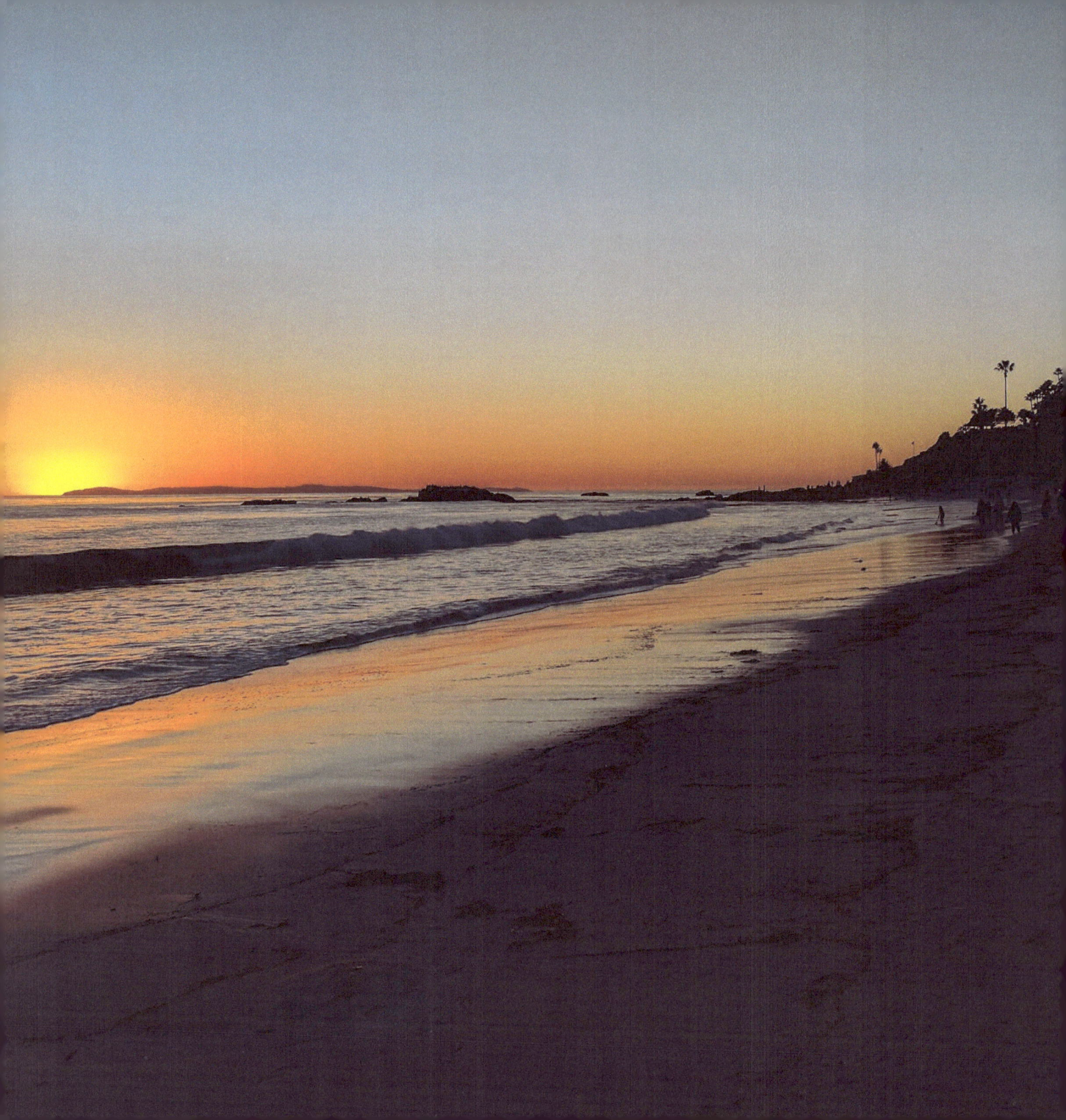

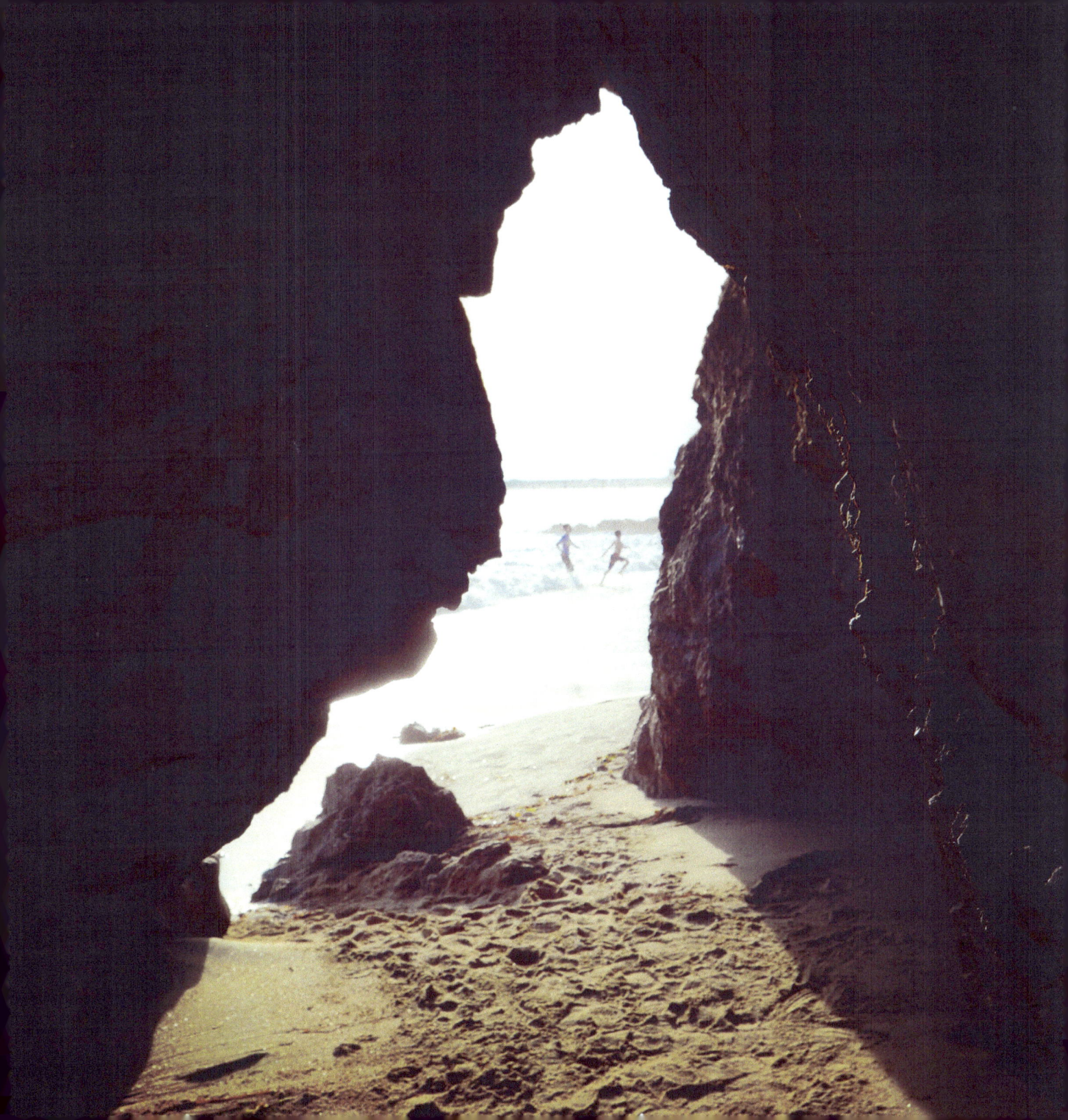

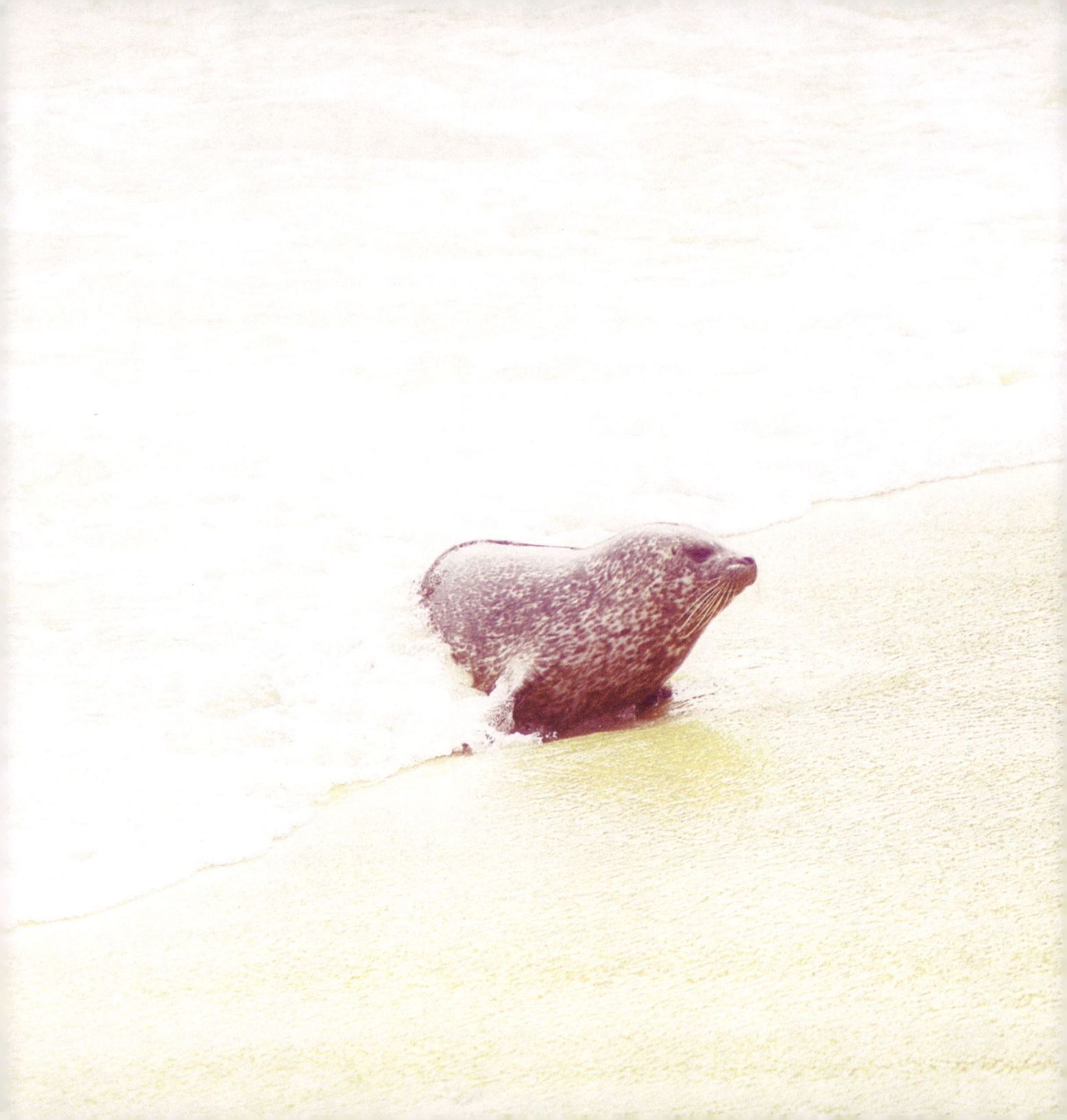